CAPED

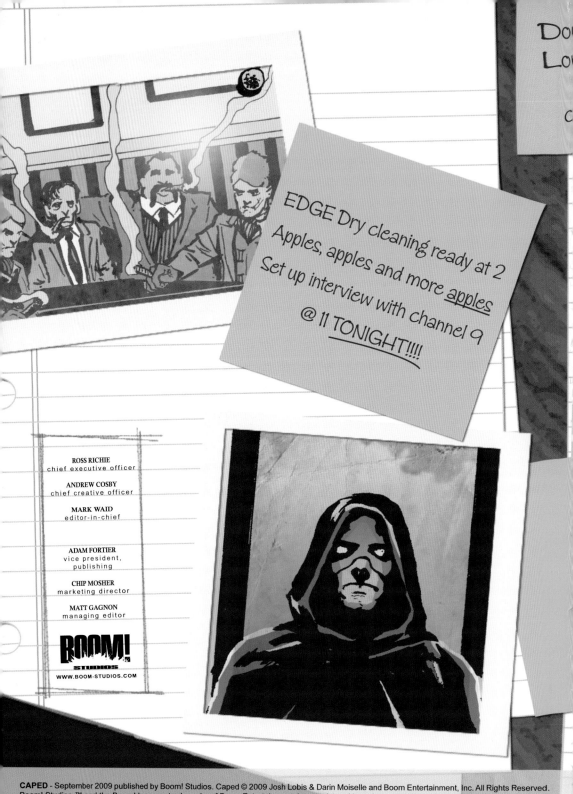

EDGE Dry cleaning ready at 2
Apples, apples and more apples
Set up interview with channel 9
@ 11 TONIGHT!!!!

ROSS RICHIE
chief executive officer

ANDREW COSBY
chief creative officer

MARK WAID
editor-in-chief

ADAM FORTIER
vice president,
publishing

CHIP MOSHER
marketing director

MATT GAGNON
managing editor

BOOM!
STUDIOS
WWW.BOOM-STUDIOS.COM

CAPED - September 2009 published by Boom! Studios. Caped © 2009 Josh Lobis & Darin Moiselle and Boom Entertainment, Inc. All Rights Reserved. Boom! Studios ™ and the Boom! logo are trademarks of Boom Entertainment, Inc., registered in various countries and categories. All rights reserved. The characters and events depicted herein are fictional. Any similarity to actual persons, demons, anti-Christs, aliens, vampires, face-suckers or political figures, whether living, dead or undead, or to any actual or supernatural events is coincidental and unintentional. So don't come whining to us. Office of publication: 6310 San Vicente Blvd Ste 404, Los Angeles, CA 90048. Printed in Korea.

mocha chocolate

at latte

co-chip muffin w/nuts

CREATED AND WRITTEN BY
DARIN MOISELLE AND JOSH LOBIS

ART BY YAIR HERRERA
CHAPTERS 1 AND 2

ART BY SEBASTIÁN PIRIZ
CHAPTERS 3 AND 4

COLORS BY RENATO FACCINI
CHAPTERS 1 AND 2

COLORS BY DIGIKORE STUDIOS
CHAPTERS 3 AND 4

LETTERING BY JOHNNY LOWE

EDITED BY IAN BRILL

COVER BY SAUMIN PATEL

Special thanks to
Caleb Cleveland and Tony Parker

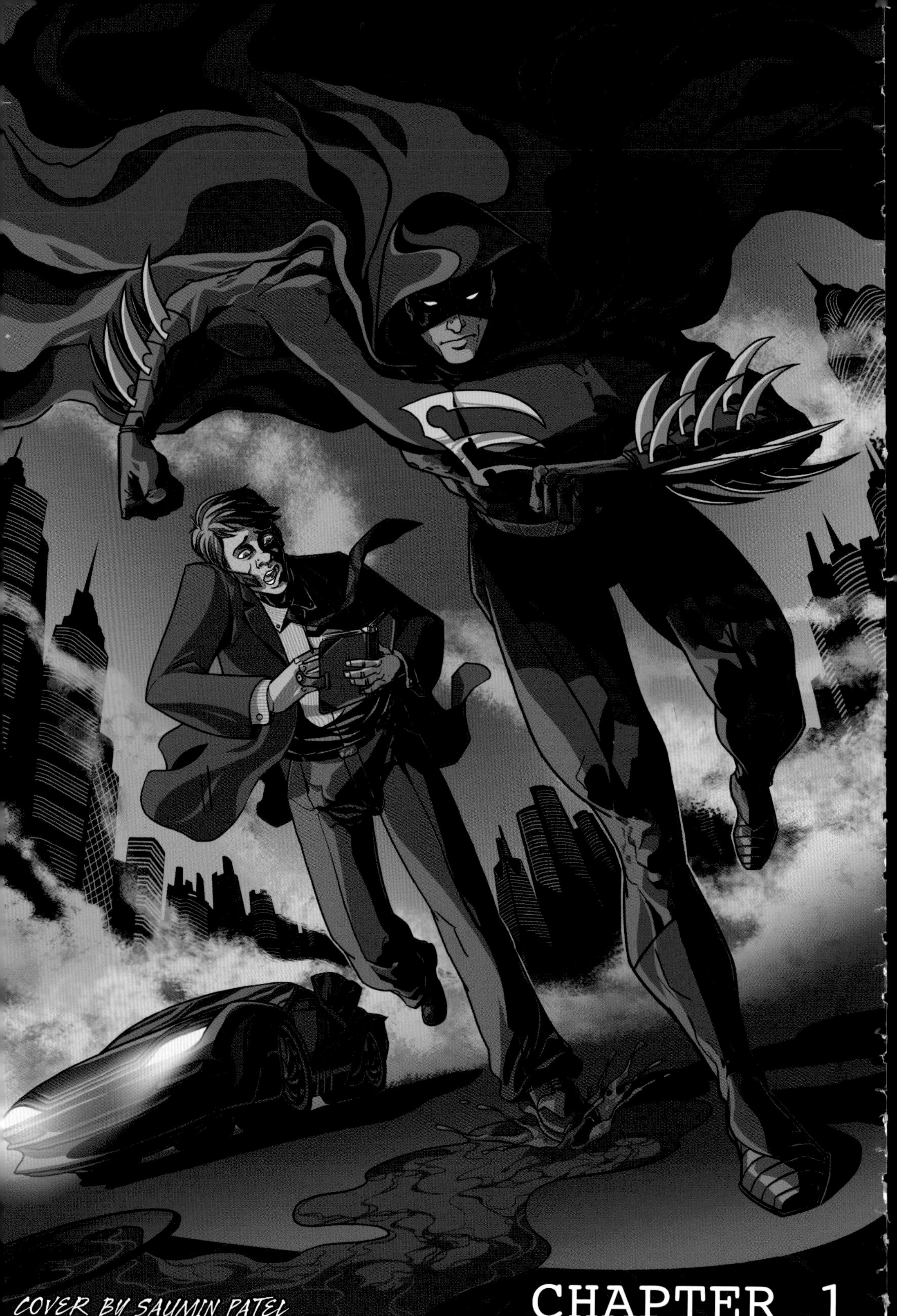

COVER BY SAUMIN PATEL

CHAPTER 1

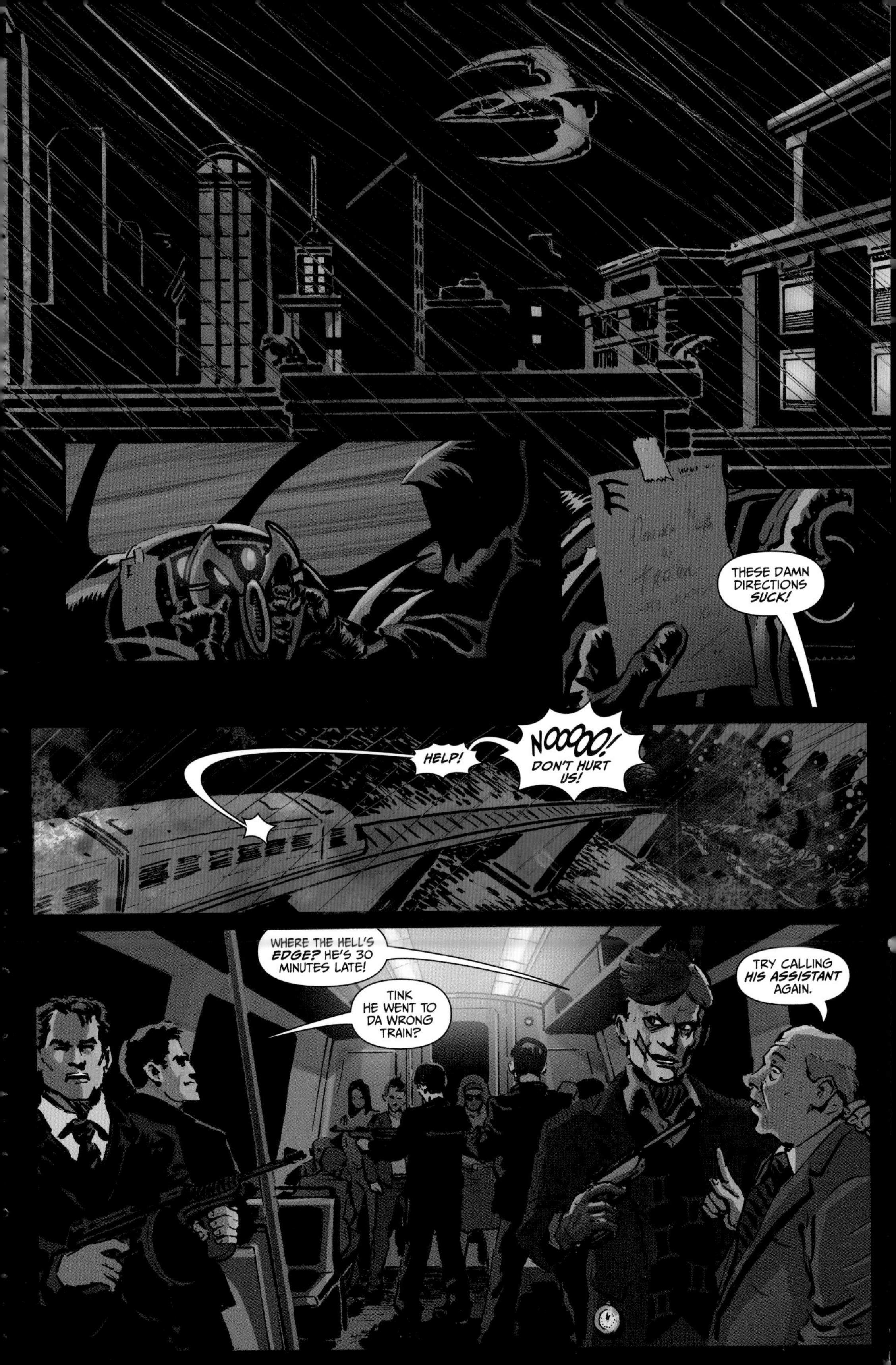
THESE DAMN DIRECTIONS SUCK!
HELP!
NOOOOO! DON'T HURT US!
WHERE THE HELL'S EDGE? HE'S 30 MINUTES LATE!
TINK HE WENT TO DA WRONG TRAIN?
TRY CALLING HIS ASSISTANT AGAIN.

EDGE'S OFFICE.

IT'S GEMINI. HE'S STILL NOT HERE!

NO! DON'T PUT ME THRU TO VOICE-MAIL!

YOU DID TELL HIM THE MAYOR'S LIFE IS IN DANGER, RIGHT?

WHISP!

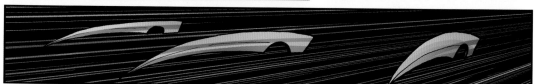

WHISP!

KLRSH!

ZWING!

SHOW YOURSELF, EDGE! OR THE VIRGIN GETS IT!

WHY DOES EVERYONE THINK I'M A VIRGIN?

CRONKITE ON CRONKITE

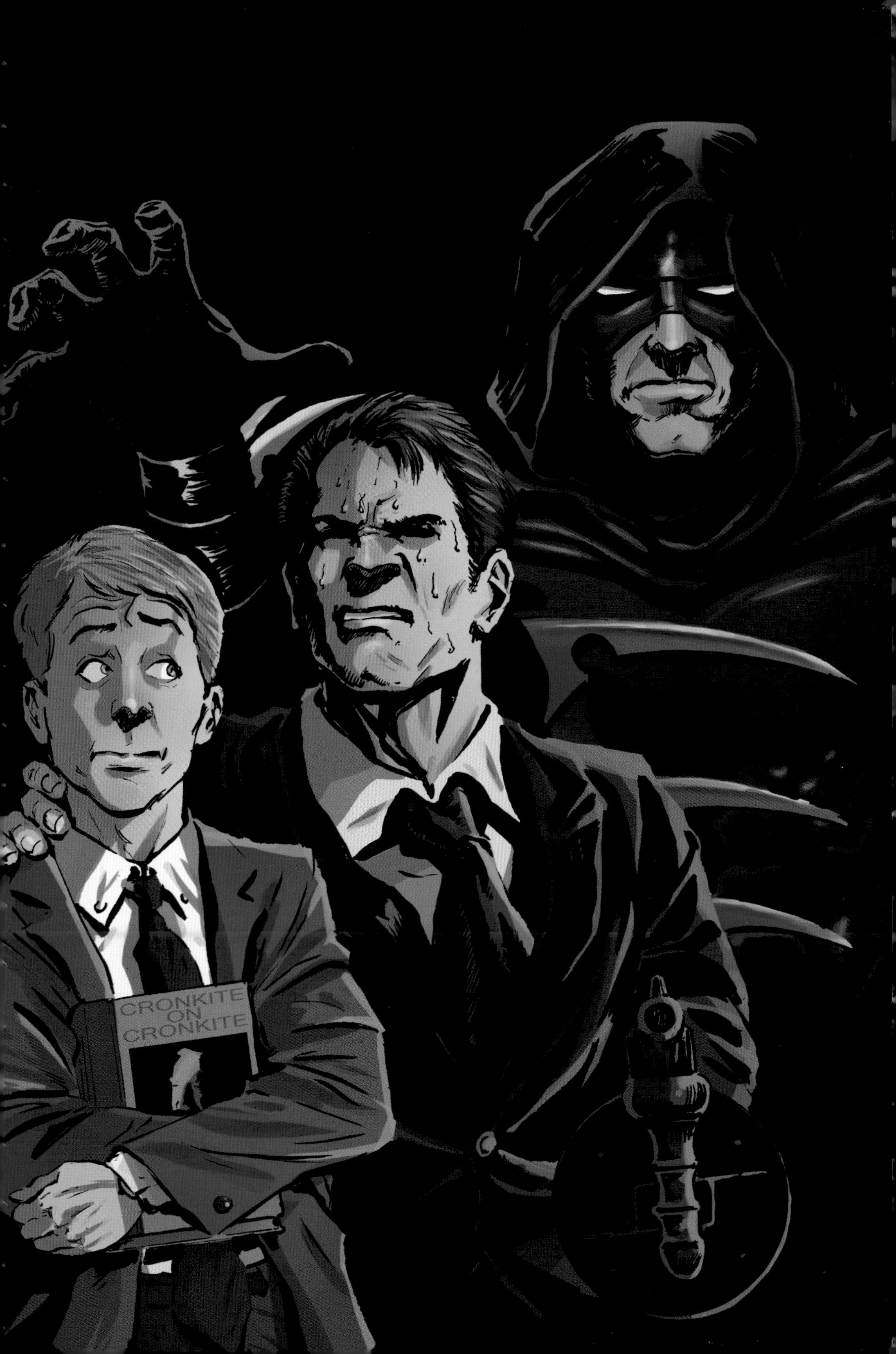
CRONKITE
ON
CRONKITE

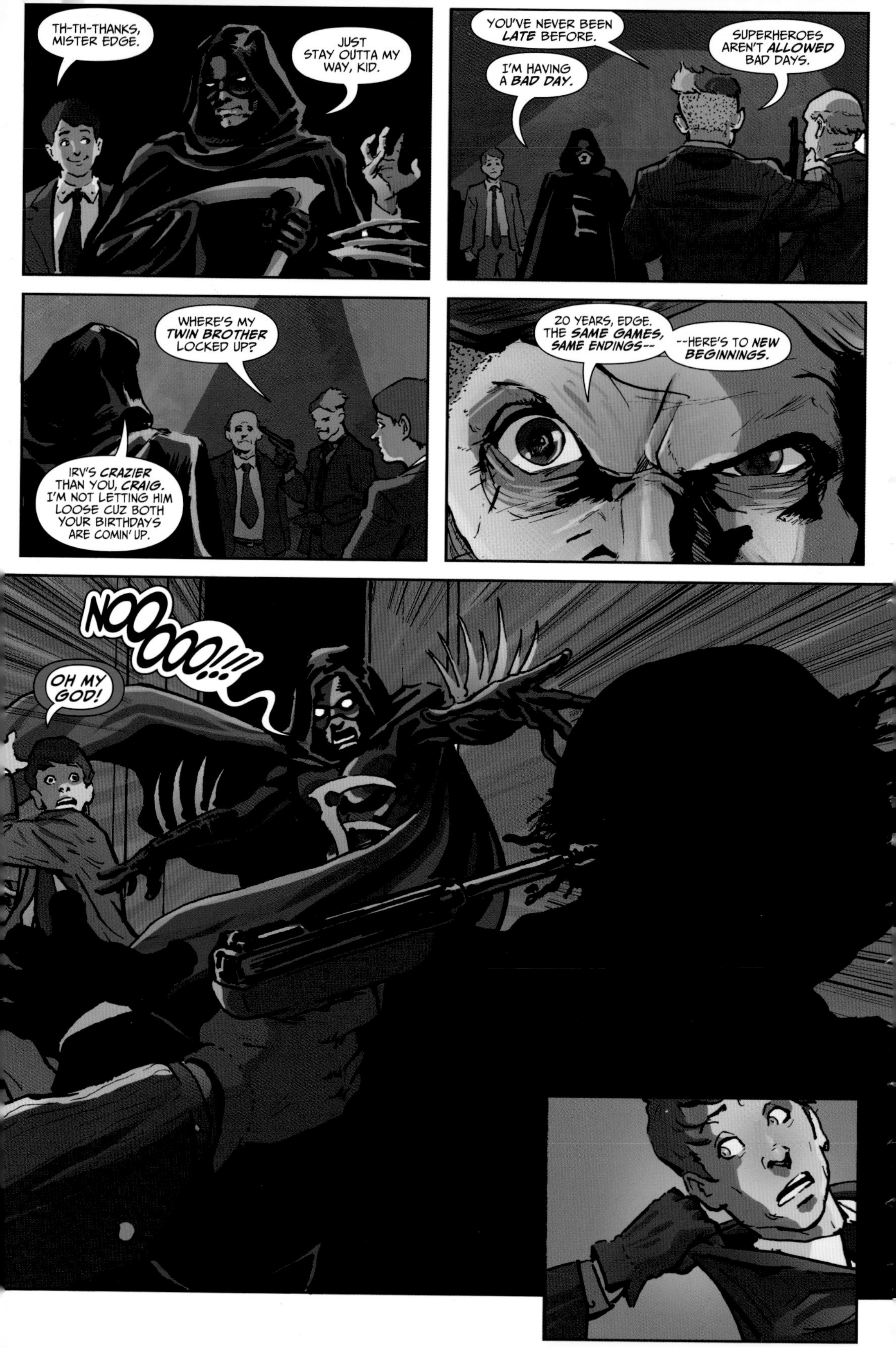
TH-TH-THANKS, MISTER EDGE.
JUST STAY OUTTA MY WAY, KID.
YOU'VE NEVER BEEN *LATE* BEFORE.
I'M HAVING A *BAD DAY.*
SUPERHEROES AREN'T *ALLOWED* BAD DAYS.
WHERE'S MY *TWIN BROTHER* LOCKED UP?
IRV'S *CRAZIER* THAN YOU, *CRAIG.* I'M NOT LETTING HIM LOOSE CUZ BOTH YOUR BIRTHDAYS ARE COMIN' UP.
20 YEARS, EDGE. THE *SAME GAMES, SAME ENDINGS--*
--HERE'S TO *NEW BEGINNINGS.*
NOOOOO!!!
OH MY GOD!

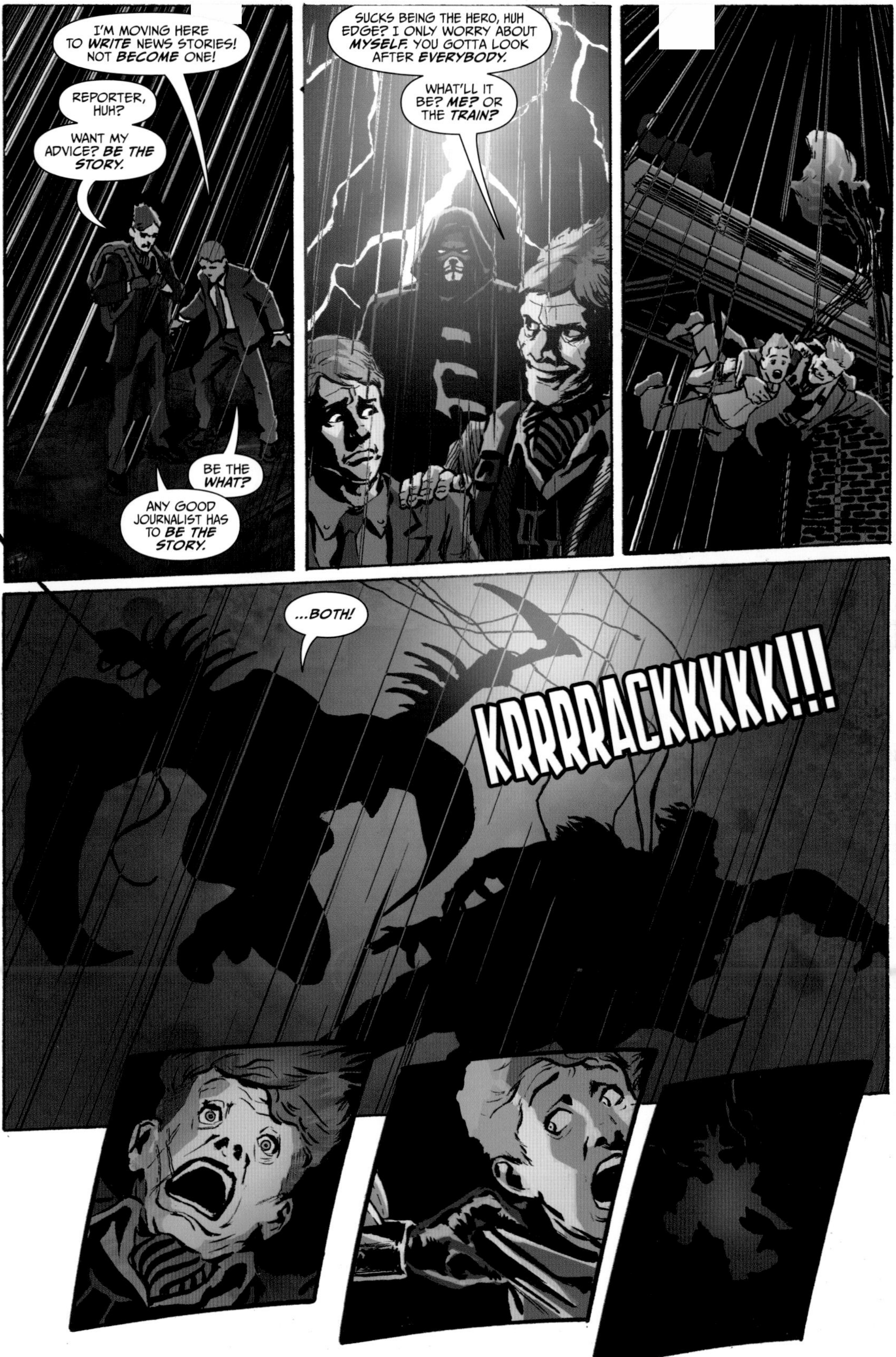
I'M MOVING HERE TO WRITE NEWS STORIES! NOT BECOME ONE!
REPORTER, HUH?
WANT MY ADVICE? BE THE STORY.
BE THE WHAT?
ANY GOOD JOURNALIST HAS TO BE THE STORY.
SUCKS BEING THE HERO, HUH EDGE? I ONLY WORRY ABOUT MYSELF. YOU GOTTA LOOK AFTER EVERYBODY.
WHAT'LL IT BE? ME? OR THE TRAIN?
...BOTH!
KRRRRACKKKKK!!!

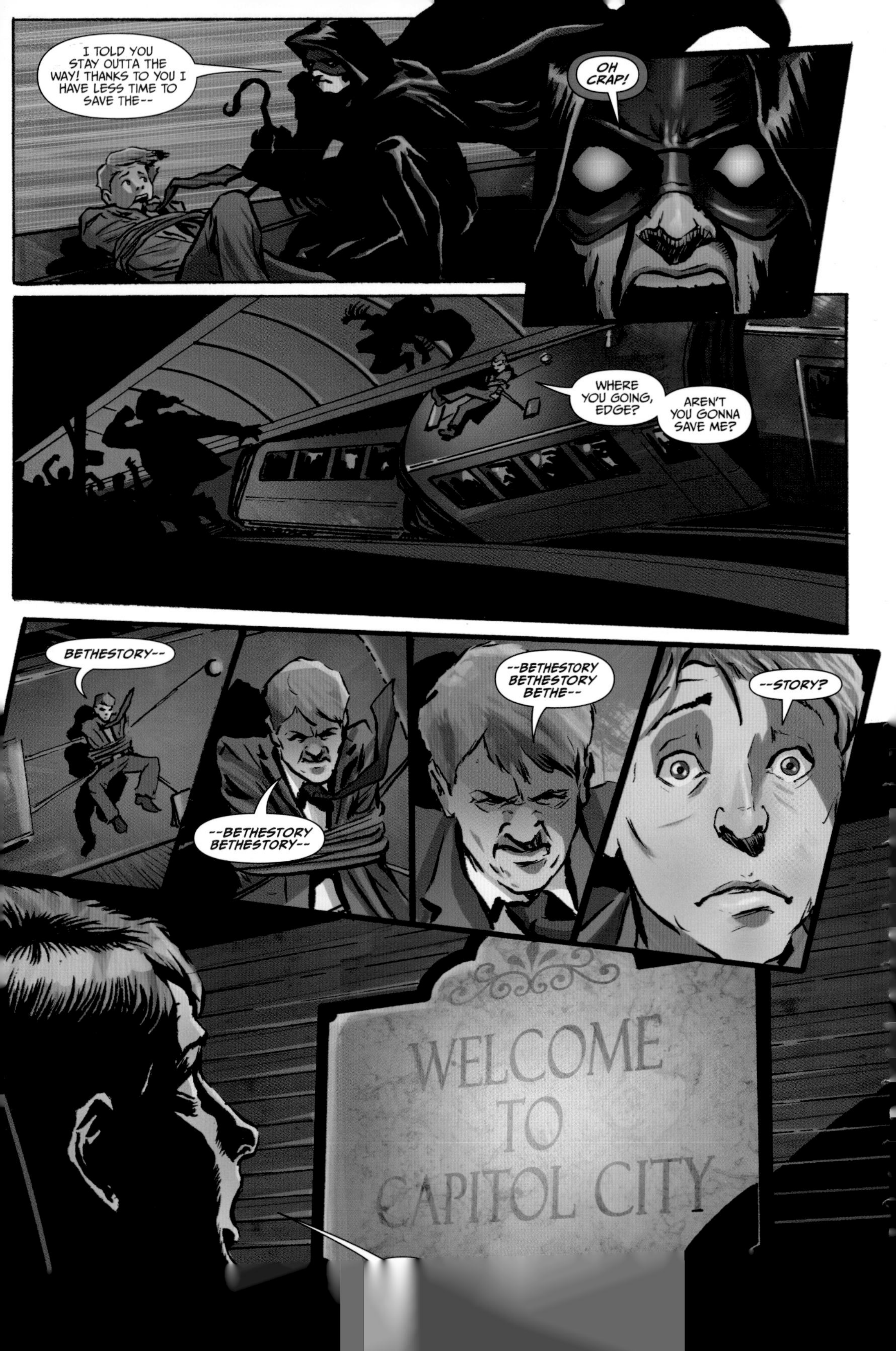
I TOLD YOU STAY OUTTA THE WAY! THANKS TO YOU I HAVE LESS TIME TO SAVE THE--
OH CRAP!
WHERE YOU GOING, EDGE?
AREN'T YOU GONNA SAVE ME?
BETHESTORY--
--BETHESTORY BETHESTORY--
--BETHESTORY BETHESTORY BETHE--
--STORY?
WELCOME TO CAPITOL CITY

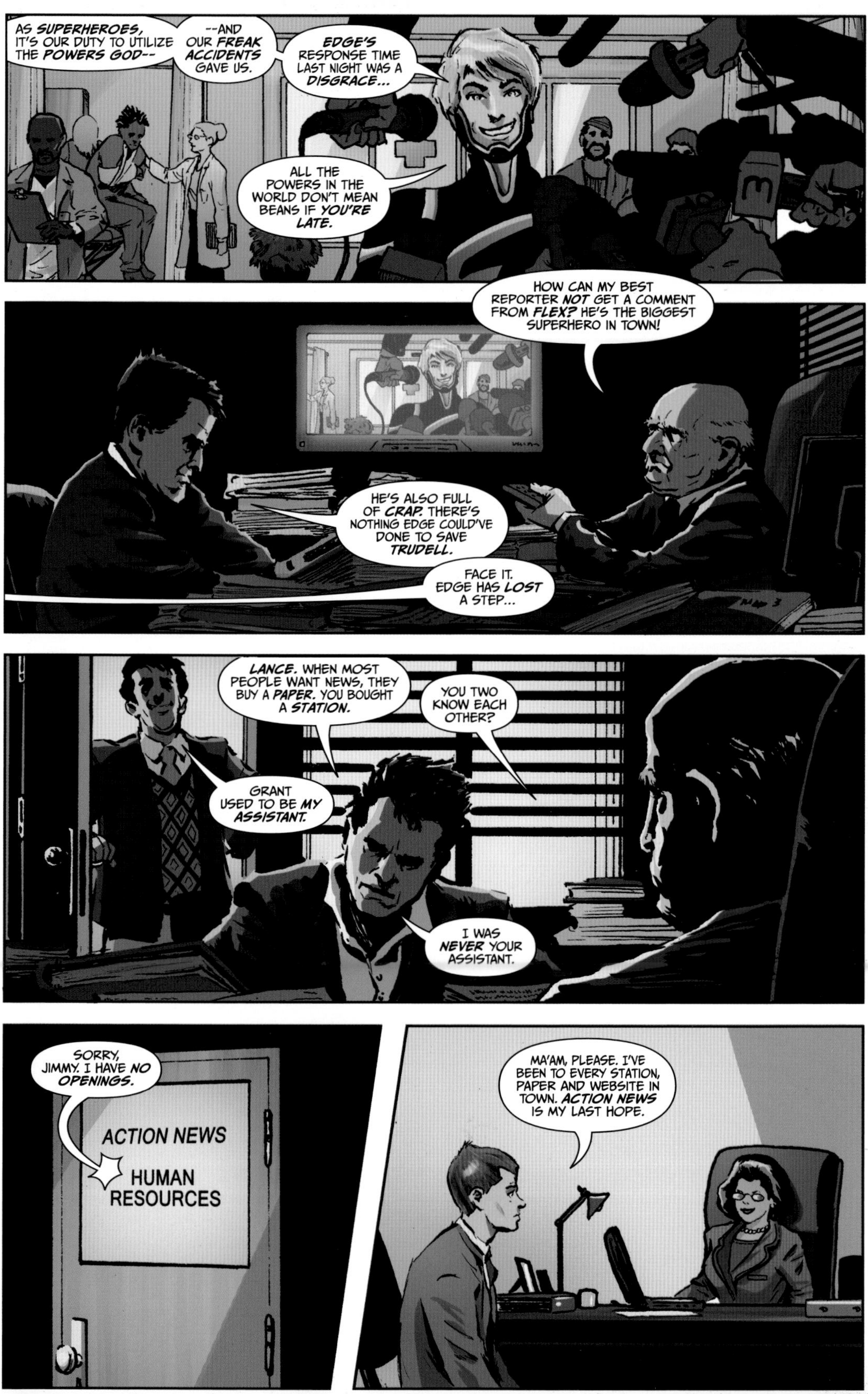

AS SUPERHEROES, IT'S OUR DUTY TO UTILIZE THE POWERS GOD--
--AND OUR FREAK ACCIDENTS GAVE US.
EDGE'S RESPONSE TIME LAST NIGHT WAS A DISGRACE...
ALL THE POWERS IN THE WORLD DON'T MEAN BEANS IF YOU'RE LATE.
HOW CAN MY BEST REPORTER NOT GET A COMMENT FROM FLEX? HE'S THE BIGGEST SUPERHERO IN TOWN!
HE'S ALSO FULL OF CRAP. THERE'S NOTHING EDGE COULD'VE DONE TO SAVE TRUDELL.
FACE IT. EDGE HAS LOST A STEP...
LANCE. WHEN MOST PEOPLE WANT NEWS, THEY BUY A PAPER. YOU BOUGHT A STATION.
YOU TWO KNOW EACH OTHER?
GRANT USED TO BE MY ASSISTANT.
I WAS NEVER YOUR ASSISTANT.
SORRY, JIMMY. I HAVE NO OPENINGS.
ACTION NEWS
HUMAN RESOURCES
MA'AM, PLEASE. I'VE BEEN TO EVERY STATION, PAPER AND WEBSITE IN TOWN. ACTION NEWS IS MY LAST HOPE.

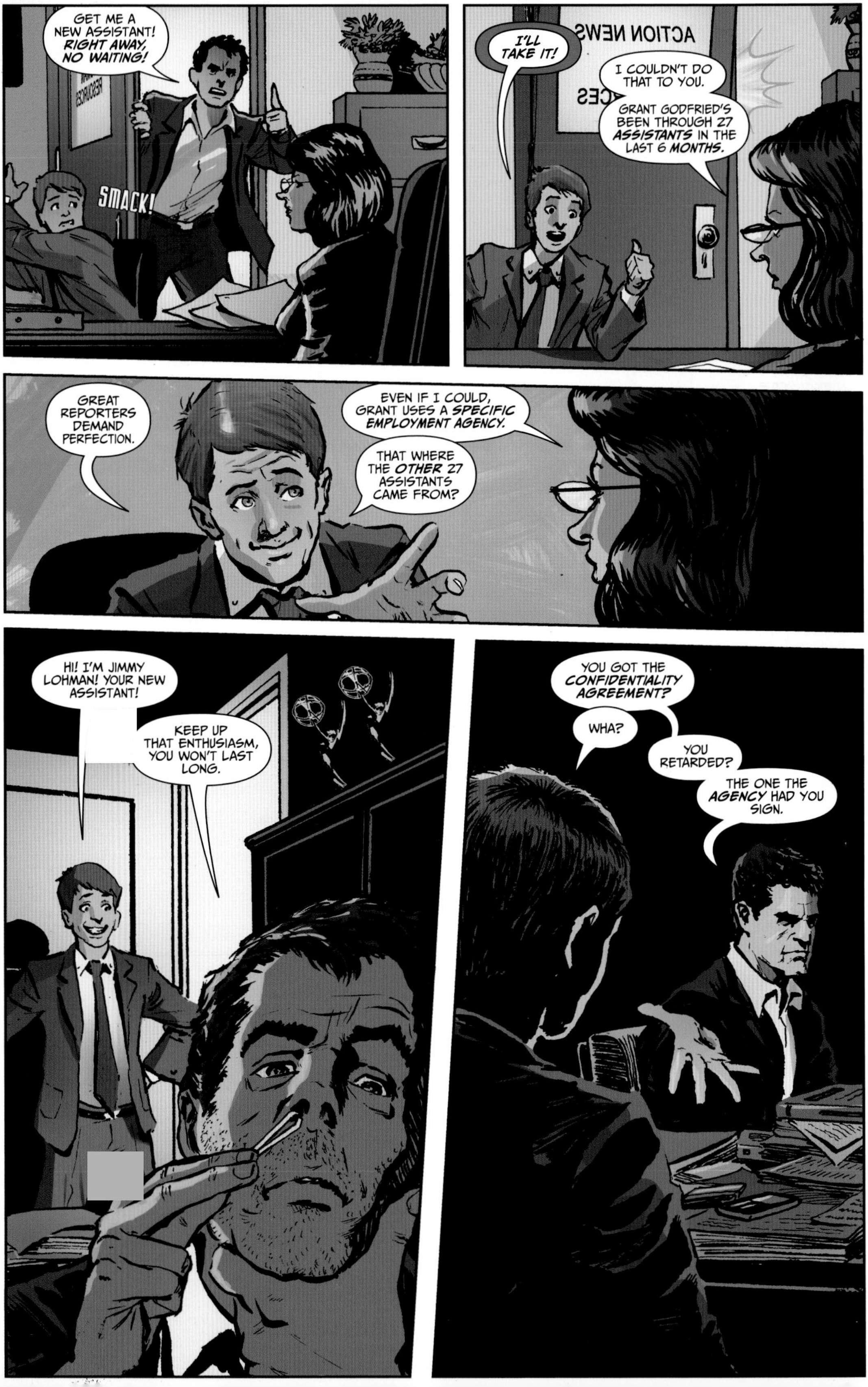
GET ME A NEW ASSISTANT! RIGHT AWAY, NO WAITING!
SMACK!
I'LL TAKE IT!
I COULDN'T DO THAT TO YOU.
GRANT GODFRIED'S BEEN THROUGH 27 ASSISTANTS IN THE LAST 6 MONTHS.
ACTION NEWS
GREAT REPORTERS DEMAND PERFECTION.
EVEN IF I COULD, GRANT USES A SPECIFIC EMPLOYMENT AGENCY.
THAT WHERE THE OTHER 27 ASSISTANTS CAME FROM?
HI! I'M JIMMY LOHMAN! YOUR NEW ASSISTANT!
KEEP UP THAT ENTHUSIASM, YOU WON'T LAST LONG.
YOU GOT THE CONFIDENTIALITY AGREEMENT?
WHA?
YOU RETARDED?
THE ONE THE AGENCY HAD YOU SIGN.

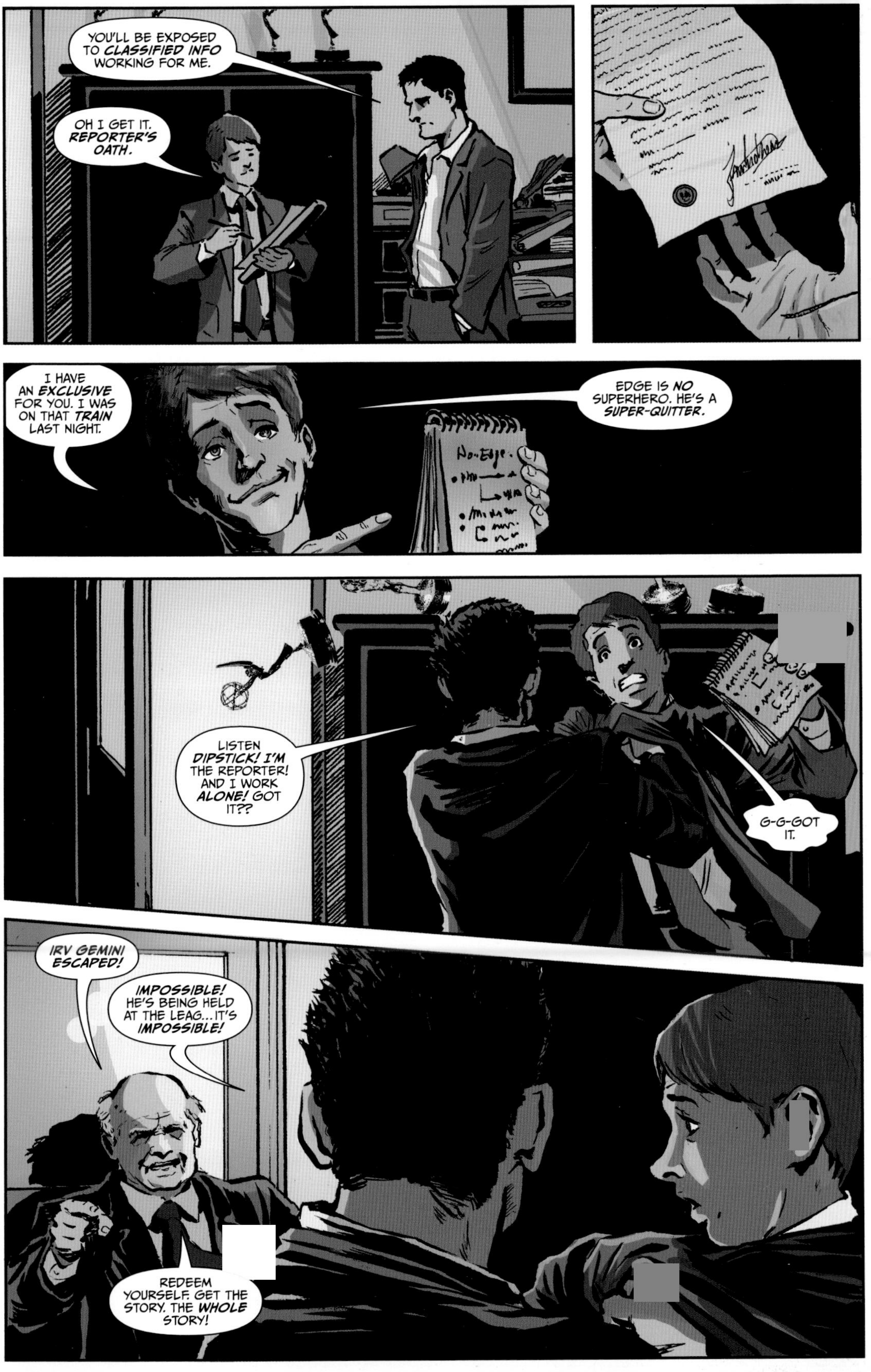
YOU'LL BE EXPOSED TO CLASSIFIED INFO WORKING FOR ME.
OH I GET IT. REPORTER'S OATH.
I HAVE AN EXCLUSIVE FOR YOU. I WAS ON THAT TRAIN LAST NIGHT.
EDGE IS NO SUPERHERO. HE'S A SUPER-QUITTER.
LISTEN DIPSTICK! I'M THE REPORTER! AND I WORK ALONE! GOT IT??
G-G-GOT IT.
IRV GEMINI ESCAPED!
IMPOSSIBLE! HE'S BEING HELD AT THE LEAG... IT'S IMPOSSIBLE!
REDEEM YOURSELF. GET THE STORY. THE WHOLE STORY!

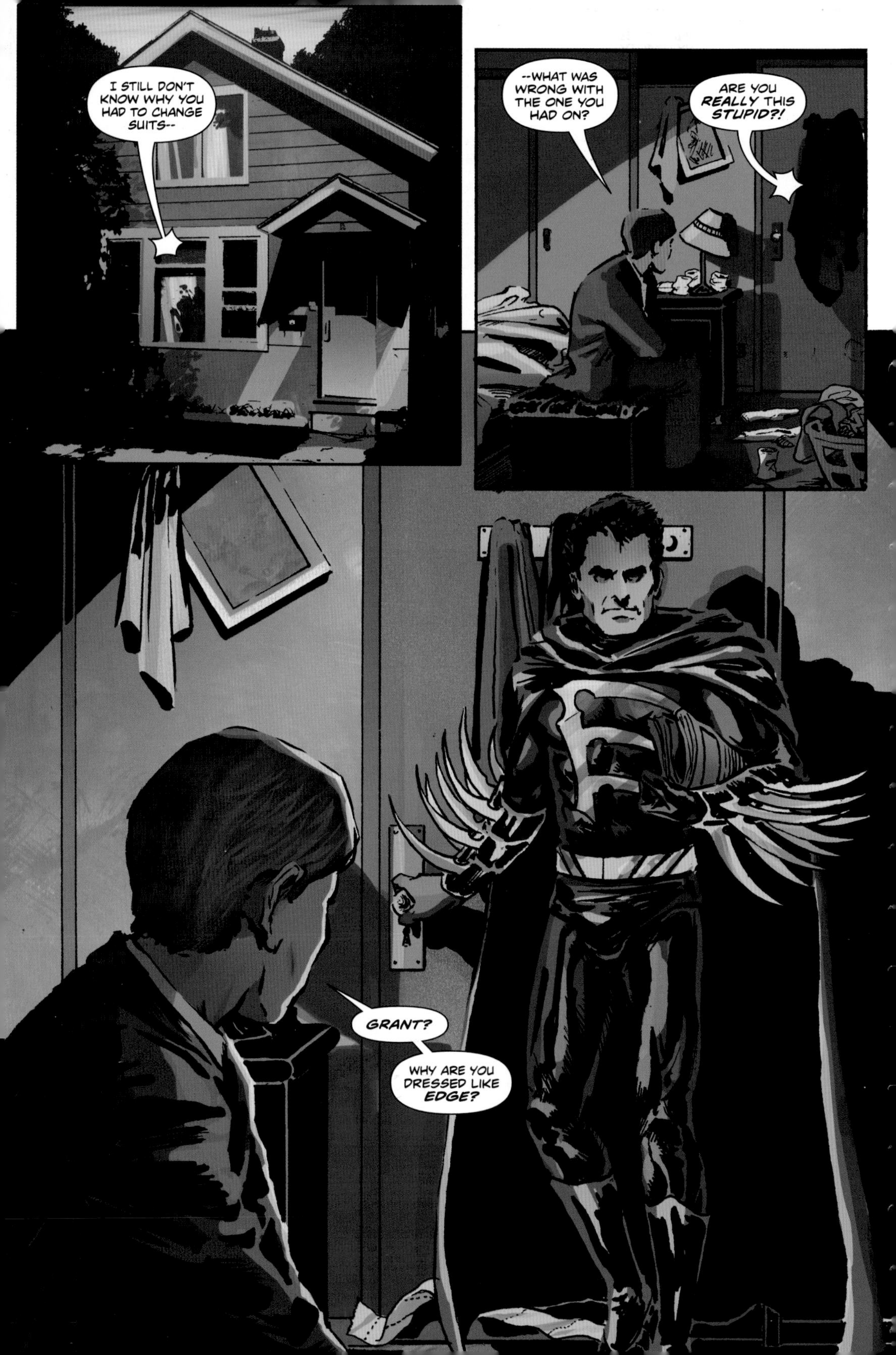
I STILL DON'T KNOW WHY YOU HAD TO CHANGE SUITS--
--WHAT WAS WRONG WITH THE ONE YOU HAD ON?
ARE YOU *REALLY* THIS *STUPID?!*
GRANT?
WHY ARE YOU DRESSED LIKE *EDGE?*

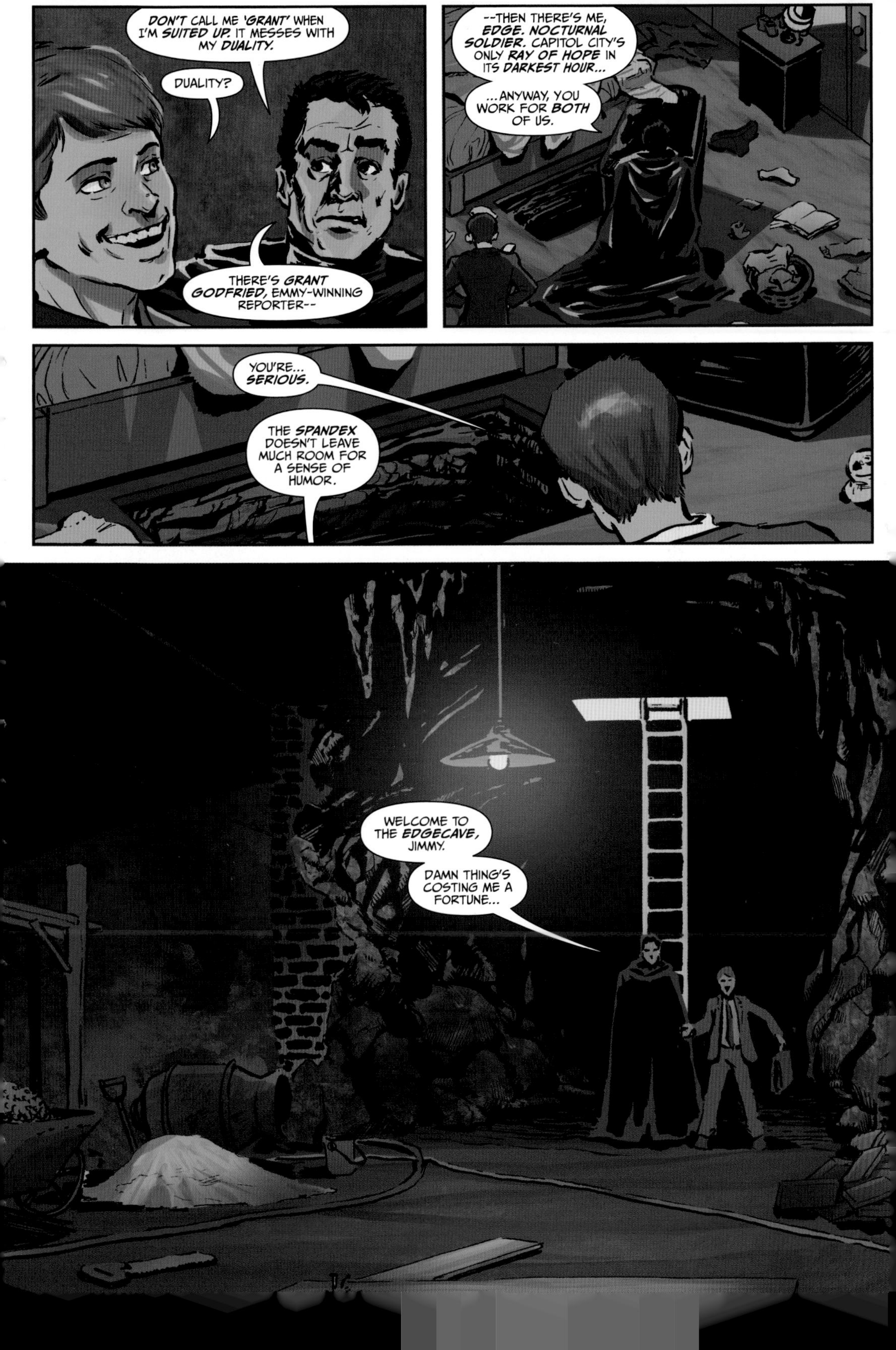
DON'T CALL ME 'GRANT' WHEN I'M SUITED UP. IT MESSES WITH MY DUALITY.
DUALITY?
THERE'S GRANT GODFRIED, EMMY-WINNING REPORTER--
--THEN THERE'S ME, EDGE. NOCTURNAL SOLDIER. CAPITOL CITY'S ONLY RAY OF HOPE IN ITS DARKEST HOUR...
...ANYWAY, YOU WORK FOR BOTH OF US.
YOU'RE... SERIOUS.
THE SPANDEX DOESN'T LEAVE MUCH ROOM FOR A SENSE OF HUMOR.
WELCOME TO THE EDGECAVE, JIMMY.
DAMN THING'S COSTING ME A FORTUNE...

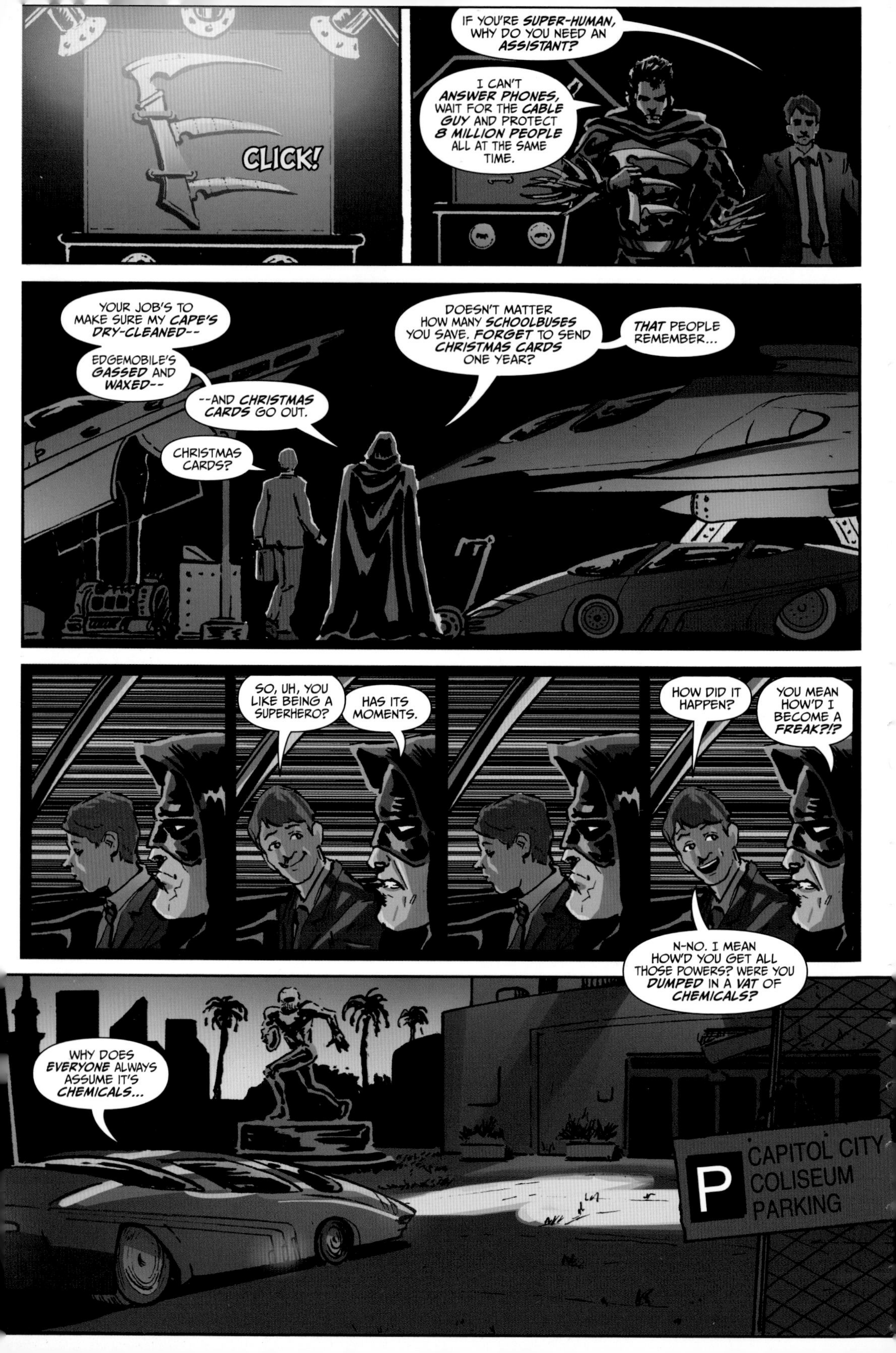
CLICK!
IF YOU'RE SUPER-HUMAN, WHY DO YOU NEED AN ASSISTANT?
I CAN'T ANSWER PHONES, WAIT FOR THE CABLE GUY AND PROTECT 8 MILLION PEOPLE ALL AT THE SAME TIME.
YOUR JOB'S TO MAKE SURE MY CAPE'S DRY-CLEANED--
EDGEMOBILE'S GASSED AND WAXED--
--AND CHRISTMAS CARDS GO OUT.
CHRISTMAS CARDS?
DOESN'T MATTER HOW MANY SCHOOLBUSES YOU SAVE. FORGET TO SEND CHRISTMAS CARDS ONE YEAR?
THAT PEOPLE REMEMBER...
SO, UH, YOU LIKE BEING A SUPERHERO?
HAS ITS MOMENTS.
HOW DID IT HAPPEN?
YOU MEAN HOW'D I BECOME A FREAK?!?
N-NO. I MEAN HOW'D YOU GET ALL THOSE POWERS? WERE YOU DUMPED IN A VAT OF CHEMICALS?
WHY DOES EVERYONE ALWAYS ASSUME IT'S CHEMICALS...
P
CAPITOL CITY COLISEUM PARKING

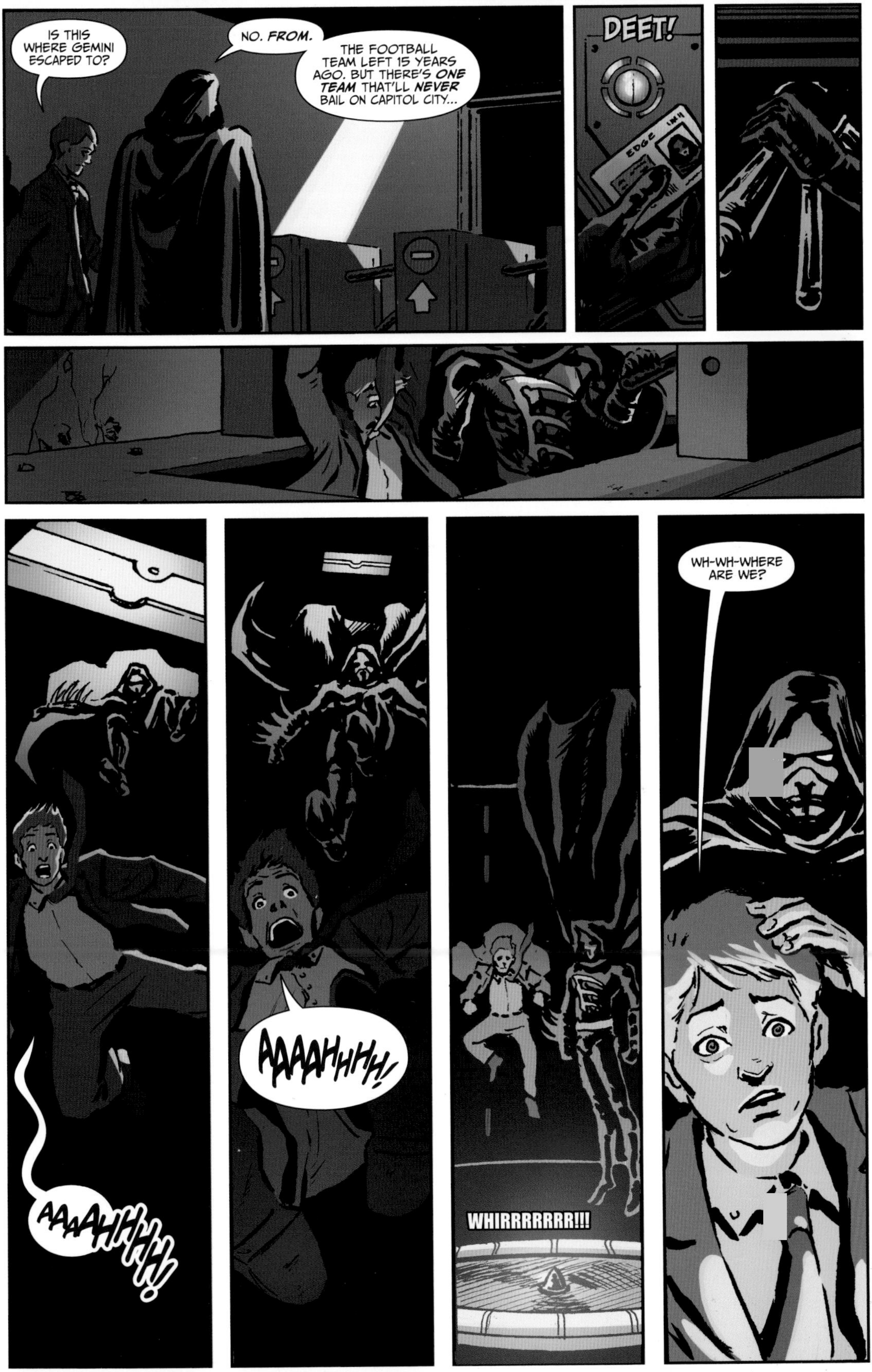
IS THIS WHERE GEMINI ESCAPED TO?
NO. *FROM.*
THE FOOTBALL TEAM LEFT 15 YEARS AGO. BUT THERE'S *ONE TEAM* THAT'LL *NEVER* BAIL ON CAPITOL CITY...
DEET!
EDGE
AAAAHHHH!
AAAAHHHH!
WHIRRRRRRR!!!
WH-WH-WHERE ARE WE?

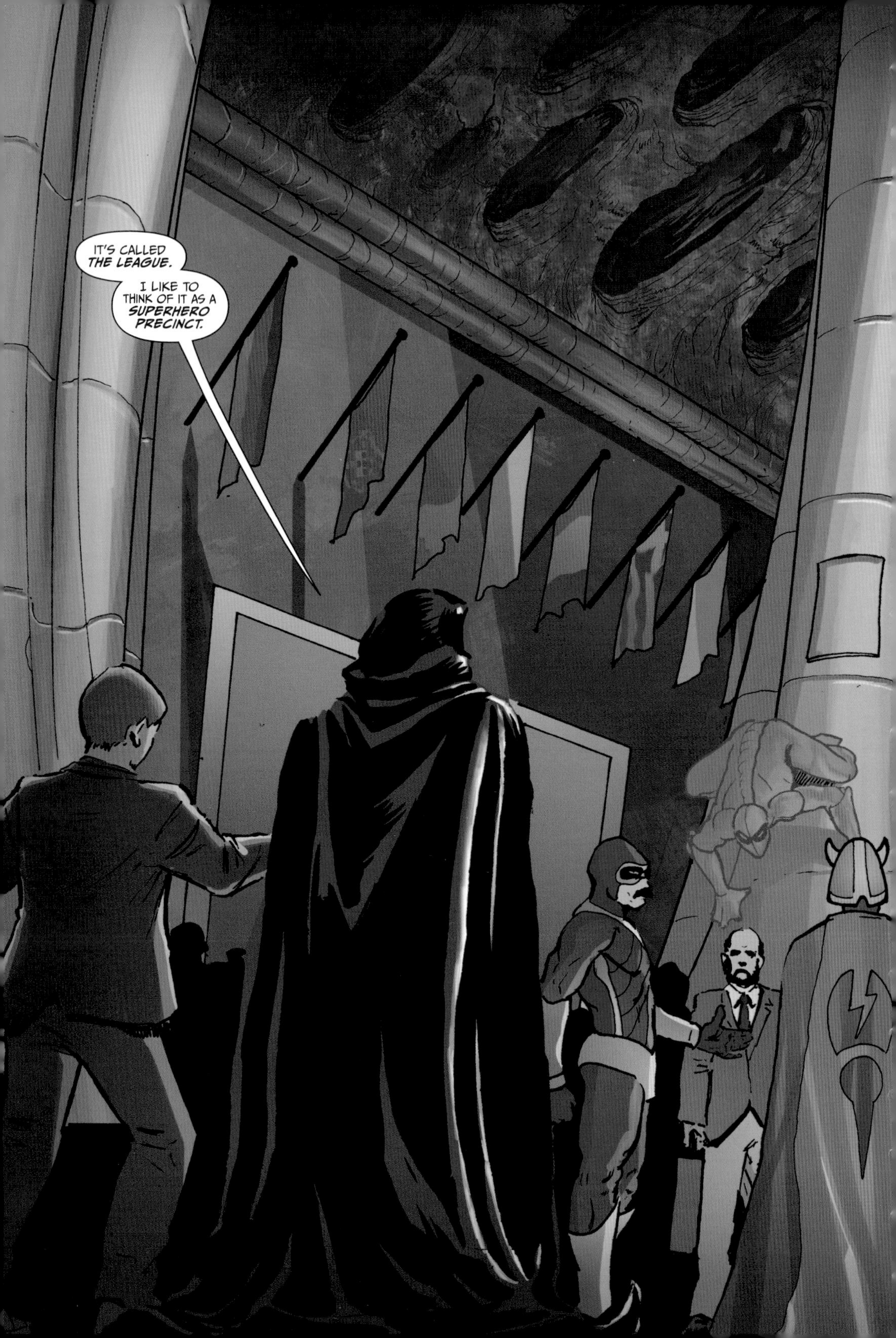
IT'S CALLED ***THE LEAGUE.***
I LIKE TO THINK OF IT AS A ***SUPERHERO PRECINCT.***

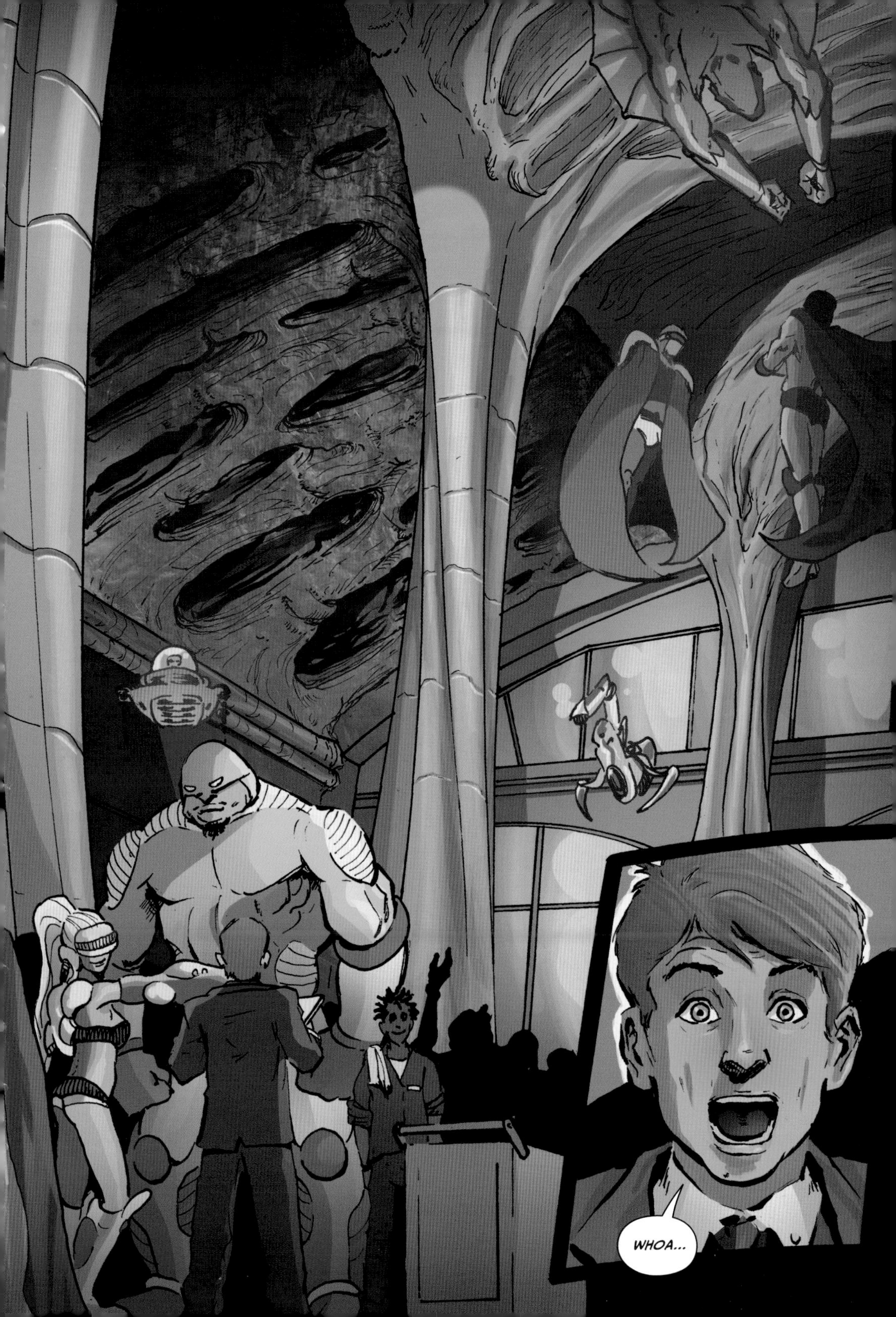
WHOA...

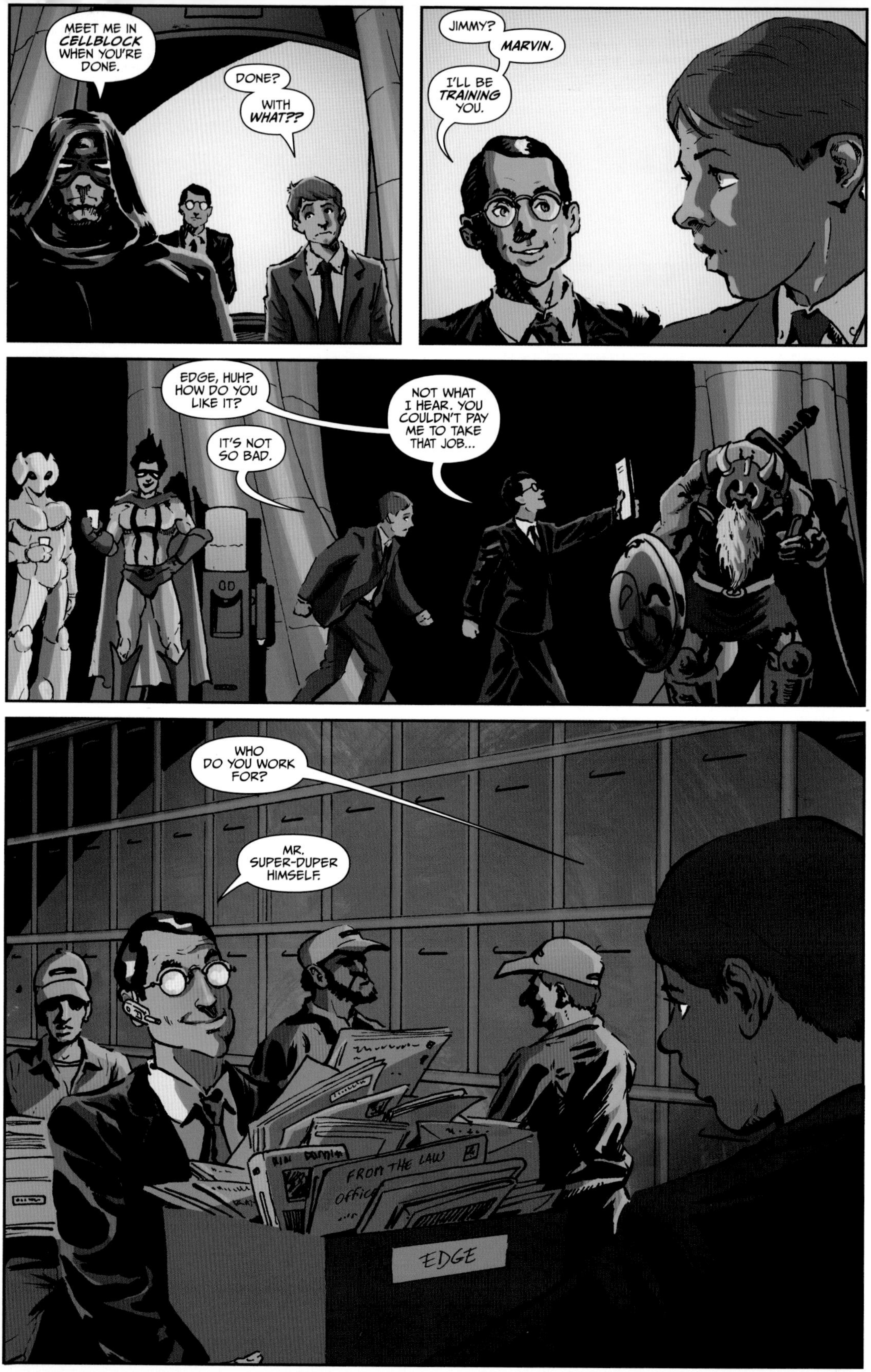
MEET ME IN CELLBLOCK WHEN YOU'RE DONE.
DONE?
WITH WHAT??
JIMMY?
MARVIN.
I'LL BE TRAINING YOU.
EDGE, HUH? HOW DO YOU LIKE IT?
IT'S NOT SO BAD.
NOT WHAT I HEAR. YOU COULDN'T PAY ME TO TAKE THAT JOB...
WHO DO YOU WORK FOR?
MR. SUPER-DUPER HIMSELF.
FROM THE LAW Office
EDGE

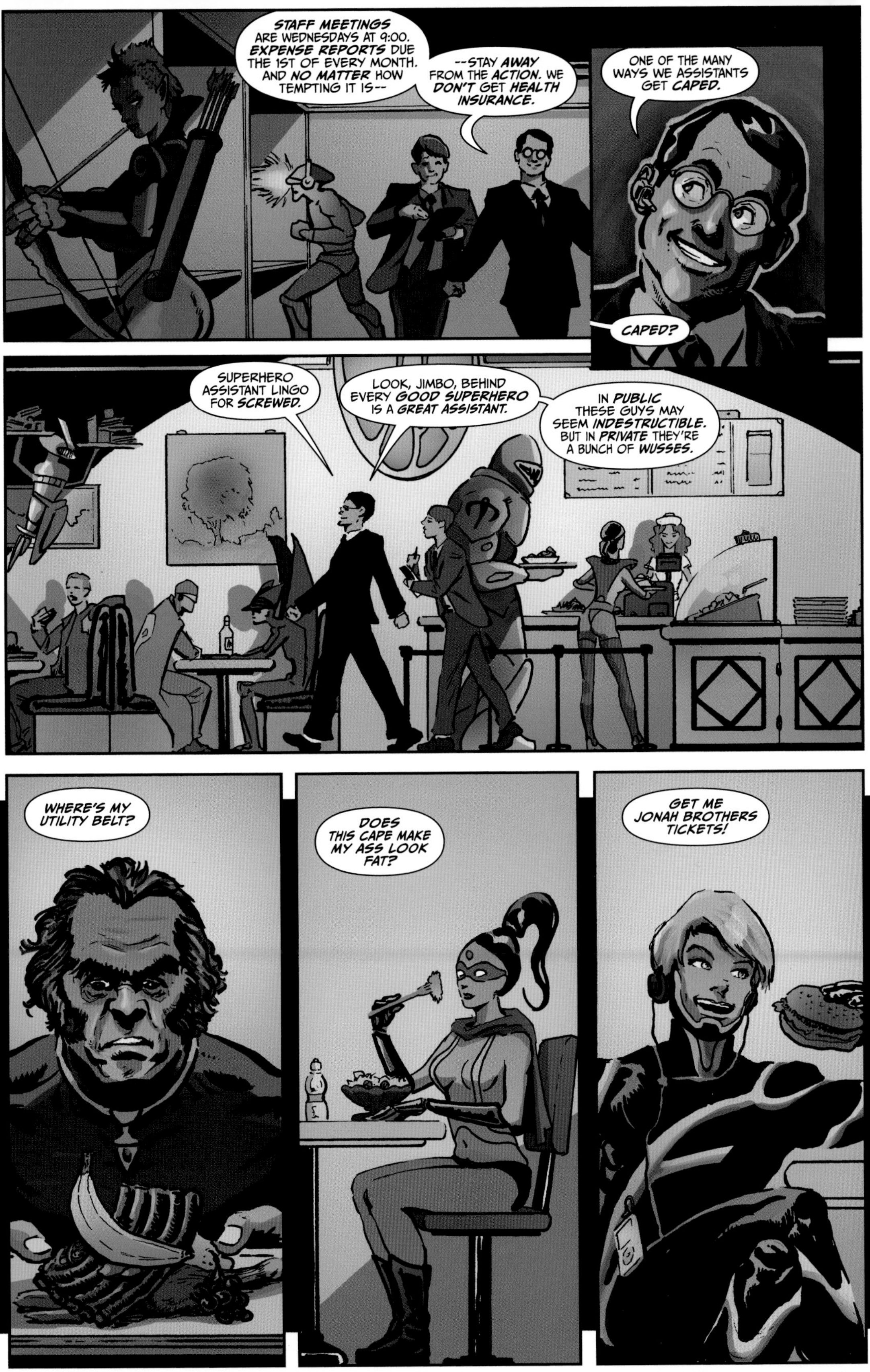
STAFF MEETINGS ARE WEDNESDAYS AT 9:00. EXPENSE REPORTS DUE THE 1ST OF EVERY MONTH. AND NO MATTER HOW TEMPTING IT IS--
--STAY AWAY FROM THE ACTION. WE DON'T GET HEALTH INSURANCE.
ONE OF THE MANY WAYS WE ASSISTANTS GET CAPED.
CAPED?
SUPERHERO ASSISTANT LINGO FOR SCREWED.
LOOK, JIMBO, BEHIND EVERY GOOD SUPERHERO IS A GREAT ASSISTANT.
IN PUBLIC THESE GUYS MAY SEEM INDESTRUCTIBLE. BUT IN PRIVATE THEY'RE A BUNCH OF WUSSES.
WHERE'S MY UTILITY BELT?
DOES THIS CAPE MAKE MY ASS LOOK FAT?
GET ME JONAH BROTHERS TICKETS!

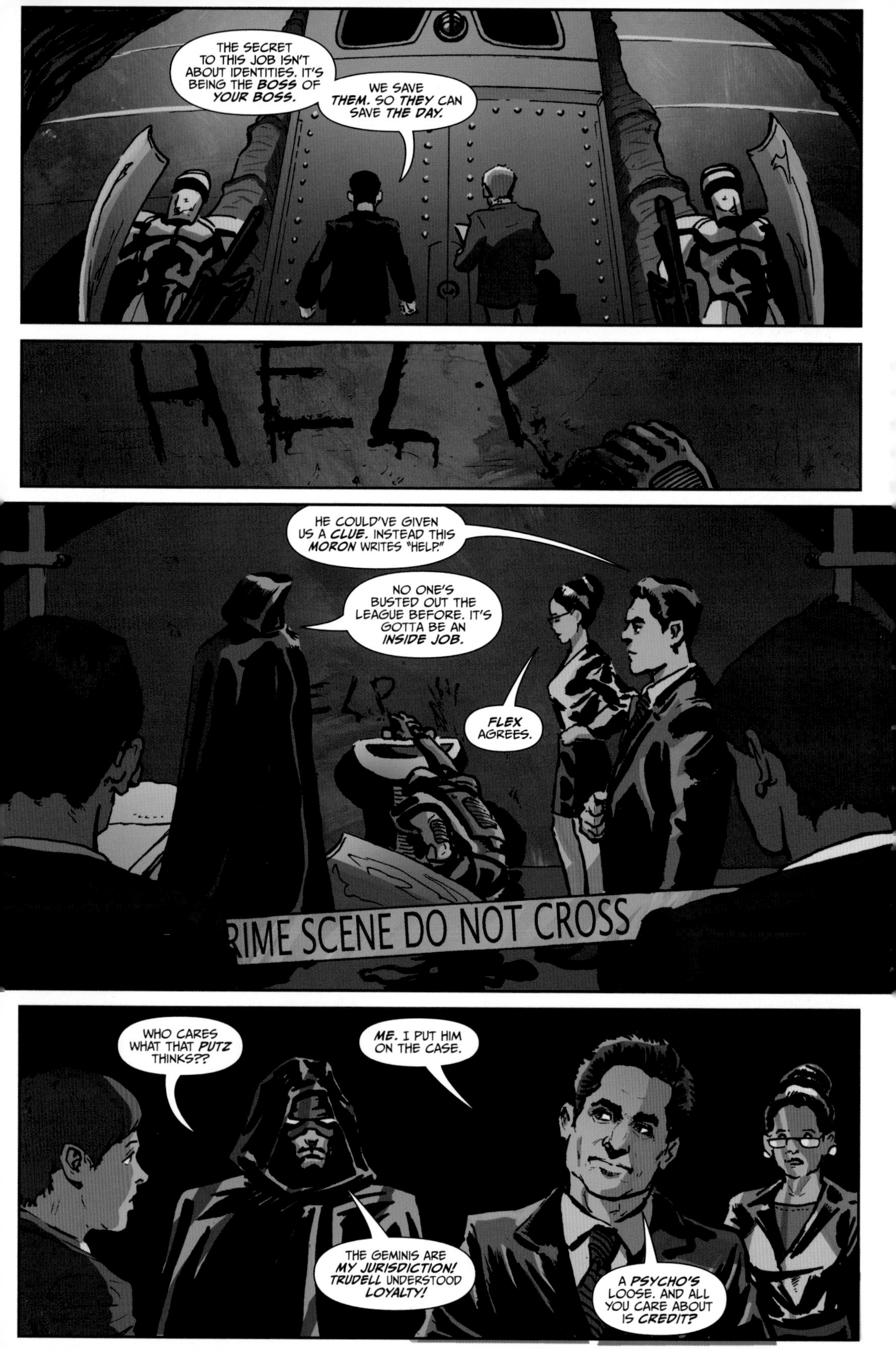
THE SECRET TO THIS JOB ISN'T ABOUT IDENTITIES. IT'S BEING THE BOSS OF YOUR BOSS.
WE SAVE THEM. SO THEY CAN SAVE THE DAY.
HELP
HE COULD'VE GIVEN US A CLUE. INSTEAD THIS MORON WRITES "HELP."
NO ONE'S BUSTED OUT THE LEAGUE BEFORE. IT'S GOTTA BE AN INSIDE JOB.
FLEX AGREES.
RIME SCENE DO NOT CROSS
WHO CARES WHAT THAT PUTZ THINKS??
ME. I PUT HIM ON THE CASE.
THE GEMINIS ARE MY JURISDICTION! TRUDELL UNDERSTOOD LOYALTY!
A PSYCHO'S LOOSE. AND ALL YOU CARE ABOUT IS CREDIT?

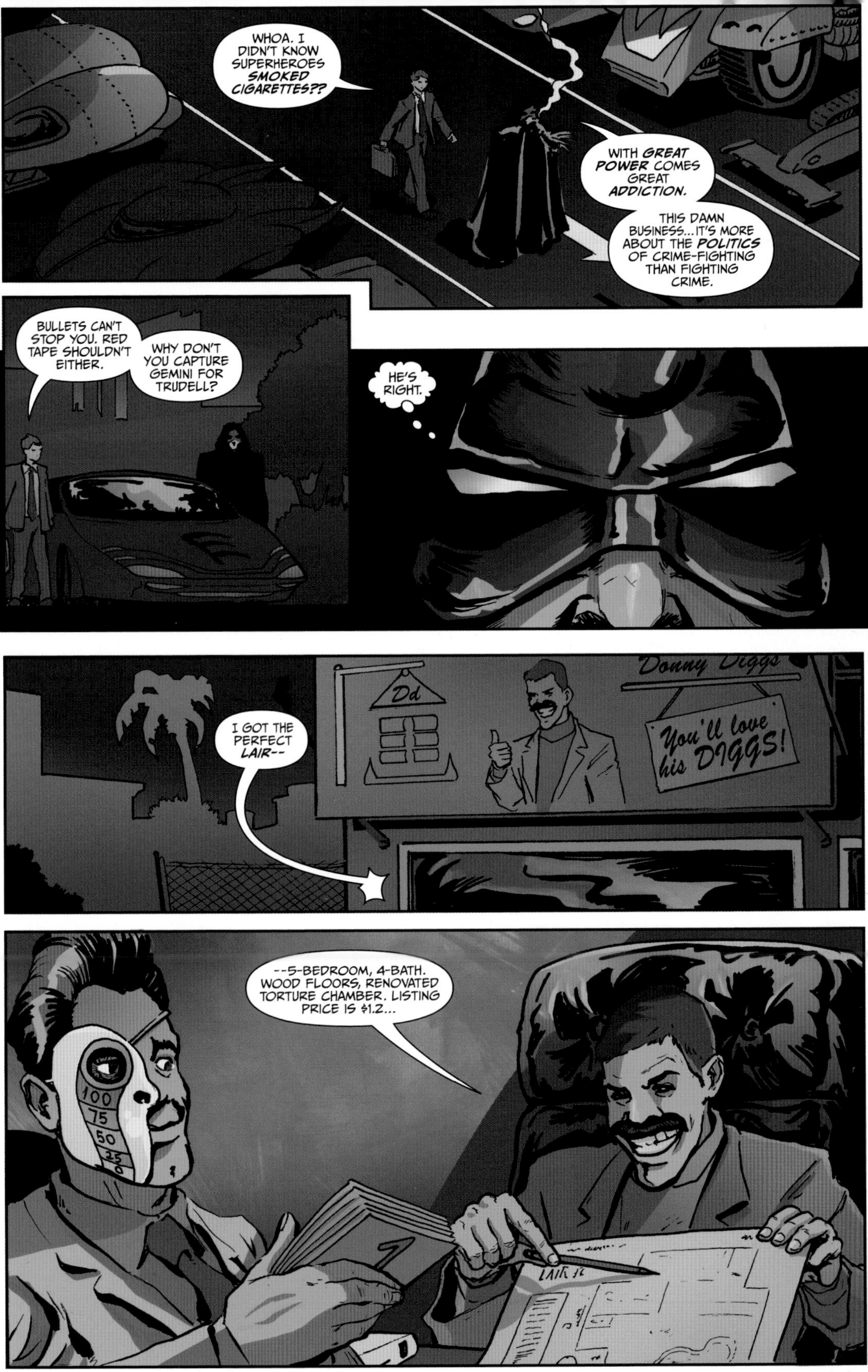
WHOA. I DIDN'T KNOW SUPERHEROES SMOKED CIGARETTES??
WITH GREAT POWER COMES GREAT ADDICTION.
THIS DAMN BUSINESS...IT'S MORE ABOUT THE POLITICS OF CRIME-FIGHTING THAN FIGHTING CRIME.
BULLETS CAN'T STOP YOU. RED TAPE SHOULDN'T EITHER.
WHY DON'T YOU CAPTURE GEMINI FOR TRUDELL?
HE'S RIGHT.
I GOT THE PERFECT LAIR--
Donny Diggs
Dd
You'll love his DIGGS!
--5-BEDROOM, 4-BATH. WOOD FLOORS, RENOVATED TORTURE CHAMBER. LISTING PRICE IS $1.2...
100
75
50
25
0

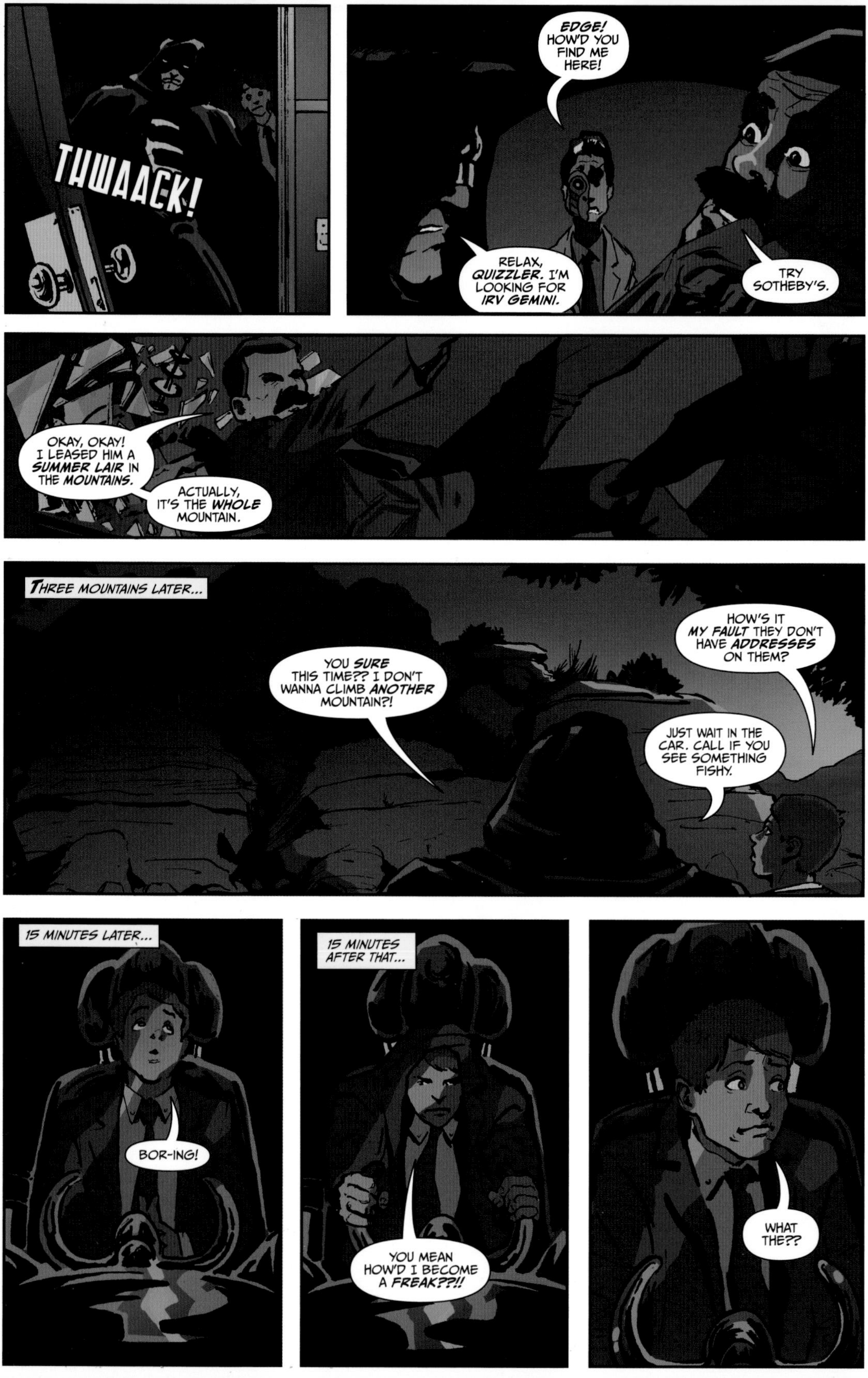
THWAACK!
EDGE! HOW'D YOU FIND ME HERE!
RELAX, QUIZZLER. I'M LOOKING FOR IRV GEMINI.
TRY SOTHEBY'S.
OKAY, OKAY! I LEASED HIM A SUMMER LAIR IN THE MOUNTAINS.
ACTUALLY, IT'S THE WHOLE MOUNTAIN.
THREE MOUNTAINS LATER...
YOU SURE THIS TIME?? I DON'T WANNA CLIMB ANOTHER MOUNTAIN?!
HOW'S IT MY FAULT THEY DON'T HAVE ADDRESSES ON THEM?
JUST WAIT IN THE CAR. CALL IF YOU SEE SOMETHING FISHY.
15 MINUTES LATER...
BOR-ING!
15 MINUTES AFTER THAT...
YOU MEAN HOW'D I BECOME A FREAK??!!
WHAT THE??

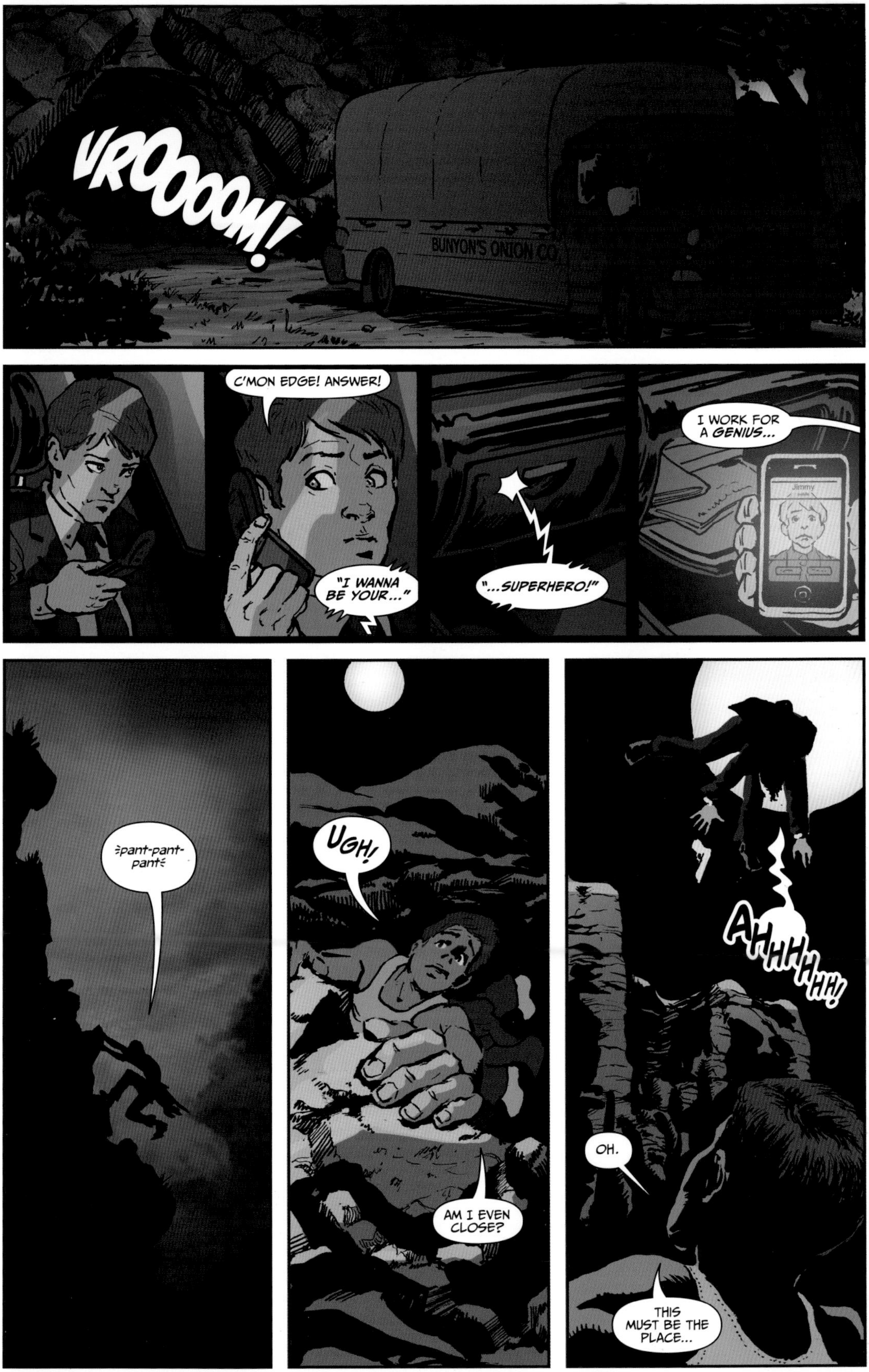
VROOOOM!
BUNYON'S ONION CO.
C'MON EDGE! ANSWER!
"I WANNA BE YOUR..."
"...SUPERHERO!"
I WORK FOR A GENIUS...
Jimmy
pant-pant-pant
UGH!
AM I EVEN CLOSE?
AHHHHHH!
OH.
THIS MUST BE THE PLACE...

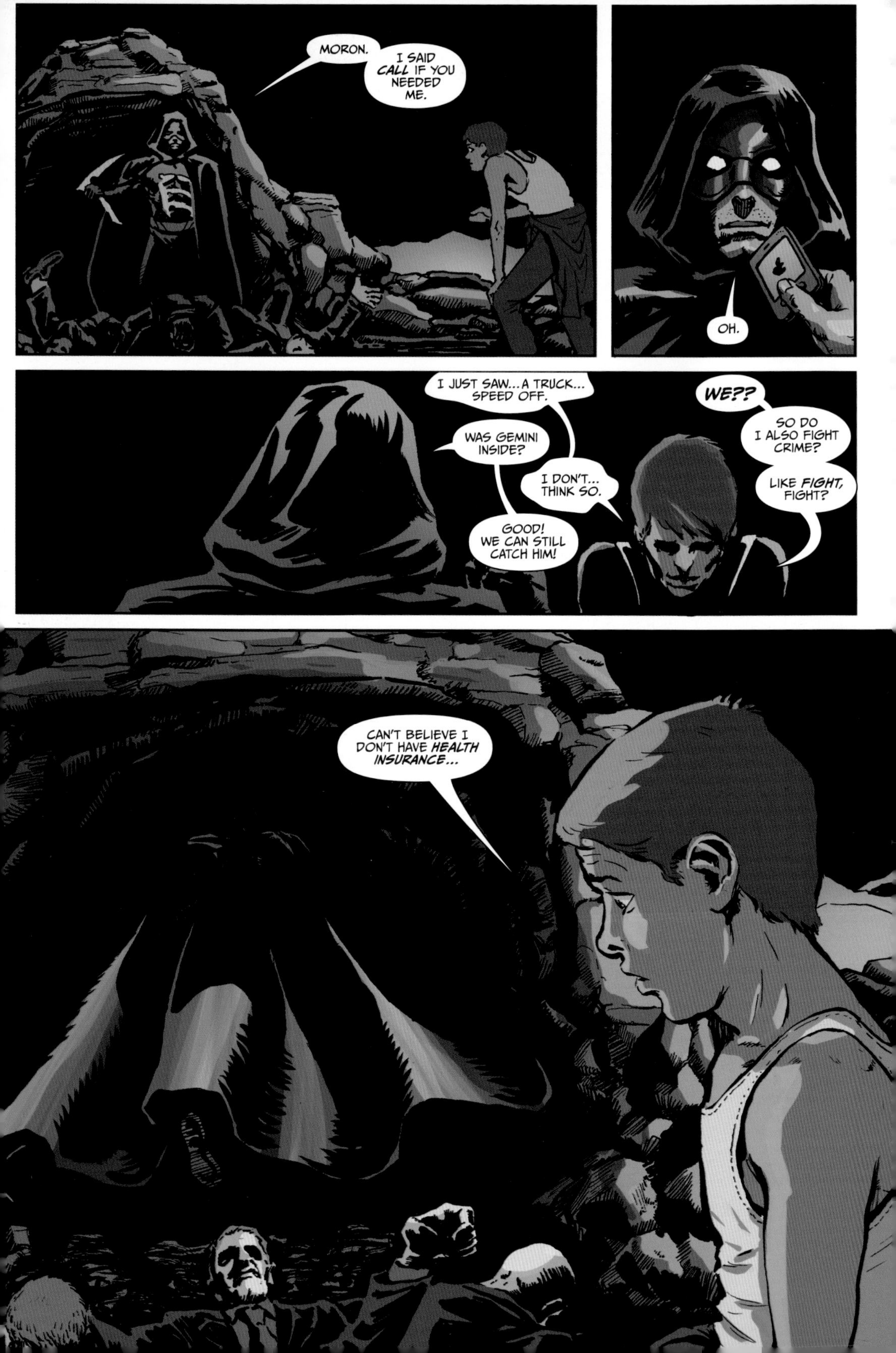
MORON.
I SAID *CALL* IF YOU NEEDED ME.
OH.
I JUST SAW... A TRUCK... SPEED OFF.
WAS GEMINI INSIDE?
I DON'T... THINK SO.
GOOD! WE CAN STILL CATCH HIM!
WE??
SO DO I ALSO FIGHT CRIME?
LIKE *FIGHT*, FIGHT?
CAN'T BELIEVE I DON'T HAVE *HEALTH INSURANCE...*

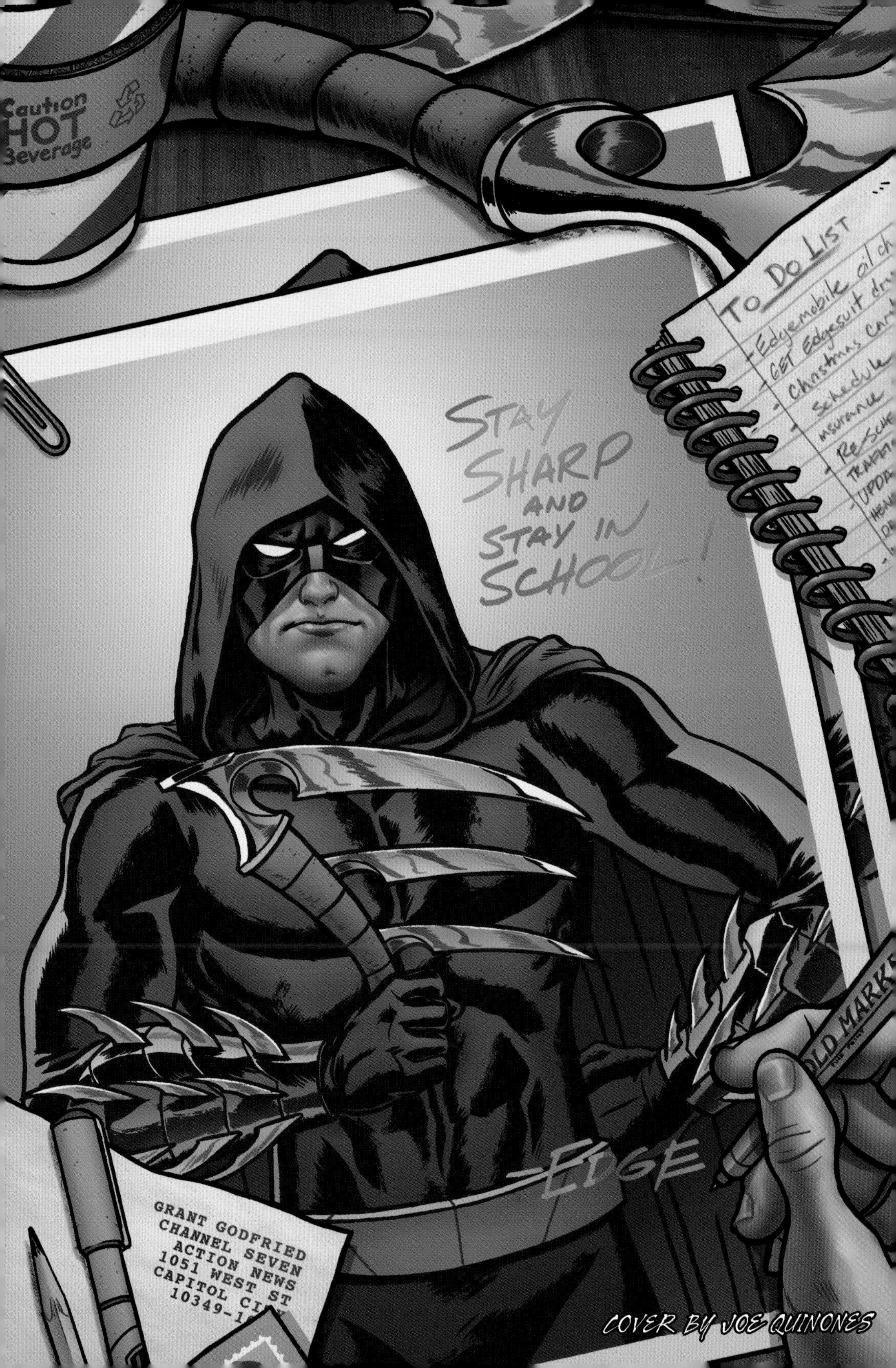
Caution HOT Beverage
TO DO LIST
STAY SHARP AND STAY IN SCHOOL!
-EDGE
GRANT GODFRIED
CHANNEL SEVEN
ACTION NEWS
1051 WEST ST
COVER BY JOE QUINONES

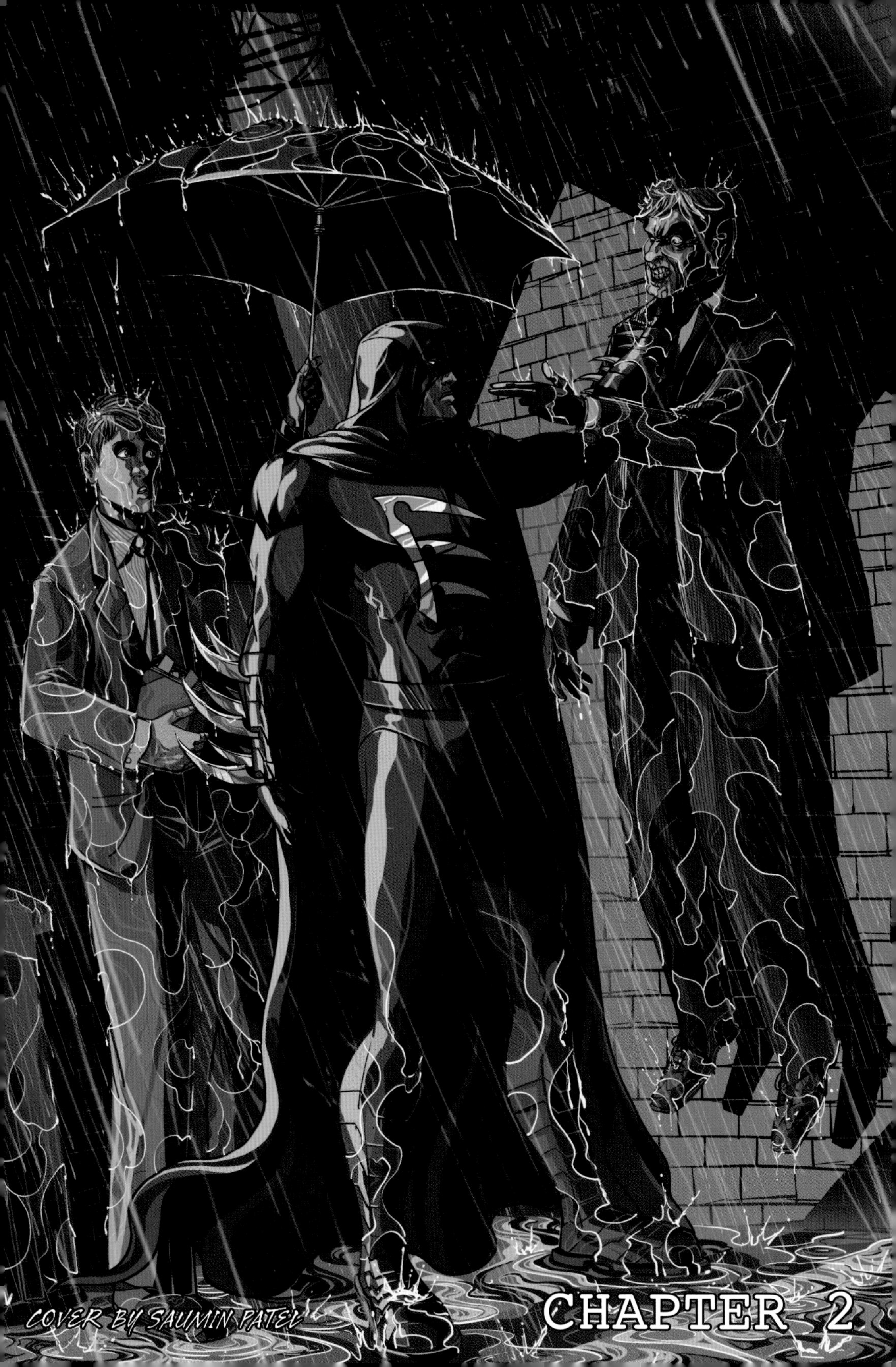
COVER BY SAUMIN PATEL
CHAPTER 2

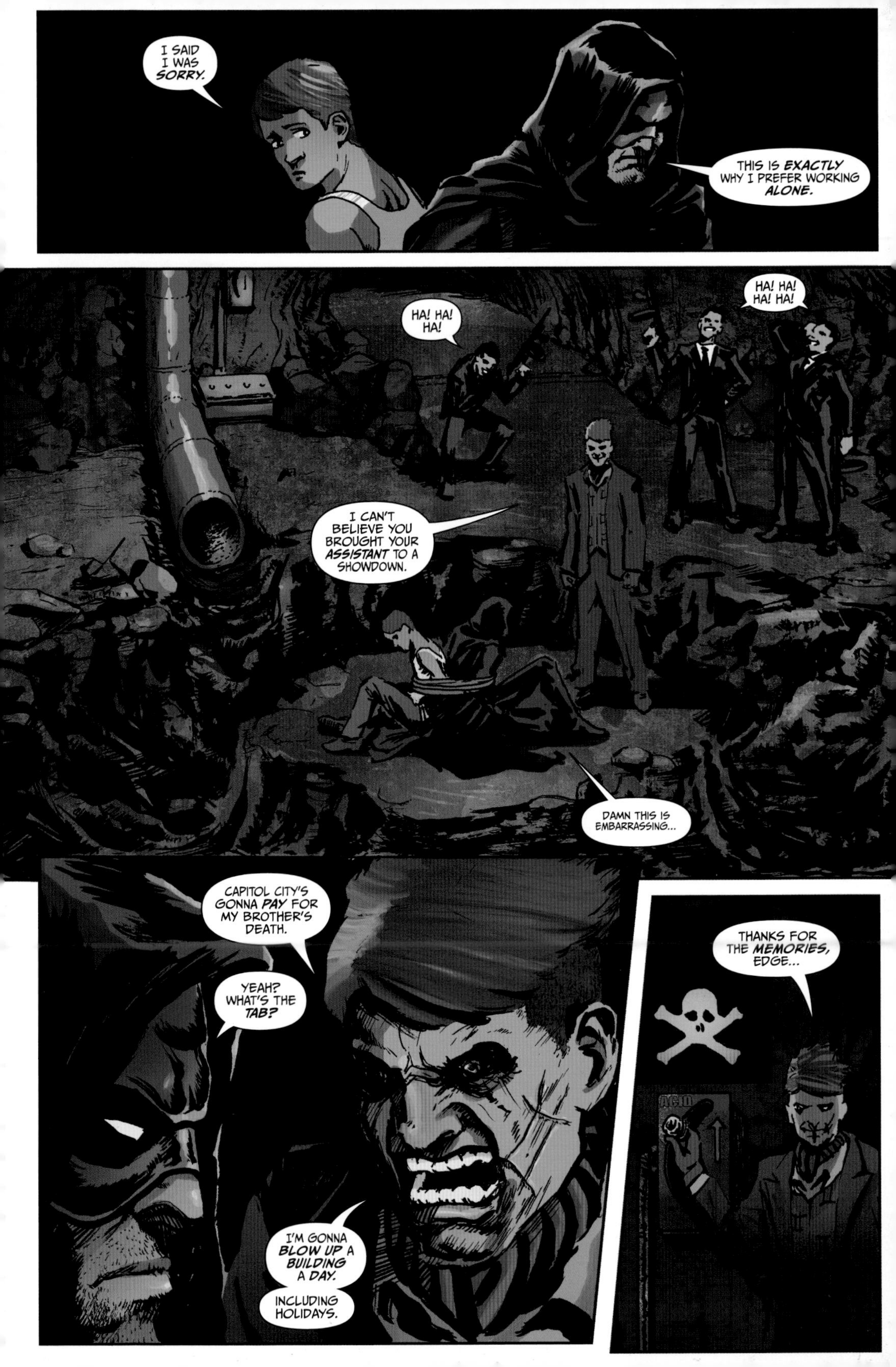
I SAID I WAS SORRY.
THIS IS EXACTLY WHY I PREFER WORKING ALONE.
HA! HA! HA!
HA! HA! HA! HA!
I CAN'T BELIEVE YOU BROUGHT YOUR ASSISTANT TO A SHOWDOWN.
DAMN THIS IS EMBARRASSING...
CAPITOL CITY'S GONNA PAY FOR MY BROTHER'S DEATH.
YEAH? WHAT'S THE TAB?
I'M GONNA BLOW UP A BUILDING A DAY.
INCLUDING HOLIDAYS.
THANKS FOR THE MEMORIES, EDGE...
ACID

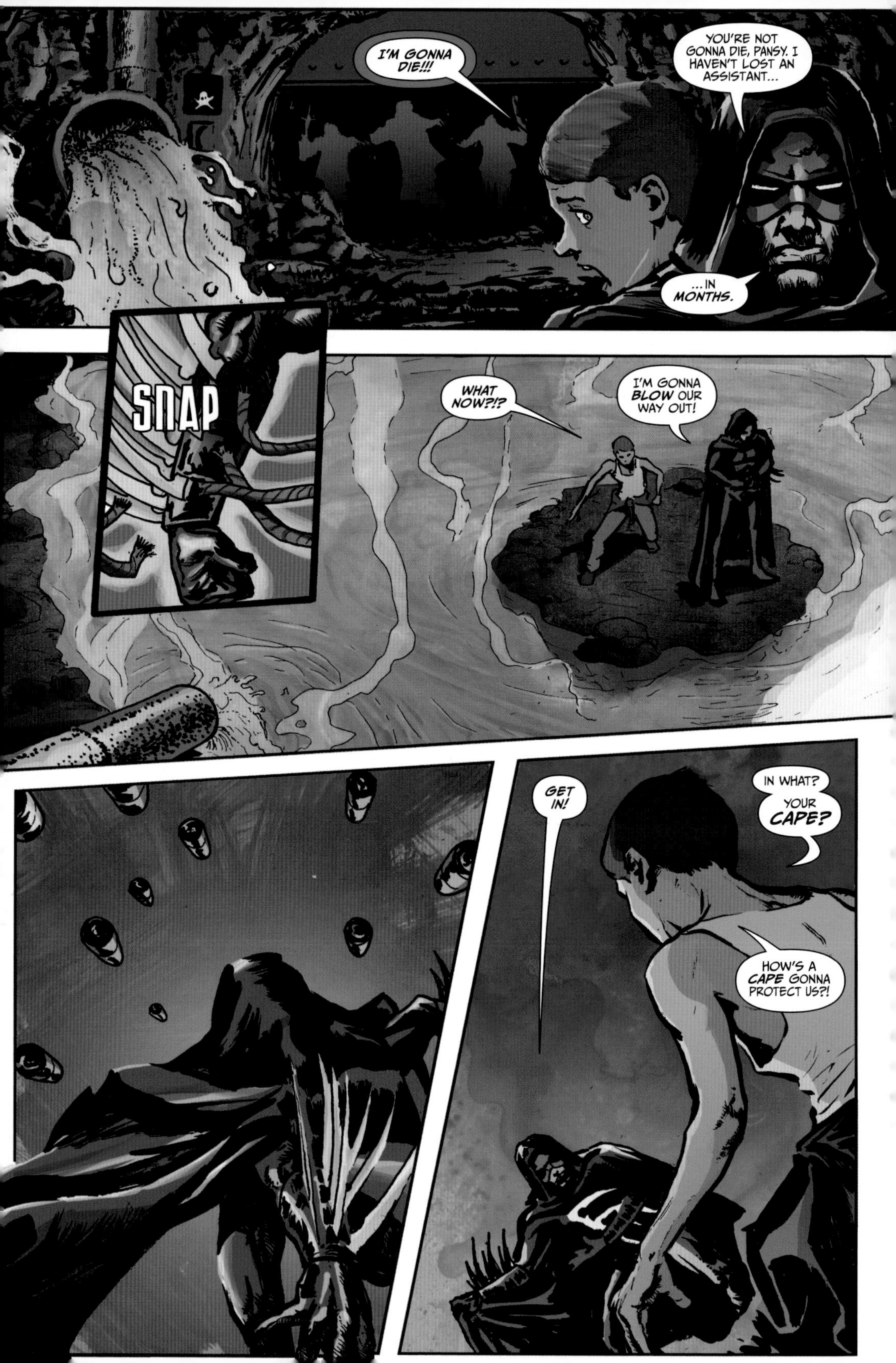
I'M GONNA DIE!!!
YOU'RE NOT GONNA DIE, PANSY. I HAVEN'T LOST AN ASSISTANT...
...IN MONTHS.
SNAP
WHAT NOW?!?
I'M GONNA BLOW OUR WAY OUT!
GET IN!
IN WHAT?
YOUR CAPE?
HOW'S A CAPE GONNA PROTECT US?!

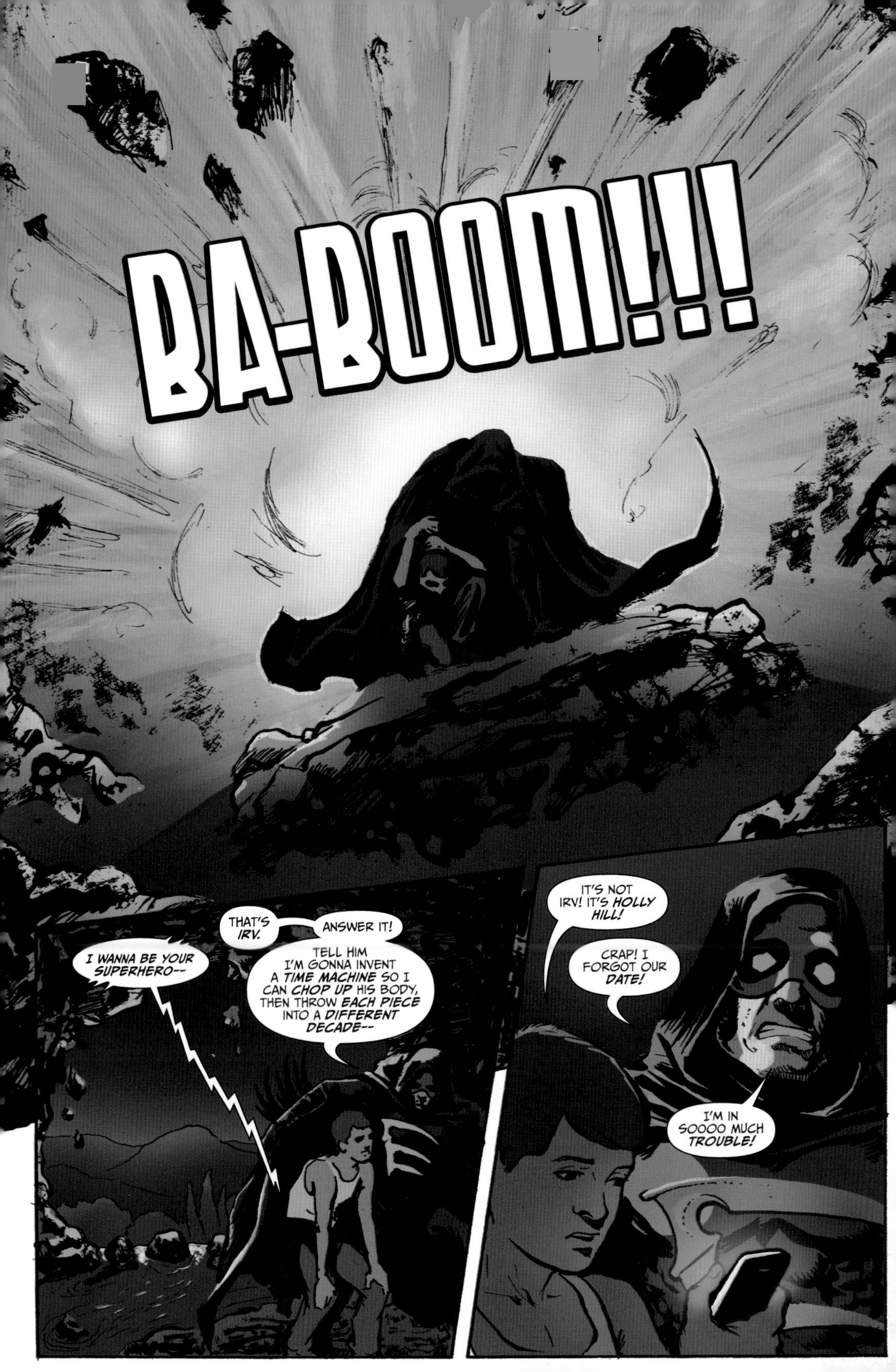
BA-BOOM!!!
I WANNA BE YOUR SUPERHERO--
THAT'S IRV.
ANSWER IT!
TELL HIM I'M GONNA INVENT A TIME MACHINE SO I CAN CHOP UP HIS BODY, THEN THROW EACH PIECE INTO A DIFFERENT DECADE--
IT'S NOT IRV! IT'S HOLLY HILL!
CRAP! I FORGOT OUR DATE!
I'M IN SOOOO MUCH TROUBLE!

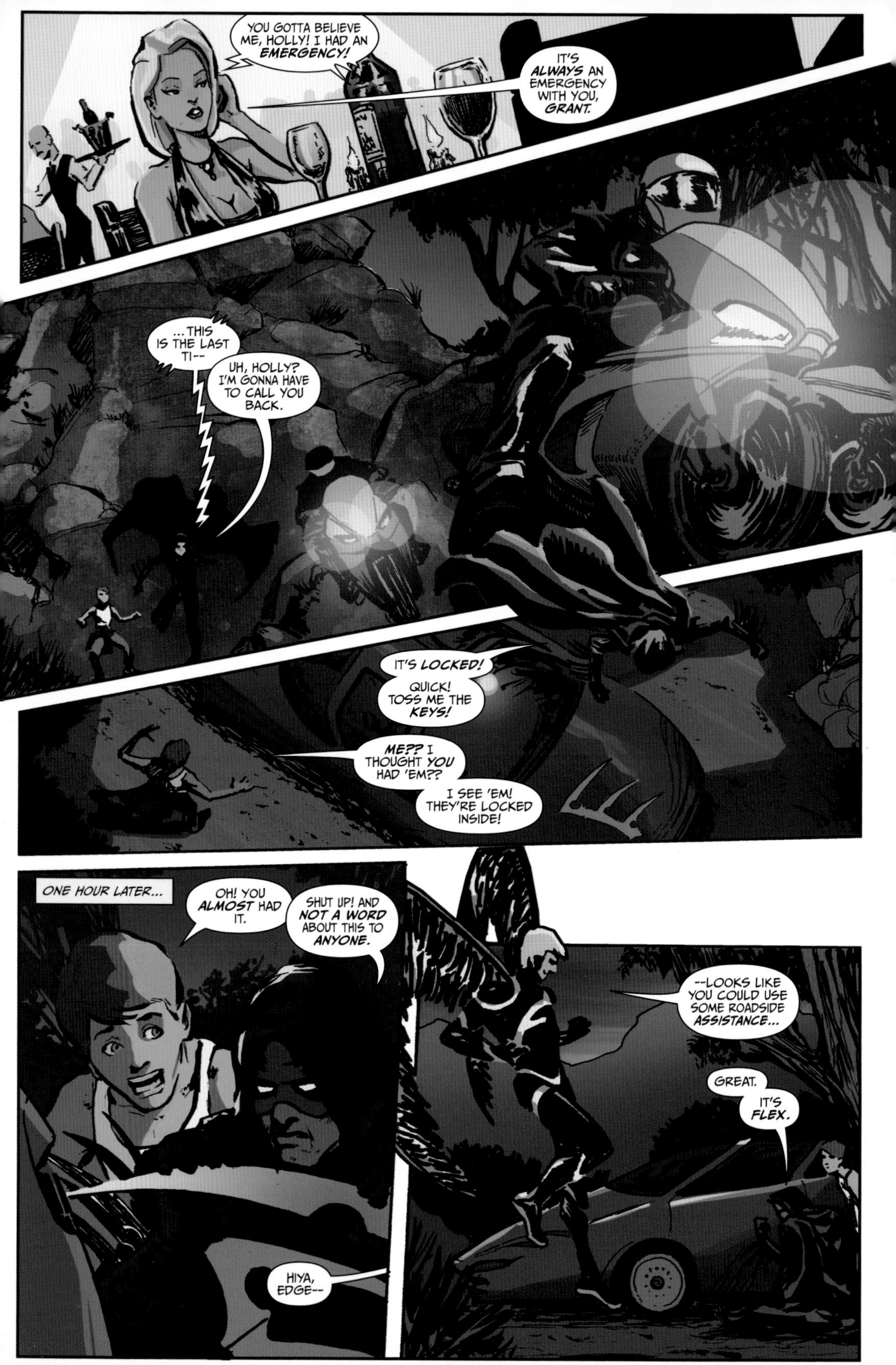
YOU GOTTA BELIEVE ME, HOLLY! I HAD AN EMERGENCY!
IT'S ALWAYS AN EMERGENCY WITH YOU, GRANT.
...THIS IS THE LAST TI--
UH, HOLLY? I'M GONNA HAVE TO CALL YOU BACK.
IT'S LOCKED!
QUICK! TOSS ME THE KEYS!
ME?? I THOUGHT YOU HAD 'EM??
I SEE 'EM! THEY'RE LOCKED INSIDE!
ONE HOUR LATER...
OH! YOU ALMOST HAD IT.
SHUT UP! AND NOT A WORD ABOUT THIS TO ANYONE.
HIYA, EDGE--
--LOOKS LIKE YOU COULD USE SOME ROADSIDE ASSISTANCE...
GREAT. IT'S FLEX.

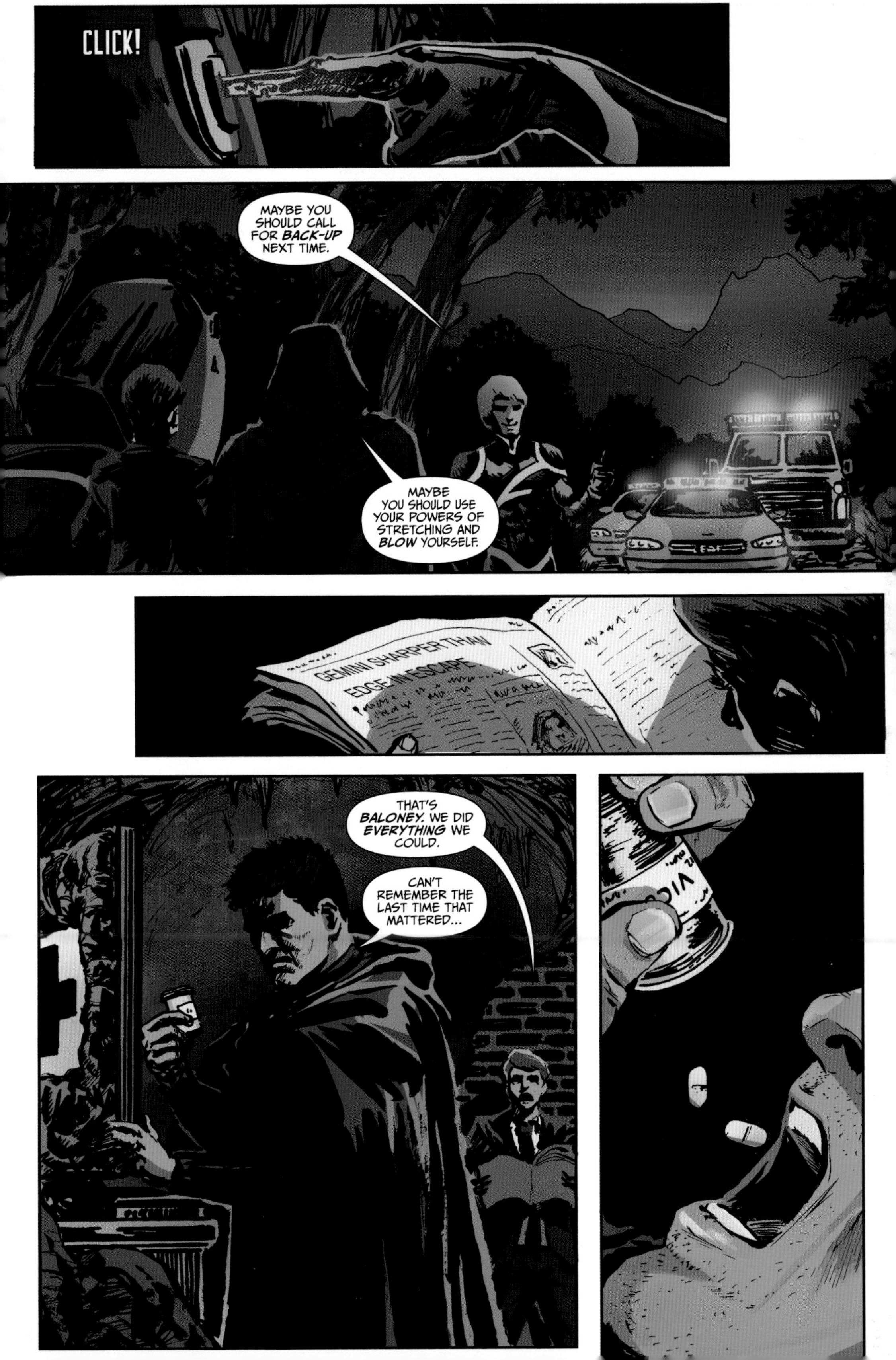
CLICK!
MAYBE YOU SHOULD CALL FOR BACK-UP NEXT TIME.
MAYBE YOU SHOULD USE YOUR POWERS OF STRETCHING AND BLOW YOURSELF.
GEMINI SHARPER THAN EDGE IN ESCAPE
THAT'S BALONEY. WE DID EVERYTHING WE COULD.
CAN'T REMEMBER THE LAST TIME THAT MATTERED...

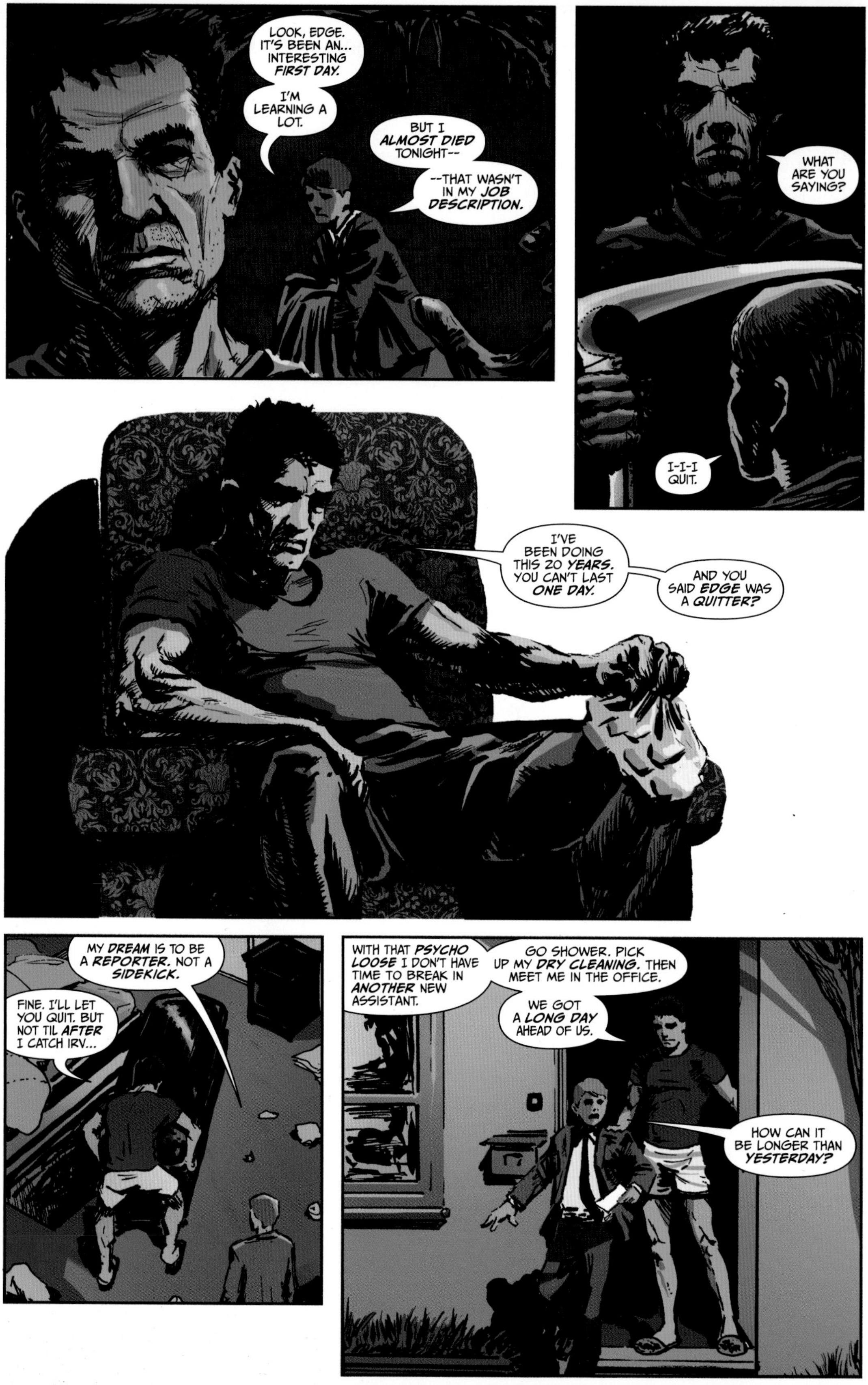
LOOK, EDGE. IT'S BEEN AN... INTERESTING FIRST DAY.
I'M LEARNING A LOT.
BUT I ALMOST DIED TONIGHT--
--THAT WASN'T IN MY JOB DESCRIPTION.
WHAT ARE YOU SAYING?
I-I-I QUIT.
I'VE BEEN DOING THIS 20 YEARS. YOU CAN'T LAST ONE DAY.
AND YOU SAID EDGE WAS A QUITTER?
MY DREAM IS TO BE A REPORTER. NOT A SIDEKICK.
FINE. I'LL LET YOU QUIT. BUT NOT TIL AFTER I CATCH IRV...
WITH THAT PSYCHO LOOSE I DON'T HAVE TIME TO BREAK IN ANOTHER NEW ASSISTANT.
GO SHOWER. PICK UP MY DRY CLEANING. THEN MEET ME IN THE OFFICE.
WE GOT A LONG DAY AHEAD OF US.
HOW CAN IT BE LONGER THAN YESTERDAY?

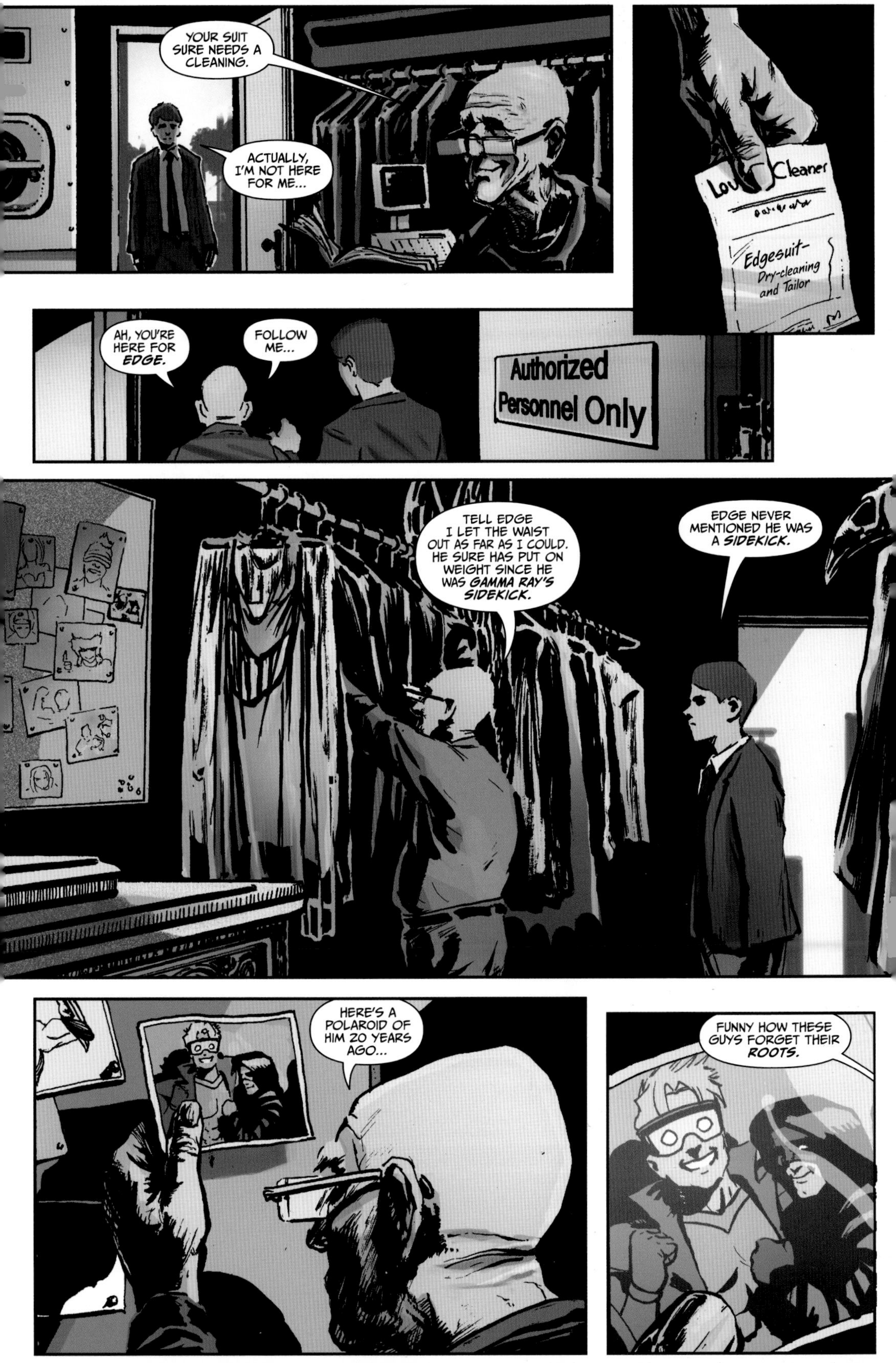
YOUR SUIT SURE NEEDS A CLEANING.
ACTUALLY, I'M NOT HERE FOR ME...
Cleaner
Edgesuit- Dry-cleaning and Tailor
AH, YOU'RE HERE FOR EDGE.
FOLLOW ME...
Authorized Personnel Only
TELL EDGE I LET THE WAIST OUT AS FAR AS I COULD. HE SURE HAS PUT ON WEIGHT SINCE HE WAS GAMMA RAY'S SIDEKICK.
EDGE NEVER MENTIONED HE WAS A SIDEKICK.
HERE'S A POLAROID OF HIM 20 YEARS AGO...
FUNNY HOW THESE GUYS FORGET THEIR ROOTS.

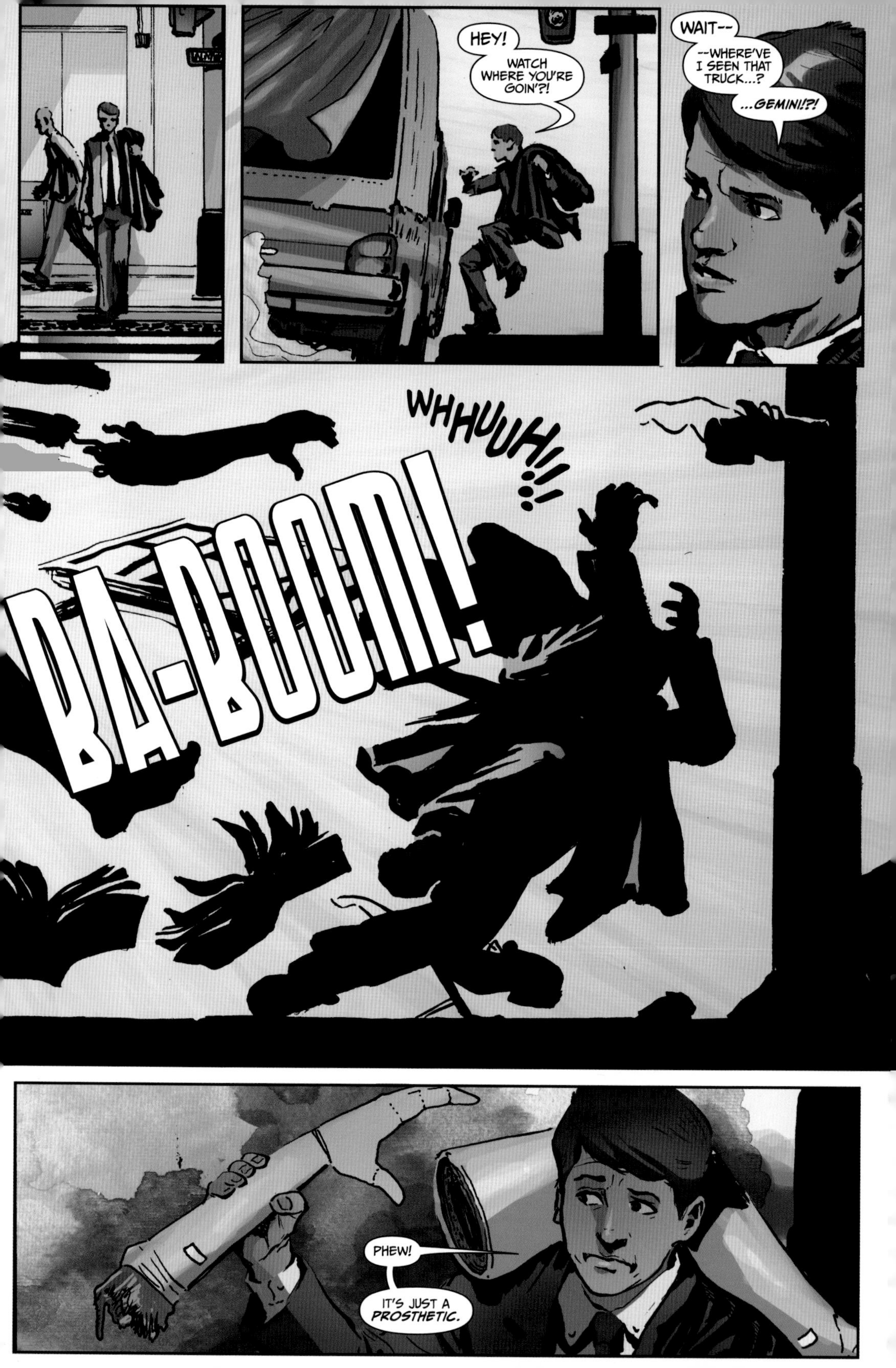
HEY!
WATCH WHERE YOU'RE GOIN'?!
WAIT--
--WHERE'VE I SEEN THAT TRUCK...?
...GEMINI!?!
WHHUUUH!!!
BA-BOOM!
PHEW!
IT'S JUST A PROSTHETIC.

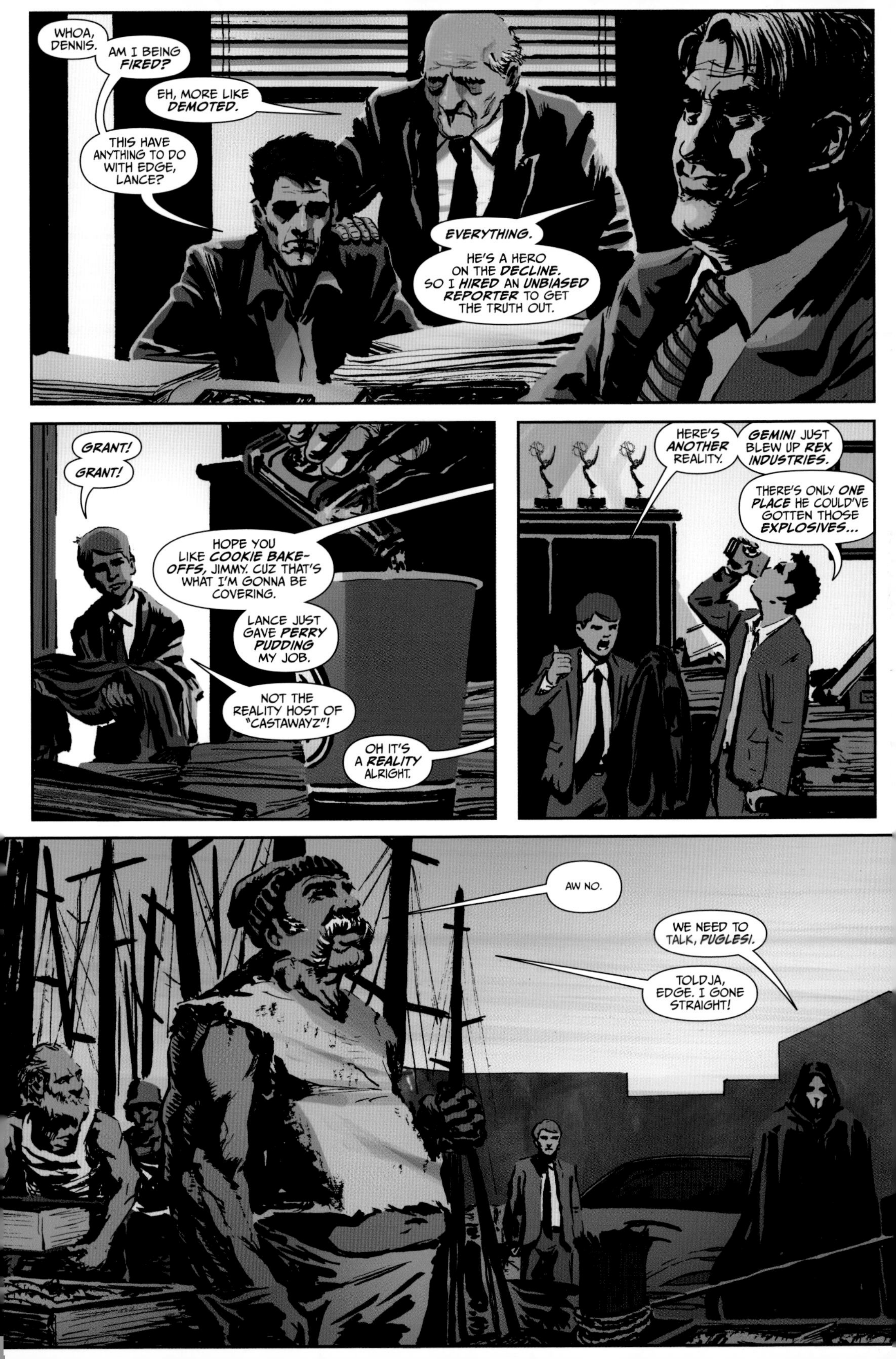
WHOA, DENNIS.
AM I BEING *FIRED?*
EH, MORE LIKE *DEMOTED.*
THIS HAVE ANYTHING TO DO WITH EDGE, LANCE?
EVERYTHING.
HE'S A HERO ON THE *DECLINE.* SO I *HIRED* AN *UNBIASED REPORTER* TO GET THE TRUTH OUT.
GRANT!
GRANT!
HOPE YOU LIKE *COOKIE BAKE-OFFS,* JIMMY. CUZ THAT'S WHAT I'M GONNA BE COVERING.
LANCE JUST GAVE *PERRY PUDDING* MY JOB.
NOT THE REALITY HOST OF "CASTAWAYZ"!
OH IT'S A *REALITY* ALRIGHT.
HERE'S *ANOTHER* REALITY.
GEMINI JUST BLEW UP *REX INDUSTRIES.*
THERE'S ONLY *ONE PLACE* HE COULD'VE GOTTEN THOSE *EXPLOSIVES...*
AW NO.
WE NEED TO TALK, *PUGLESI.*
TOLDJA, EDGE. I GONE STRAIGHT!

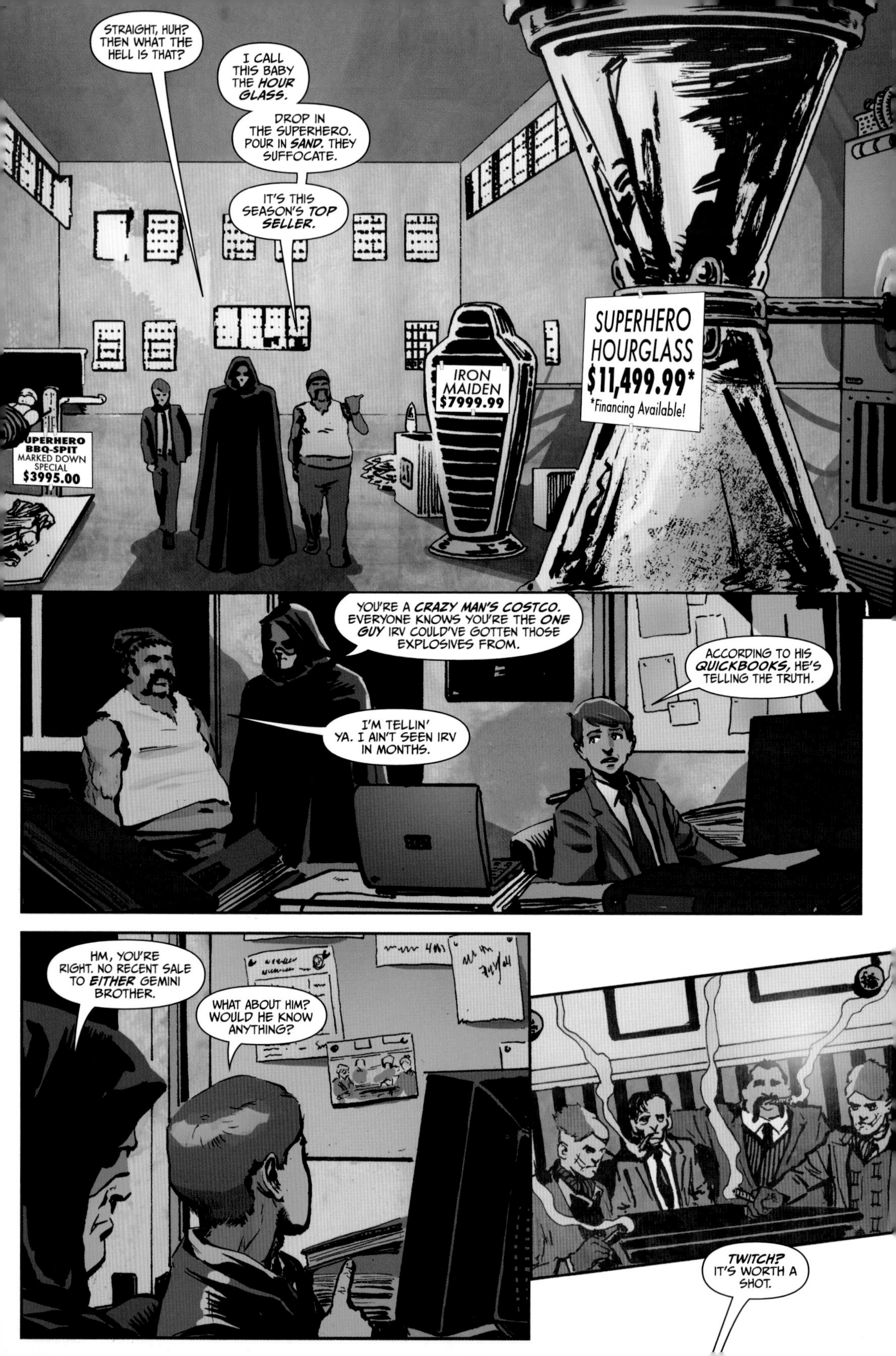
STRAIGHT, HUH? THEN WHAT THE HELL IS THAT?
I CALL THIS BABY THE HOUR GLASS.
DROP IN THE SUPERHERO. POUR IN SAND. THEY SUFFOCATE.
IT'S THIS SEASON'S TOP SELLER.
SUPERHERO HOURGLASS $11,499.99* *Financing Available!
IRON MAIDEN $7999.99
SUPERHERO BBQ-SPIT MARKED DOWN SPECIAL $3995.00
YOU'RE A CRAZY MAN'S COSTCO. EVERYONE KNOWS YOU'RE THE ONE GUY IRV COULD'VE GOTTEN THOSE EXPLOSIVES FROM.
I'M TELLIN' YA. I AIN'T SEEN IRV IN MONTHS.
ACCORDING TO HIS QUICKBOOKS, HE'S TELLING THE TRUTH.
HM, YOU'RE RIGHT. NO RECENT SALE TO EITHER GEMINI BROTHER.
WHAT ABOUT HIM? WOULD HE KNOW ANYTHING?
TWITCH? IT'S WORTH A SHOT.

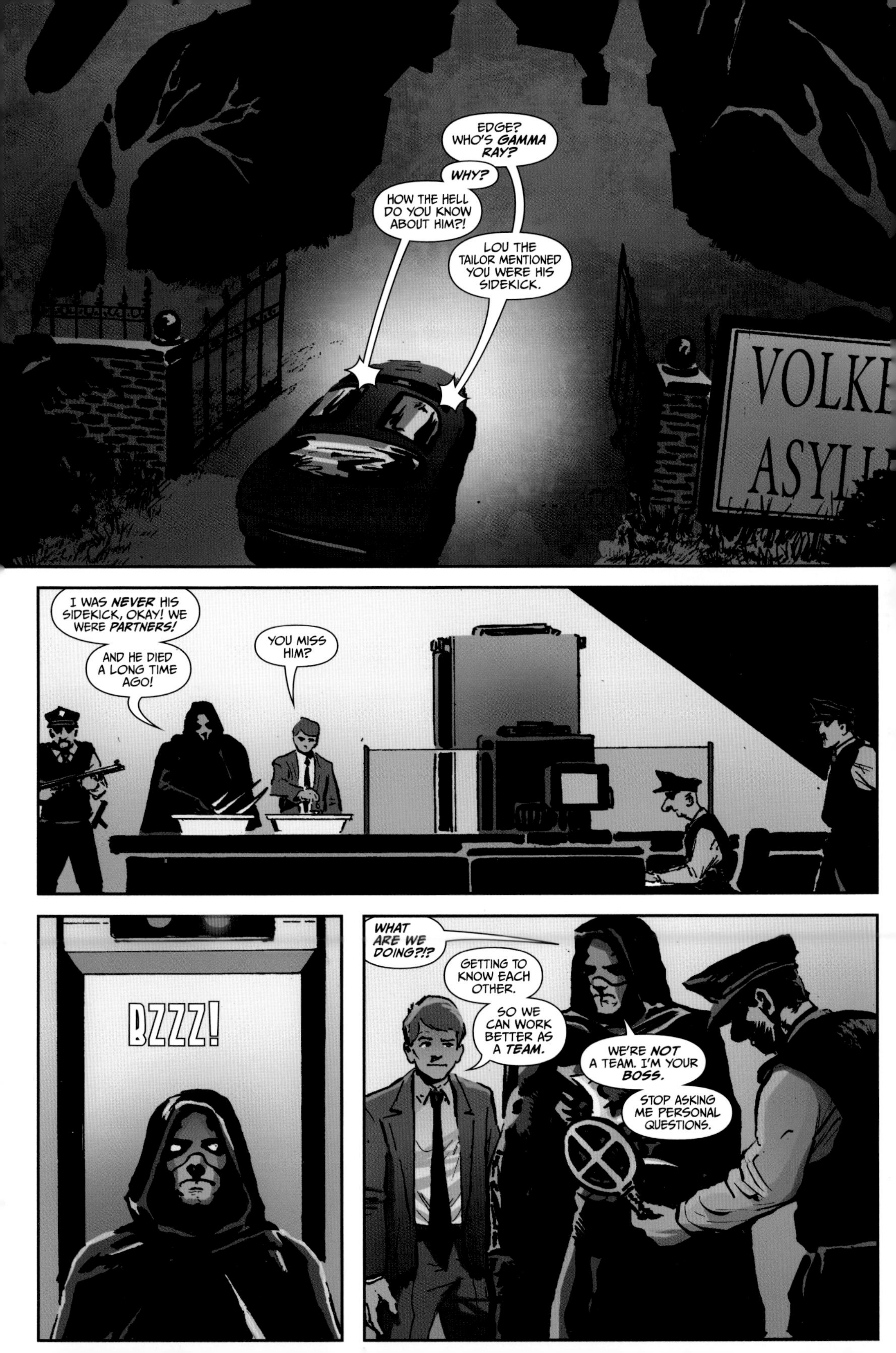
EDGE? WHO'S *GAMMA RAY?*
WHY?
HOW THE HELL DO YOU KNOW ABOUT HIM?!
LOU THE TAILOR MENTIONED YOU WERE HIS SIDEKICK.
VOLKE
ASYL
I WAS *NEVER* HIS SIDEKICK, OKAY! WE WERE *PARTNERS!*
AND HE DIED A LONG TIME AGO!
YOU MISS HIM?
BZZZ!
WHAT ARE WE DOING?!?
GETTING TO KNOW EACH OTHER.
SO WE CAN WORK BETTER AS A *TEAM.*
WE'RE *NOT* A TEAM. I'M YOUR *BOSS.*
STOP ASKING ME PERSONAL QUESTIONS.

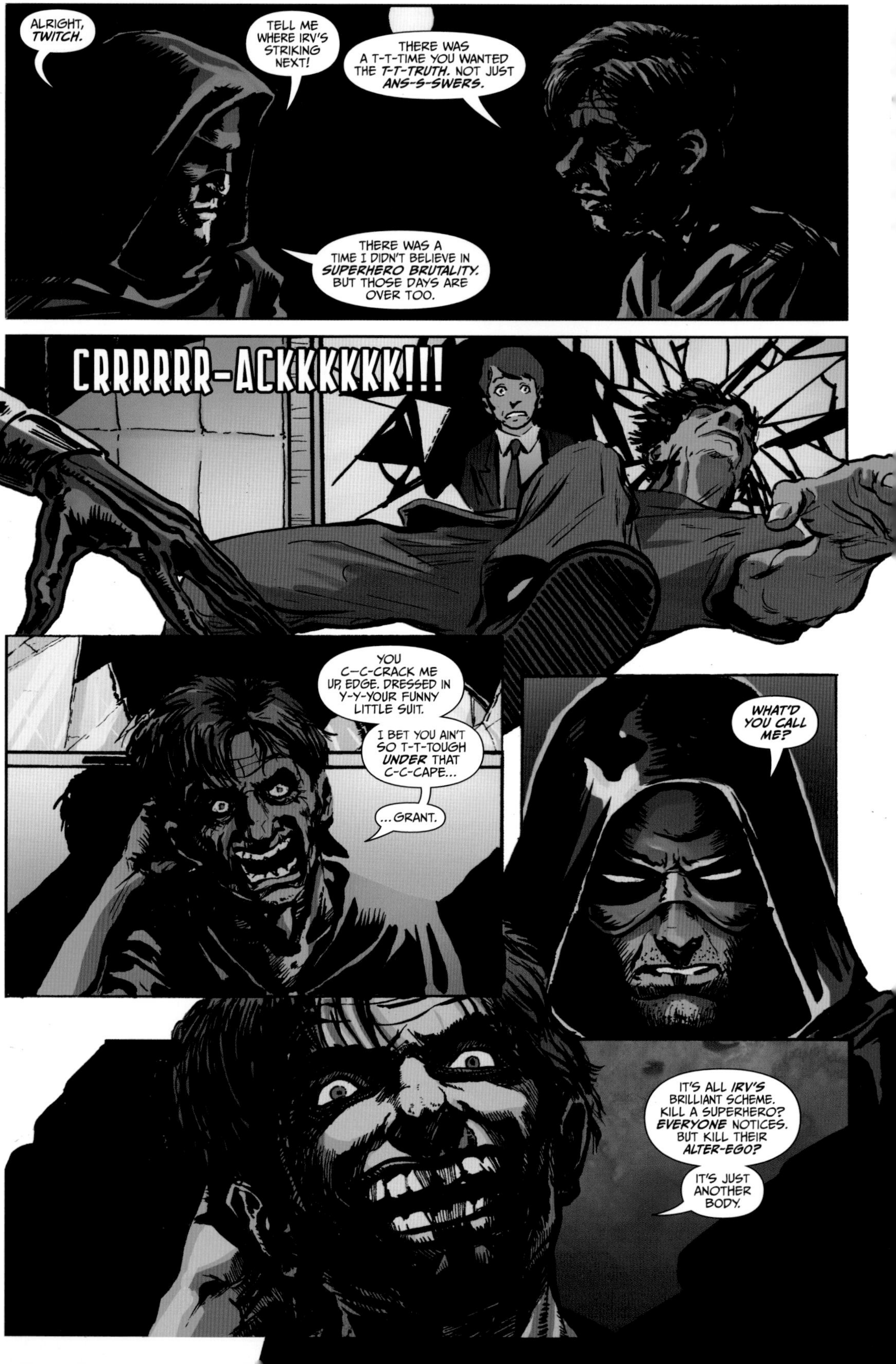
ALRIGHT, TWITCH.
TELL ME WHERE IRV'S STRIKING NEXT!
THERE WAS A T-T-TIME YOU WANTED THE T-T-TRUTH. NOT JUST ANS-S-SWERS.
THERE WAS A TIME I DIDN'T BELIEVE IN SUPERHERO BRUTALITY. BUT THOSE DAYS ARE OVER TOO.
CRRRRRR-ACKKKKKK!!!
YOU C-C-CRACK ME UP, EDGE. DRESSED IN Y-Y-YOUR FUNNY LITTLE SUIT.
I BET YOU AIN'T SO T-T-TOUGH UNDER THAT C-C-CAPE...
...GRANT.
WHAT'D YOU CALL ME?
IT'S ALL IRV'S BRILLIANT SCHEME. KILL A SUPERHERO? EVERYONE NOTICES. BUT KILL THEIR ALTER-EGO?
IT'S JUST ANOTHER BODY.

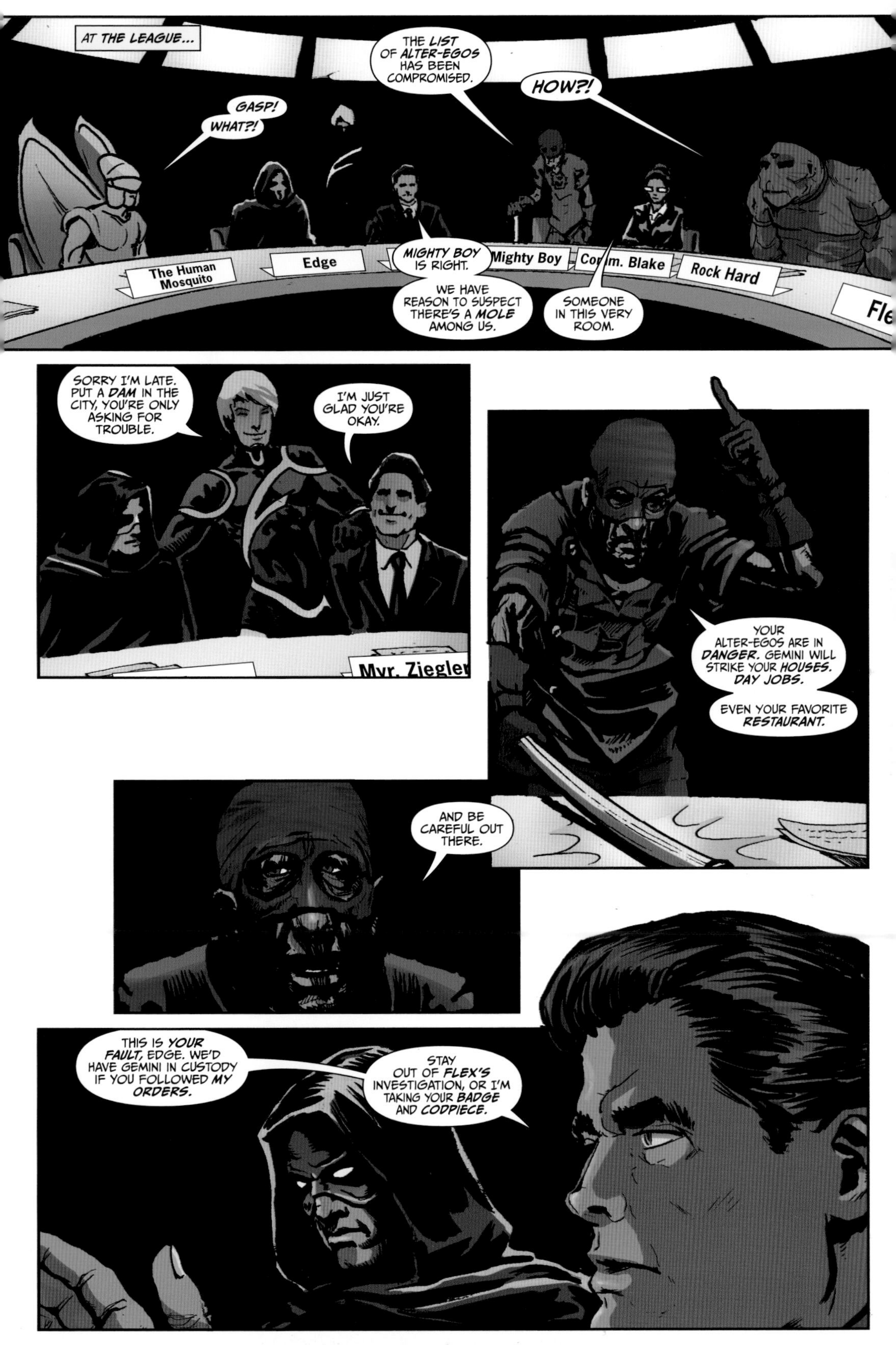
AT THE LEAGUE...
GASP!
WHAT?!
THE LIST OF ALTER-EGOS HAS BEEN COMPROMISED.
HOW?!
The Human Mosquito
Edge
Mighty Boy
Comm. Blake
Rock Hard
MIGHTY BOY IS RIGHT.
WE HAVE REASON TO SUSPECT THERE'S A MOLE AMONG US.
SOMEONE IN THIS VERY ROOM.
SORRY I'M LATE. PUT A DAM IN THE CITY, YOU'RE ONLY ASKING FOR TROUBLE.
I'M JUST GLAD YOU'RE OKAY.
Myr. Ziegler
YOUR ALTER-EGOS ARE IN DANGER. GEMINI WILL STRIKE YOUR HOUSES. DAY JOBS.
EVEN YOUR FAVORITE RESTAURANT.
AND BE CAREFUL OUT THERE.
THIS IS YOUR FAULT, EDGE. WE'D HAVE GEMINI IN CUSTODY IF YOU FOLLOWED MY ORDERS.
STAY OUT OF FLEX'S INVESTIGATION, OR I'M TAKING YOUR BADGE AND CODPIECE.

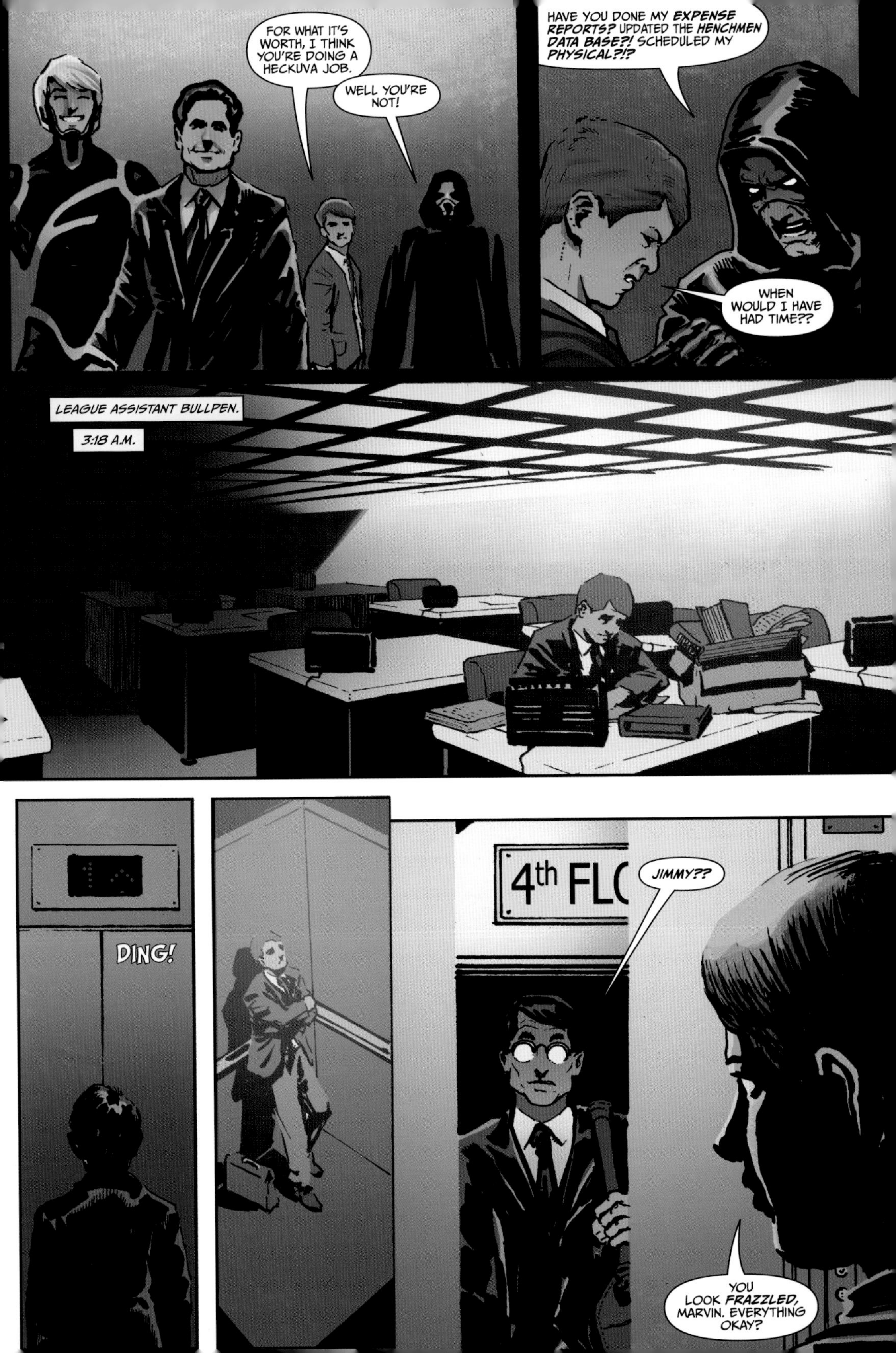
FOR WHAT IT'S WORTH, I THINK YOU'RE DOING A HECKUVA JOB.
WELL YOU'RE NOT!
HAVE YOU DONE MY EXPENSE REPORTS? UPDATED THE HENCHMEN DATA BASE?! SCHEDULED MY PHYSICAL?!?
WHEN WOULD I HAVE HAD TIME??
LEAGUE ASSISTANT BULLPEN.
3:18 A.M.
DING!
4th FLO
JIMMY??
YOU LOOK FRAZZLED, MARVIN. EVERYTHING OKAY?

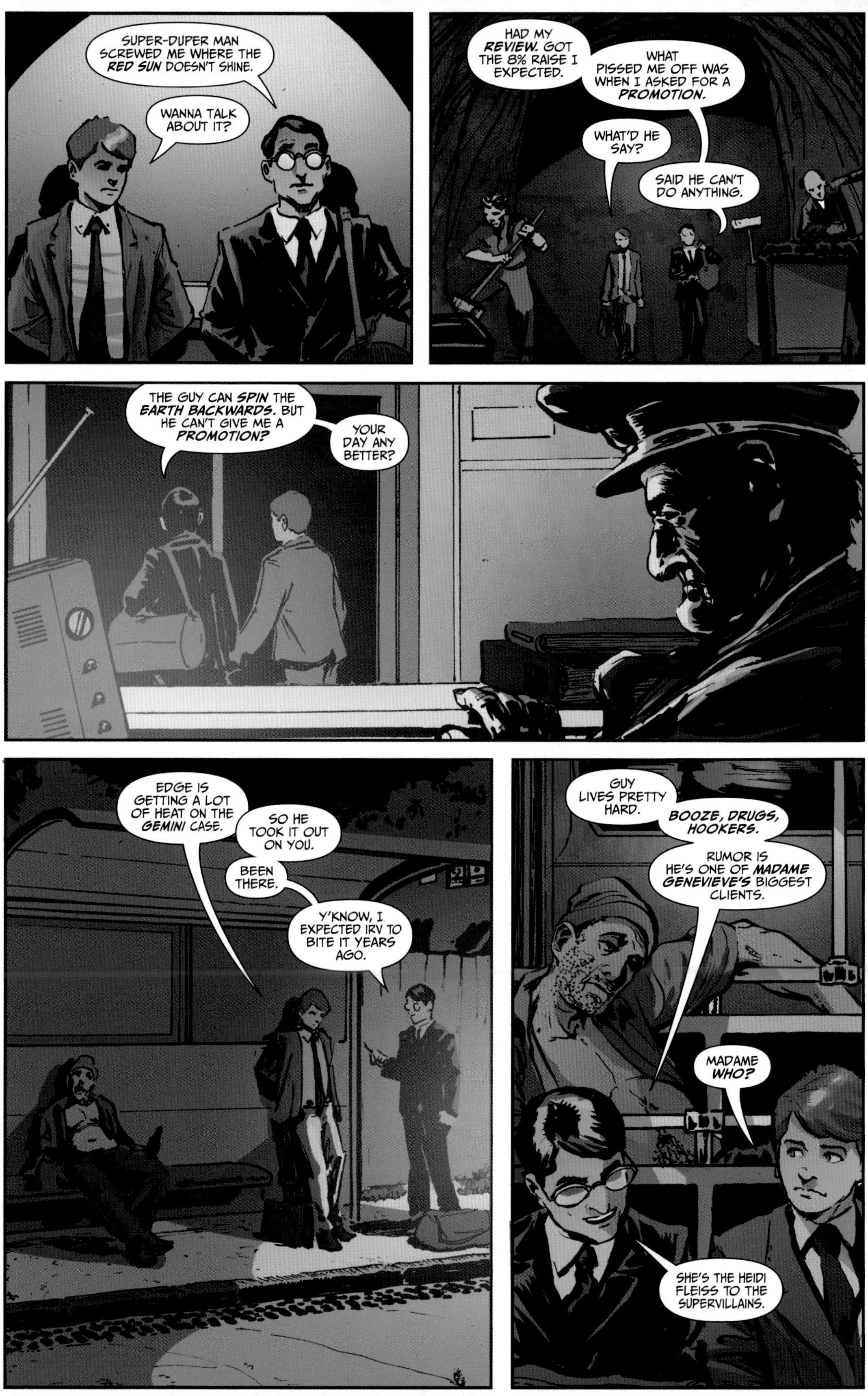
SUPER-DUPER MAN SCREWED ME WHERE THE RED SUN DOESN'T SHINE.
WANNA TALK ABOUT IT?
HAD MY REVIEW. GOT THE 8% RAISE I EXPECTED.
WHAT PISSED ME OFF WAS WHEN I ASKED FOR A PROMOTION.
WHAT'D HE SAY?
SAID HE CAN'T DO ANYTHING.
THE GUY CAN SPIN THE EARTH BACKWARDS. BUT HE CAN'T GIVE ME A PROMOTION?
YOUR DAY ANY BETTER?
EDGE IS GETTING A LOT OF HEAT ON THE GEMINI CASE.
SO HE TOOK IT OUT ON YOU.
BEEN THERE.
Y'KNOW, I EXPECTED IRV TO BITE IT YEARS AGO.
GUY LIVES PRETTY HARD.
BOOZE, DRUGS, HOOKERS.
RUMOR IS HE'S ONE OF MADAME GENEVIEVE'S BIGGEST CLIENTS.
MADAME WHO?
SHE'S THE HEIDI FLEISS TO THE SUPERVILLAINS.

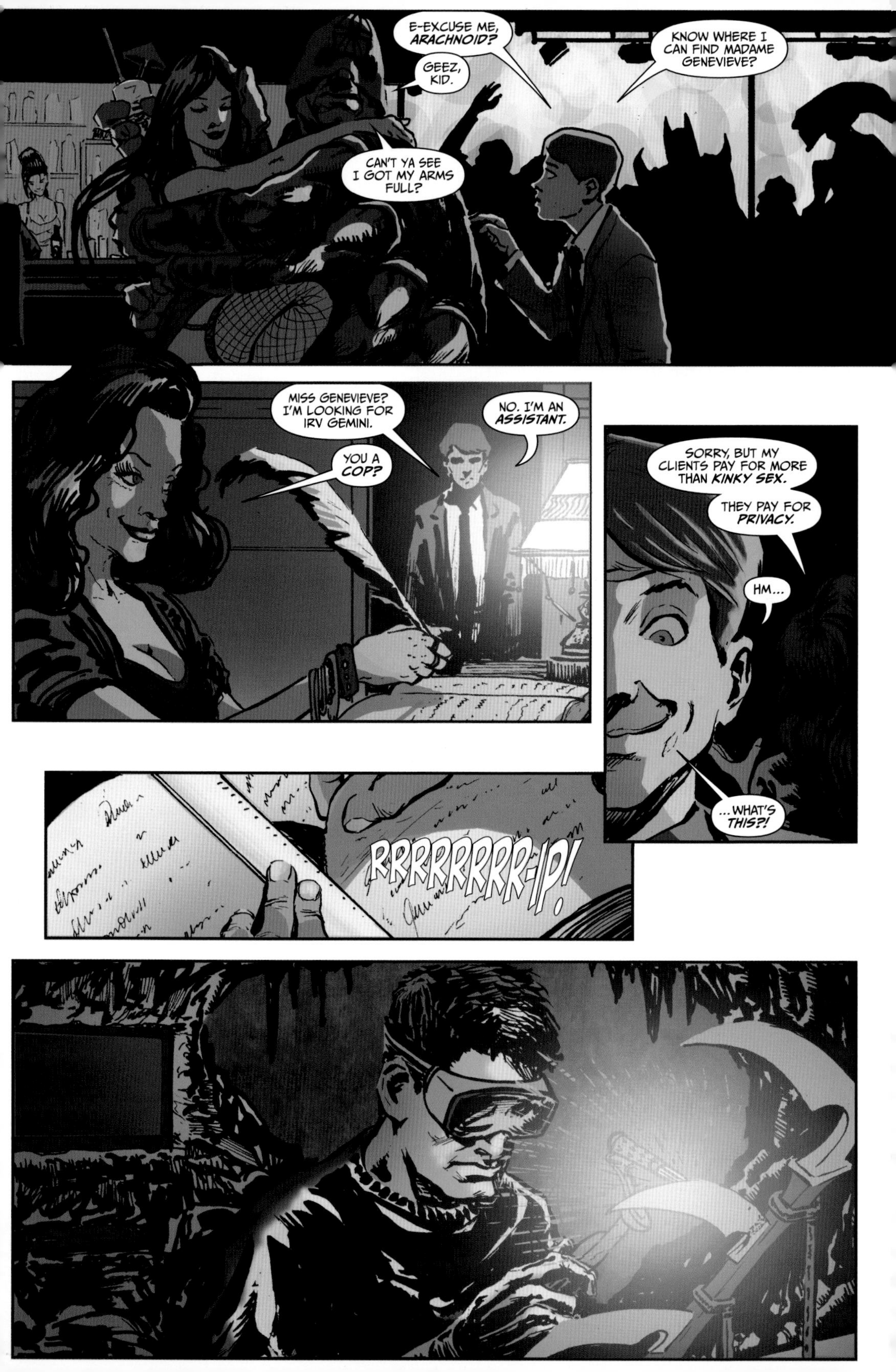
E-EXCUSE ME, ARACHNOID?
GEEZ, KID.
CAN'T YA SEE I GOT MY ARMS FULL?
KNOW WHERE I CAN FIND MADAME GENEVIEVE?
MISS GENEVIEVE? I'M LOOKING FOR IRV GEMINI.
YOU A COP?
NO. I'M AN ASSISTANT.
SORRY, BUT MY CLIENTS PAY FOR MORE THAN KINKY SEX.
THEY PAY FOR PRIVACY.
HM...
...WHAT'S THIS?!
RRRRRRRR-IP!

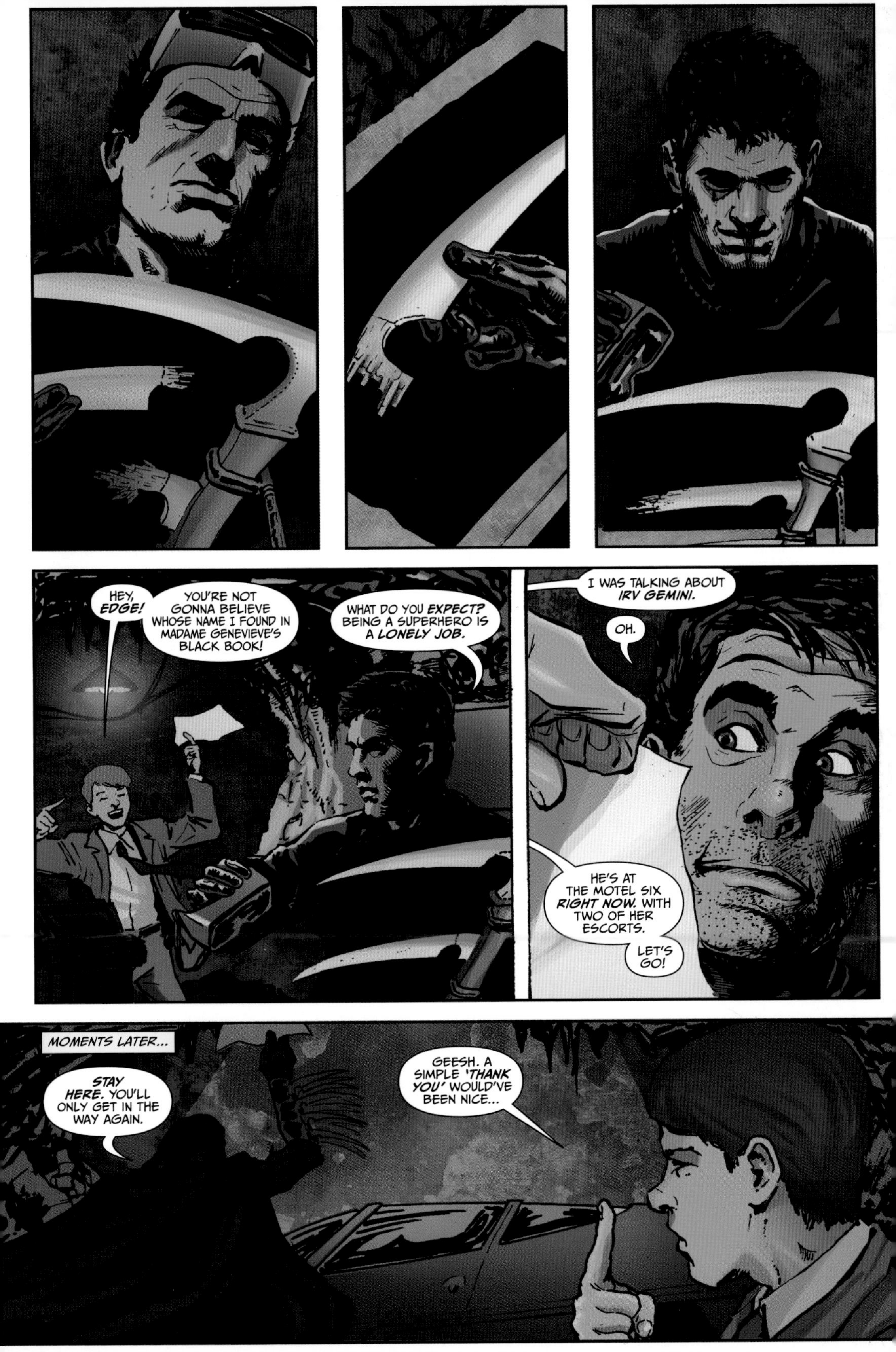
HEY, EDGE!
YOU'RE NOT GONNA BELIEVE WHOSE NAME I FOUND IN MADAME GENEVIEVE'S BLACK BOOK!
WHAT DO YOU EXPECT? BEING A SUPERHERO IS A LONELY JOB.
I WAS TALKING ABOUT IRV GEMINI.
OH.
HE'S AT THE MOTEL SIX RIGHT NOW. WITH TWO OF HER ESCORTS.
LET'S GO!
MOMENTS LATER...
STAY HERE. YOU'LL ONLY GET IN THE WAY AGAIN.
GEESH. A SIMPLE 'THANK YOU' WOULD'VE BEEN NICE...

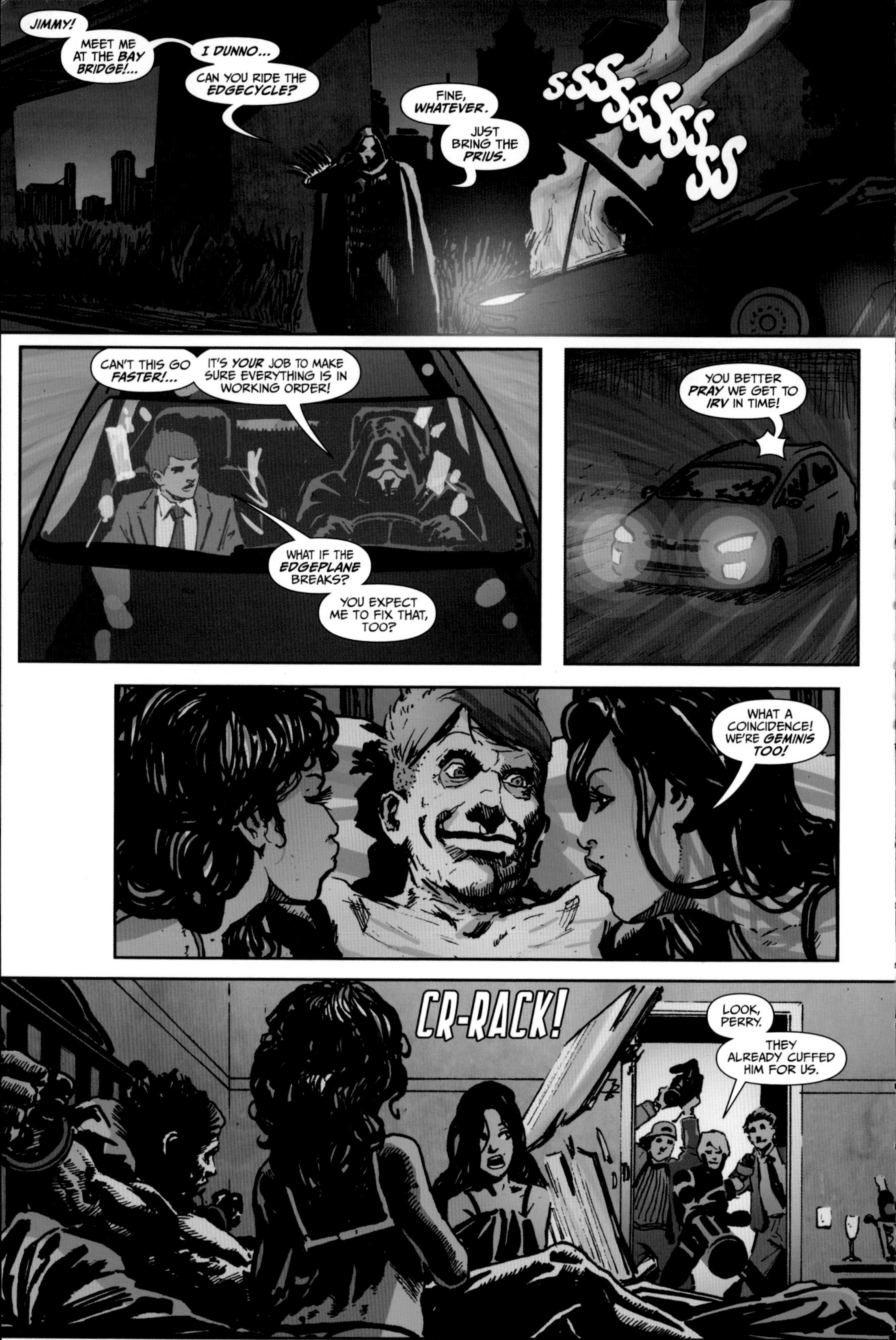
JIMMY!
MEET ME AT THE BAY BRIDGE!...
I DUNNO...
CAN YOU RIDE THE EDGECYCLE?
FINE, WHATEVER.
JUST BRING THE PRIUS.
SSSSSSSSSSSSS
CAN'T THIS GO FASTER!...
IT'S YOUR JOB TO MAKE SURE EVERYTHING IS IN WORKING ORDER!
WHAT IF THE EDGEPLANE BREAKS?
YOU EXPECT ME TO FIX THAT, TOO?
YOU BETTER PRAY WE GET TO IRV IN TIME!
WHAT A COINCIDENCE! WE'RE GEMINIS TOO!
CR-RACK!
LOOK, PERRY.
THEY ALREADY CUFFED HIM FOR US.

NO Vacancy

DOESN'T ADD UP. HOW'D FLEX *KNOW* IRV WAS HERE?

YOU ARE *SO FIRED!*

LATER THAT NIGHT...

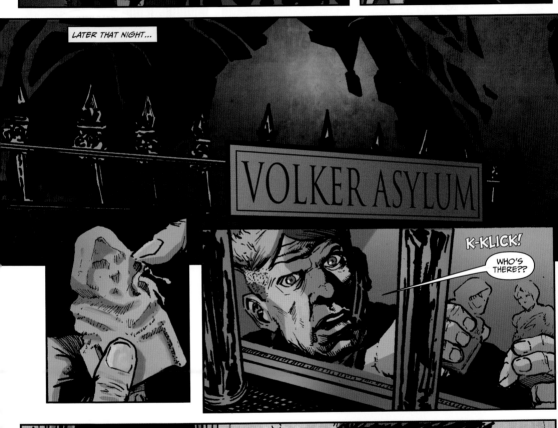

VOLKER ASYLUM

K-KLICK!

WHO'S THERE??

FLEX?! WHAT'RE YOU DOING HERE...SO *LATE?*

A GUY COULD GO CRAZY IN THIS ASYLUM.

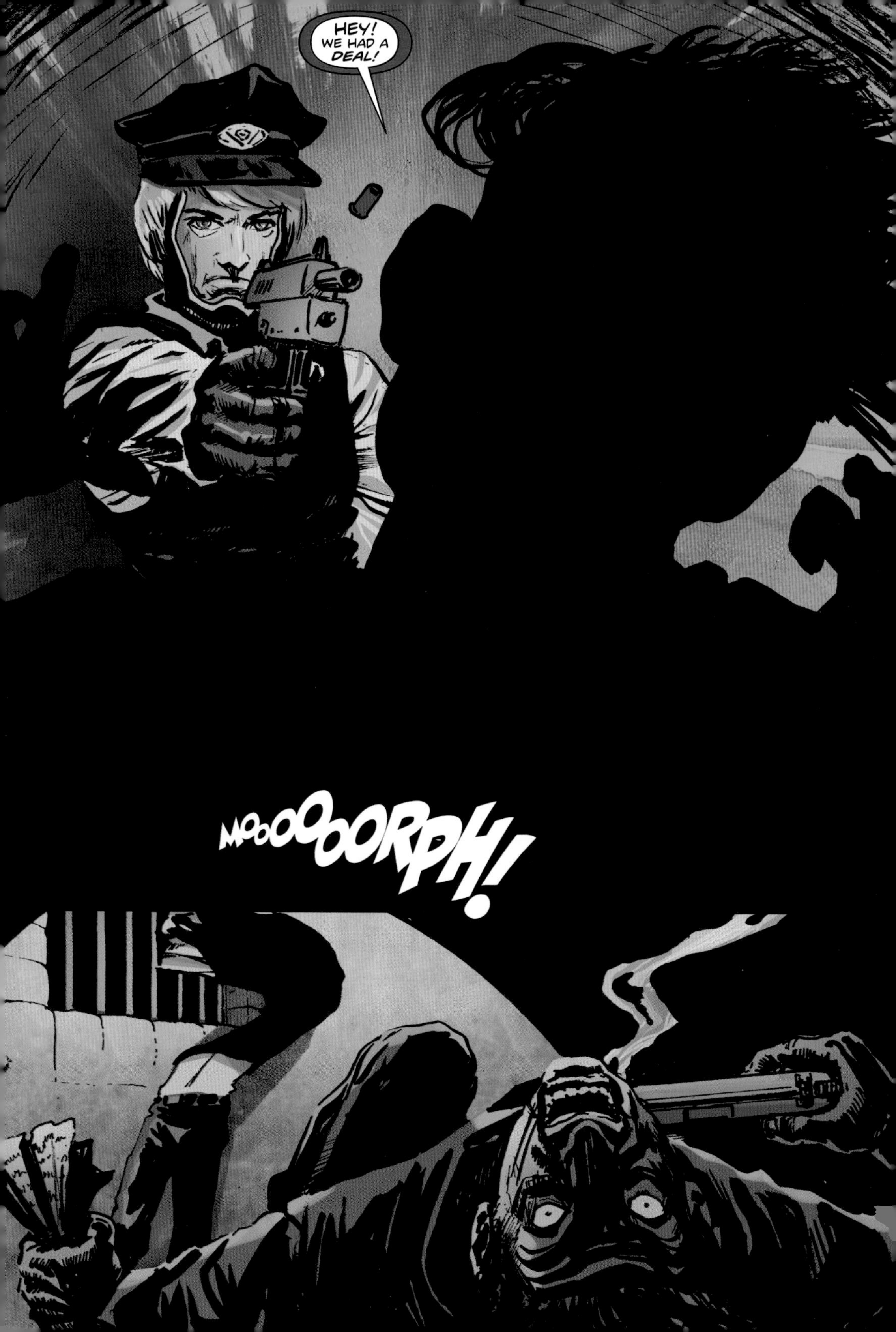
HEY! WE HAD A DEAL!
MOOOOOORPH!

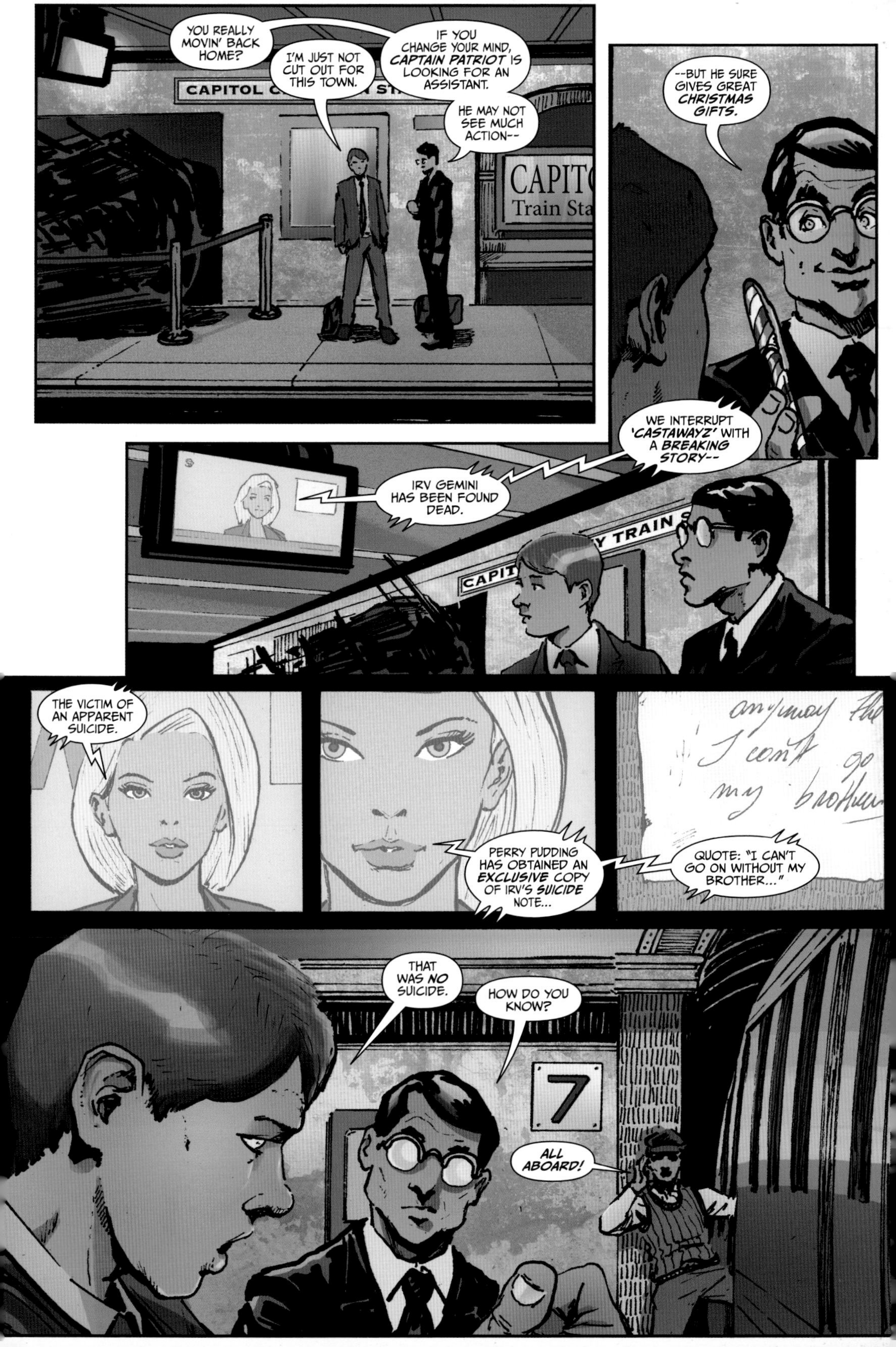
YOU REALLY MOVIN' BACK HOME?
I'M JUST NOT CUT OUT FOR THIS TOWN.
IF YOU CHANGE YOUR MIND, *CAPTAIN PATRIOT* IS LOOKING FOR AN ASSISTANT.
HE MAY NOT SEE MUCH ACTION--
--BUT HE SURE GIVES GREAT *CHRISTMAS GIFTS.*
WE INTERRUPT *'CASTAWAYZ'* WITH A *BREAKING STORY*--
IRV GEMINI HAS BEEN FOUND DEAD.
THE VICTIM OF AN APPARENT SUICIDE.
PERRY PUDDING HAS OBTAINED AN *EXCLUSIVE* COPY OF IRV'S *SUICIDE* NOTE...
QUOTE: "I CAN'T GO ON WITHOUT MY BROTHER..."
THAT WAS *NO* SUICIDE.
HOW DO YOU KNOW?
7
ALL ABOARD!

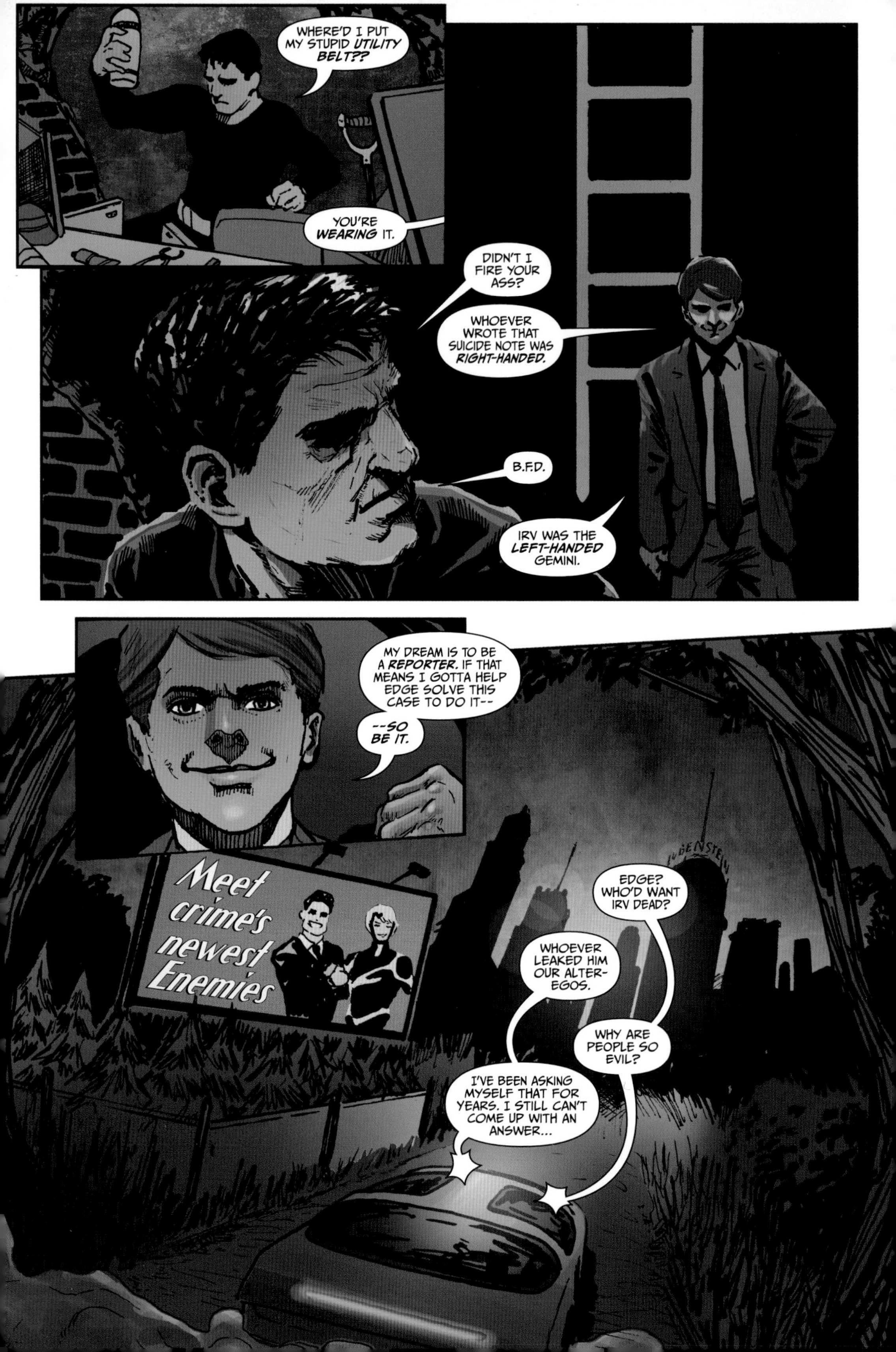

WHERE'D I PUT MY STUPID UTILITY BELT??
YOU'RE WEARING IT.
DIDN'T I FIRE YOUR ASS?
WHOEVER WROTE THAT SUICIDE NOTE WAS RIGHT-HANDED.
B.F.D.
IRV WAS THE LEFT-HANDED GEMINI.
MY DREAM IS TO BE A REPORTER. IF THAT MEANS I GOTTA HELP EDGE SOLVE THIS CASE TO DO IT--
--SO BE IT.
Meet crime's newest Enemies
EDGE? WHO'D WANT IRV DEAD?
WHOEVER LEAKED HIM OUR ALTER-EGOS.
WHY ARE PEOPLE SO EVIL?
I'VE BEEN ASKING MYSELF THAT FOR YEARS. I STILL CAN'T COME UP WITH AN ANSWER...

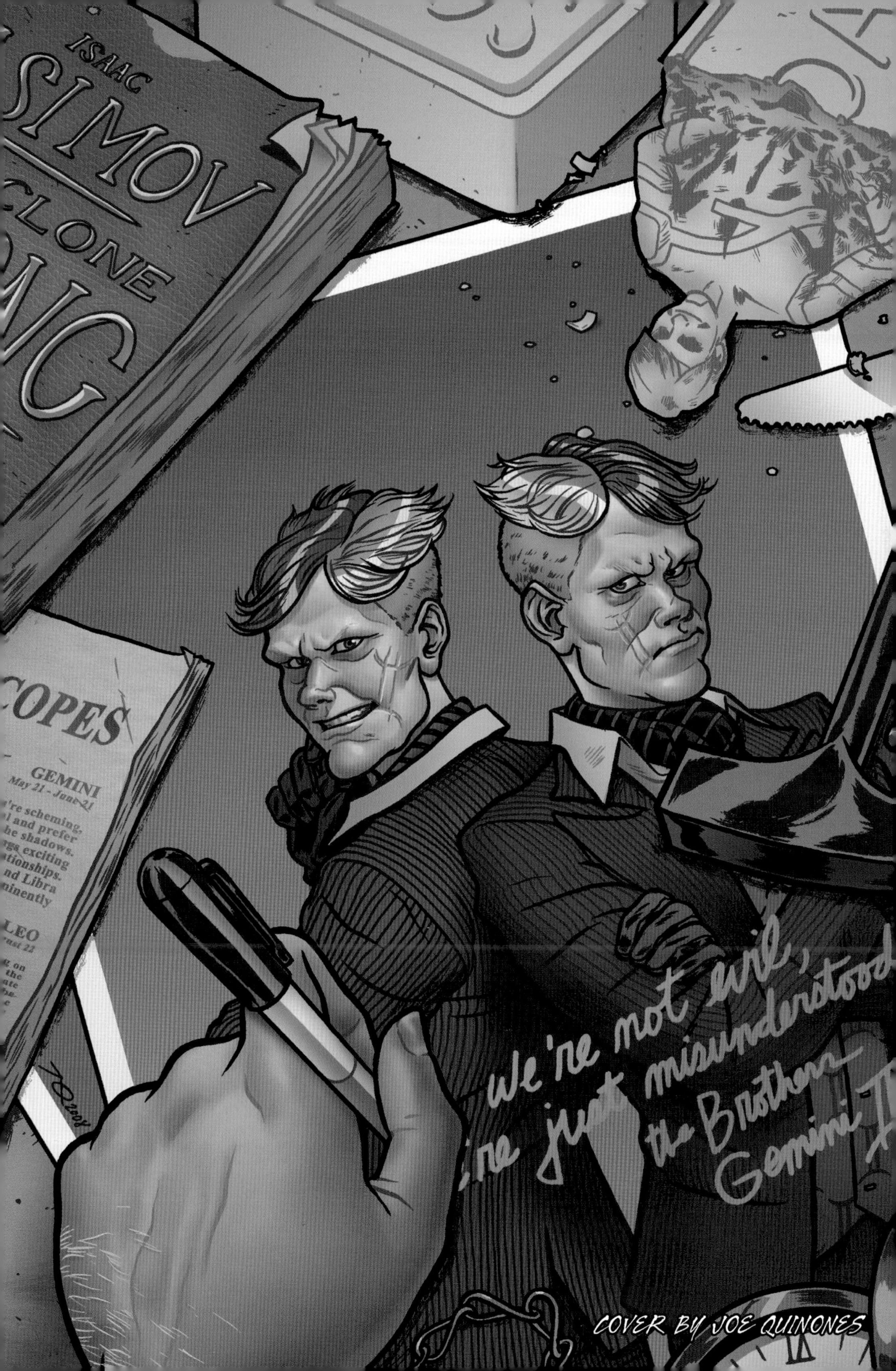
ISAAC
SIMOV
CLONE
COPES
GEMINI
May 21 - June 21
We're not evil,
the Brothers
Gemini
COVER BY JOE QUINONES

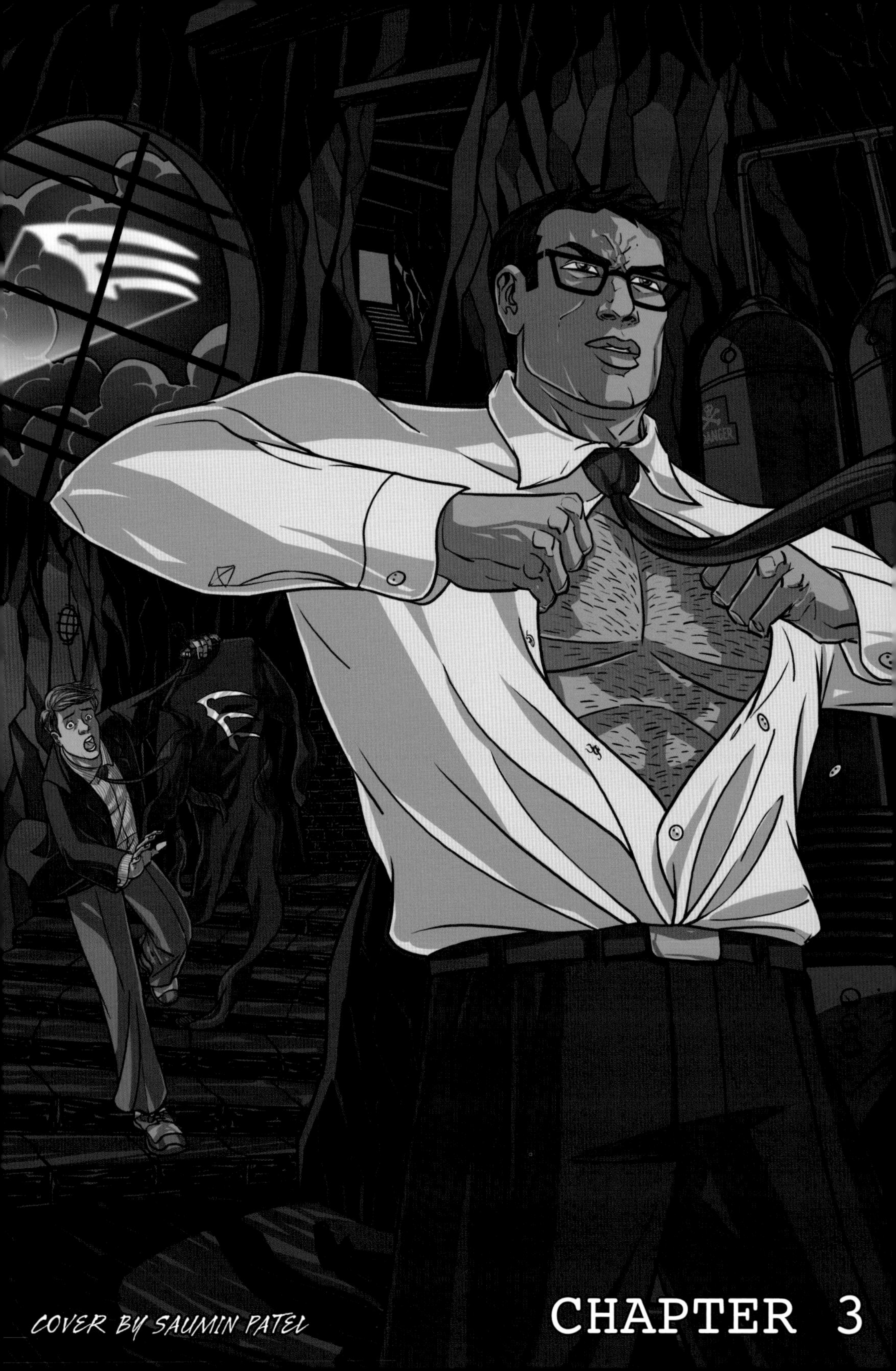
DANGER

CHAPTER 3

COVER BY SAUMIN PATEL

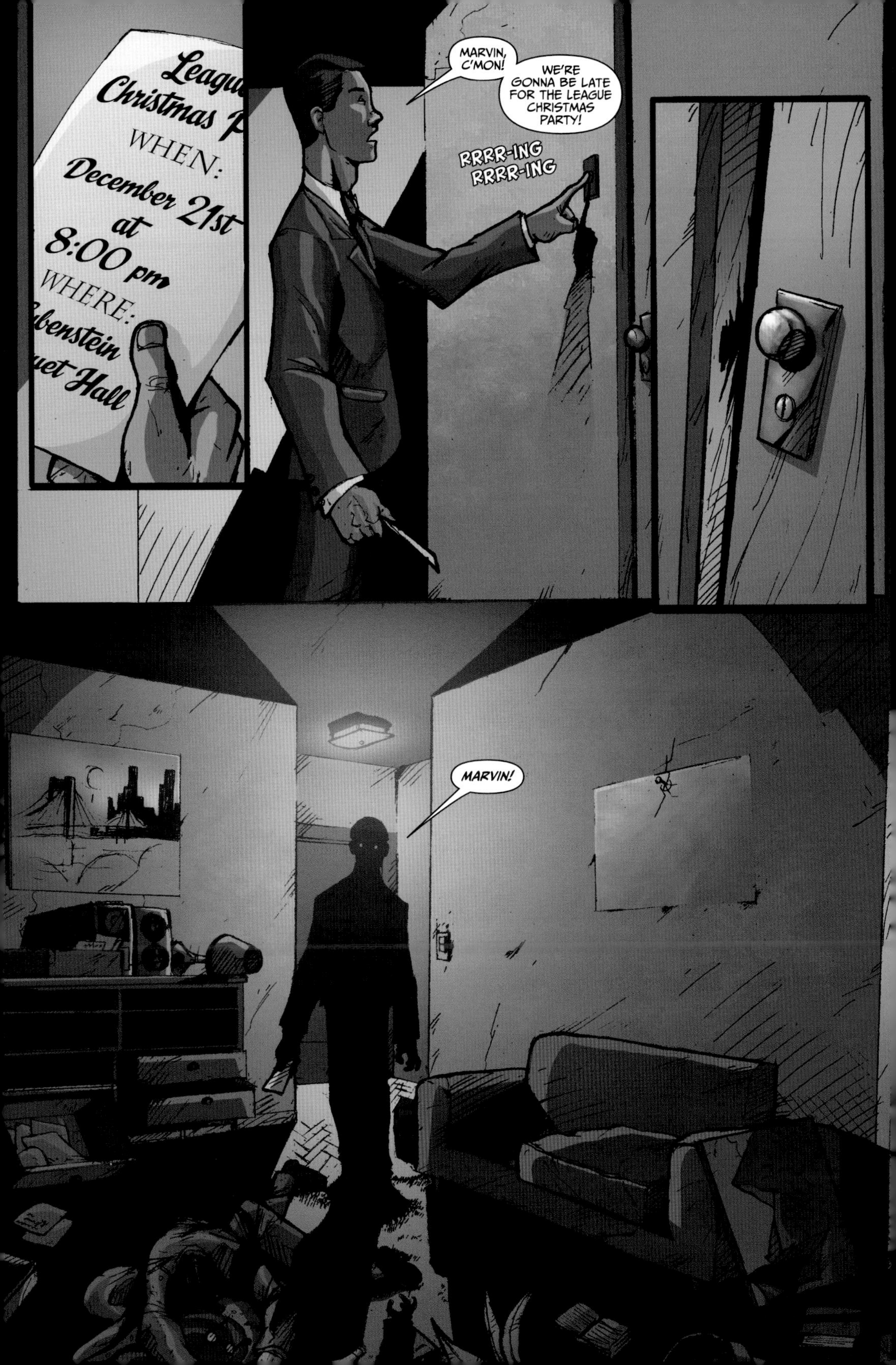
Leagu
Christmas P
WHEN:
December 21st
at
8:00 pm
WHERE:
benstein
uet-Hall
MARVIN, C'MON!
WE'RE GONNA BE LATE FOR THE LEAGUE CHRISTMAS PARTY!
RRRR-ING
RRRR-ING
MARVIN!

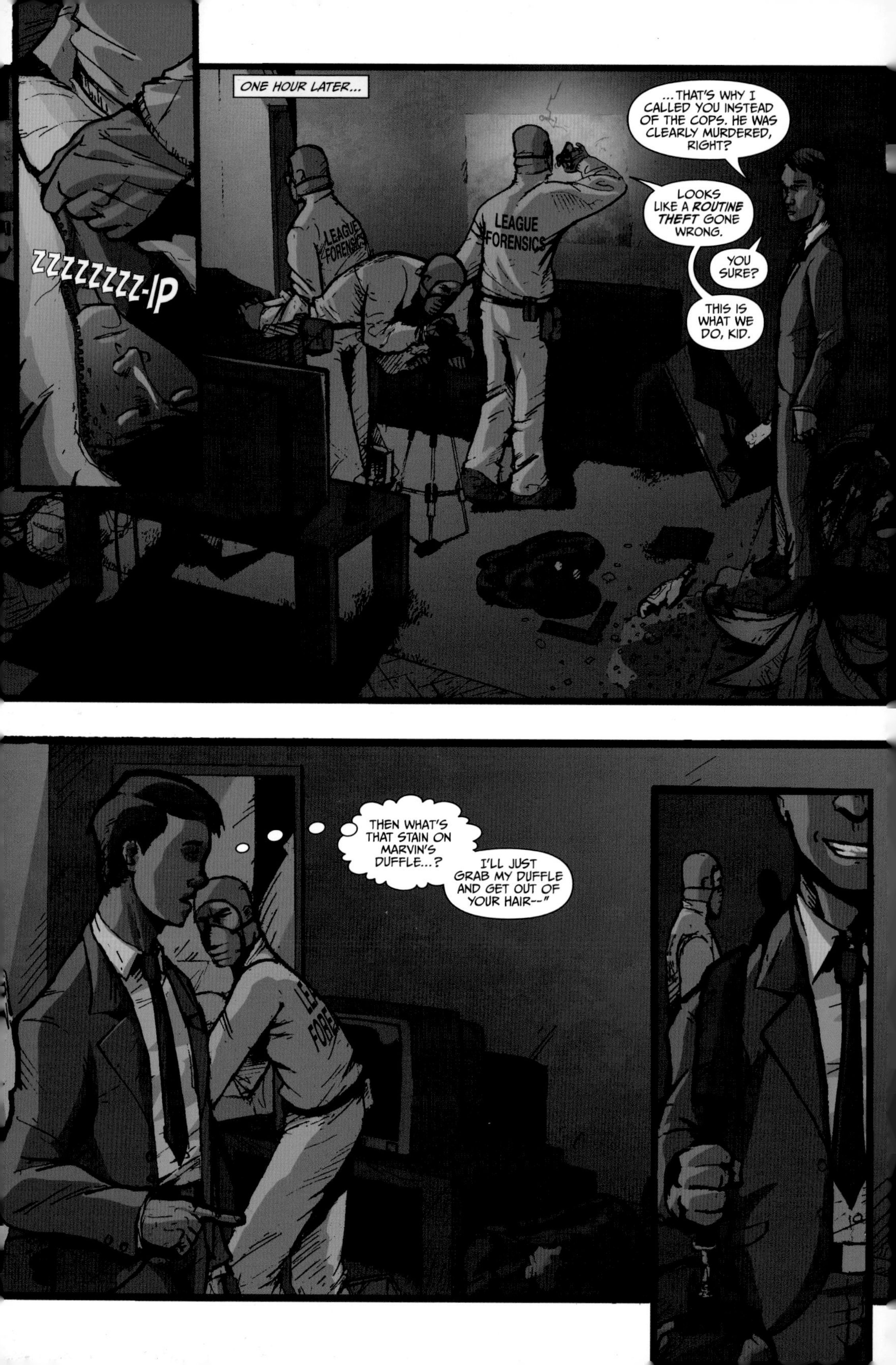
ZZZZZZZZ-IP
ONE HOUR LATER...
...THAT'S WHY I CALLED YOU INSTEAD OF THE COPS. HE WAS CLEARLY MURDERED, RIGHT?
LOOKS LIKE A ROUTINE THEFT GONE WRONG.
YOU SURE?
THIS IS WHAT WE DO, KID.
LEAGUE FORENSICS
LEAGUE FORENSICS
THEN WHAT'S THAT STAIN ON MARVIN'S DUFFLE...?
I'LL JUST GRAB MY DUFFLE AND GET OUT OF YOUR HAIR--"

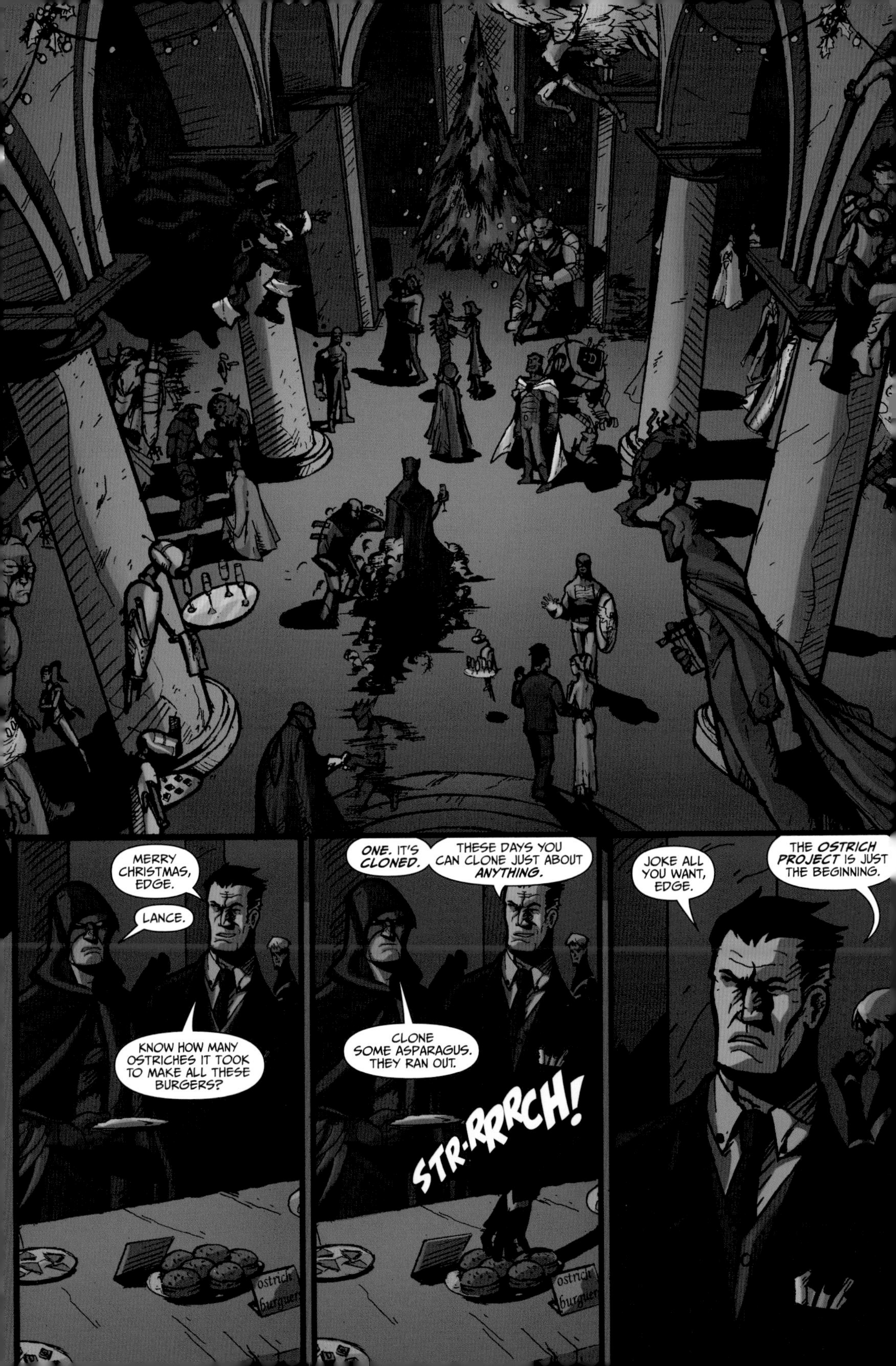
MERRY CHRISTMAS, EDGE.
LANCE.
KNOW HOW MANY OSTRICHES IT TOOK TO MAKE ALL THESE BURGERS?
ONE. IT'S *CLONED.*
THESE DAYS YOU CAN CLONE JUST ABOUT *ANYTHING.*
CLONE SOME ASPARAGUS. THEY RAN OUT.
STR-RRRCH!
JOKE ALL YOU WANT, EDGE.
THE *OSTRICH PROJECT* IS JUST THE BEGINNING.

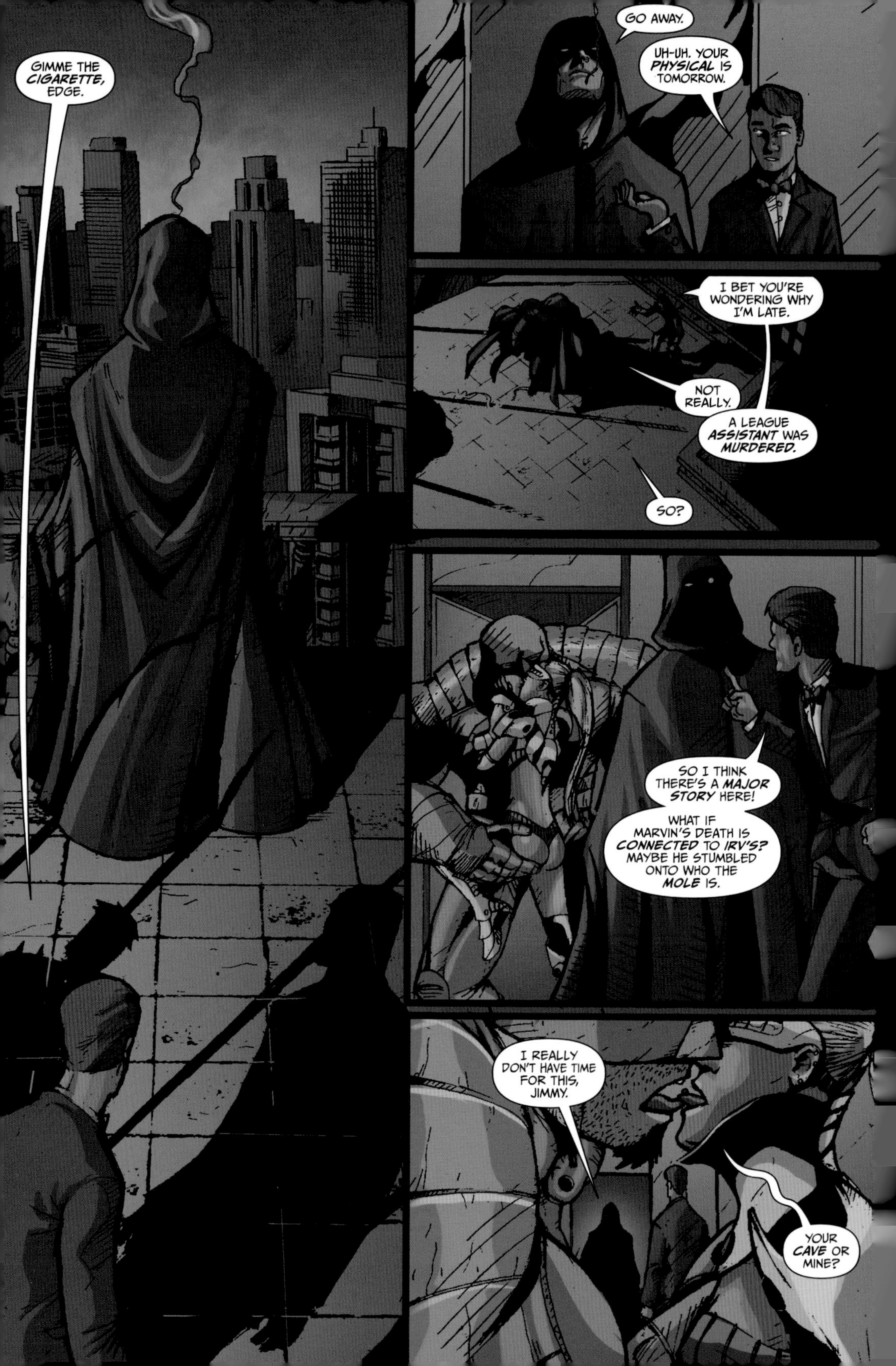
GIMME THE CIGARETTE, EDGE.
GO AWAY.
UH-UH. YOUR PHYSICAL IS TOMORROW.
I BET YOU'RE WONDERING WHY I'M LATE.
NOT REALLY.
A LEAGUE ASSISTANT WAS MURDERED.
SO?
SO I THINK THERE'S A MAJOR STORY HERE!
WHAT IF MARVIN'S DEATH IS CONNECTED TO IRV'S? MAYBE HE STUMBLED ONTO WHO THE MOLE IS.
I REALLY DON'T HAVE TIME FOR THIS, JIMMY.
YOUR CAVE OR MINE?

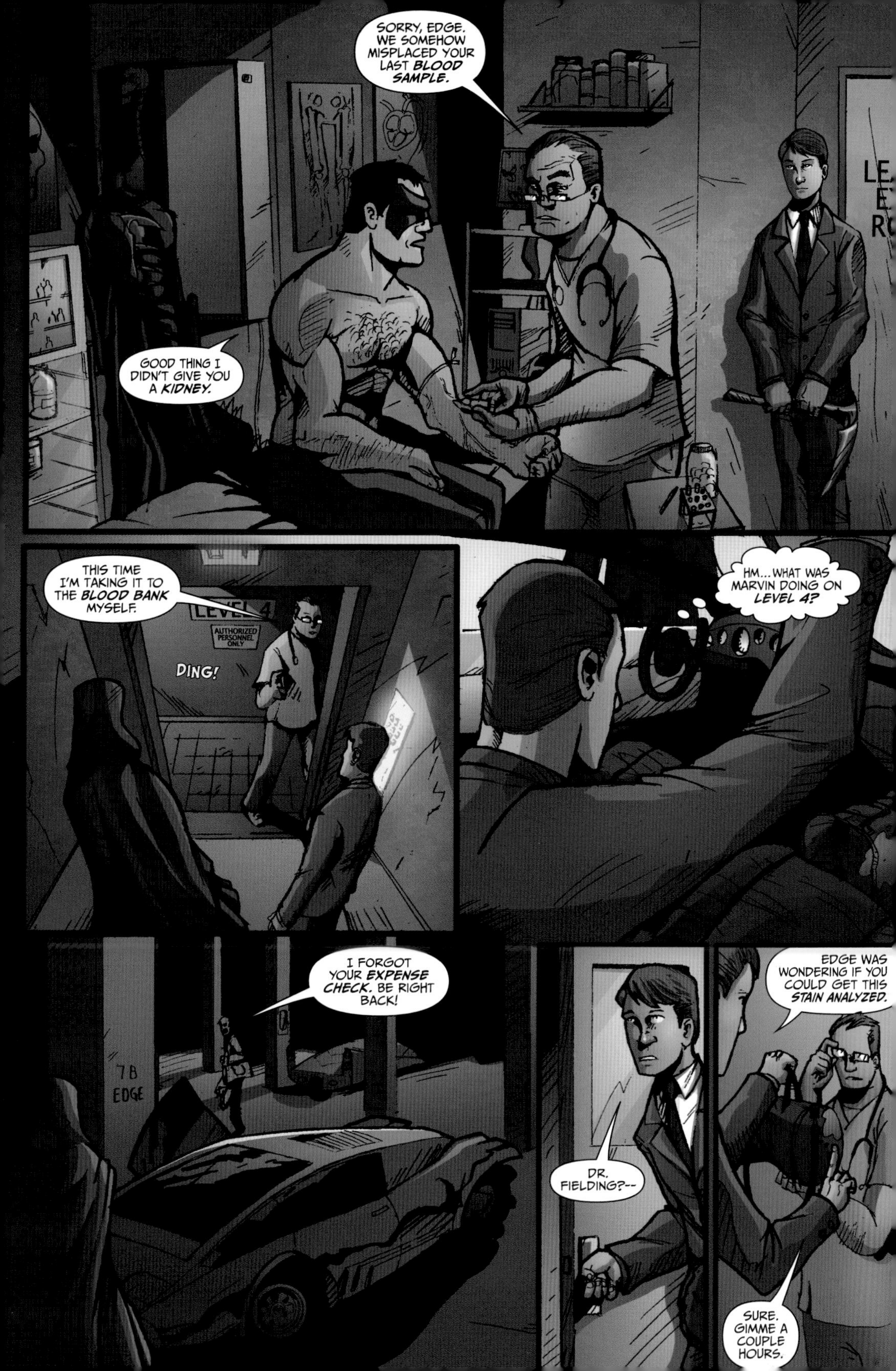
SORRY, EDGE. WE SOMEHOW MISPLACED YOUR LAST BLOOD SAMPLE.
GOOD THING I DIDN'T GIVE YOU A KIDNEY.
THIS TIME I'M TAKING IT TO THE BLOOD BANK MYSELF.
LEVEL 4
AUTHORIZED PERSONNEL ONLY
DING!
HM... WHAT WAS MARVIN DOING ON LEVEL 4?
I FORGOT YOUR EXPENSE CHECK. BE RIGHT BACK!
7B EDGE
DR. FIELDING?--
EDGE WAS WONDERING IF YOU COULD GET THIS STAIN ANALYZED.
SURE. GIMME A COUPLE HOURS.

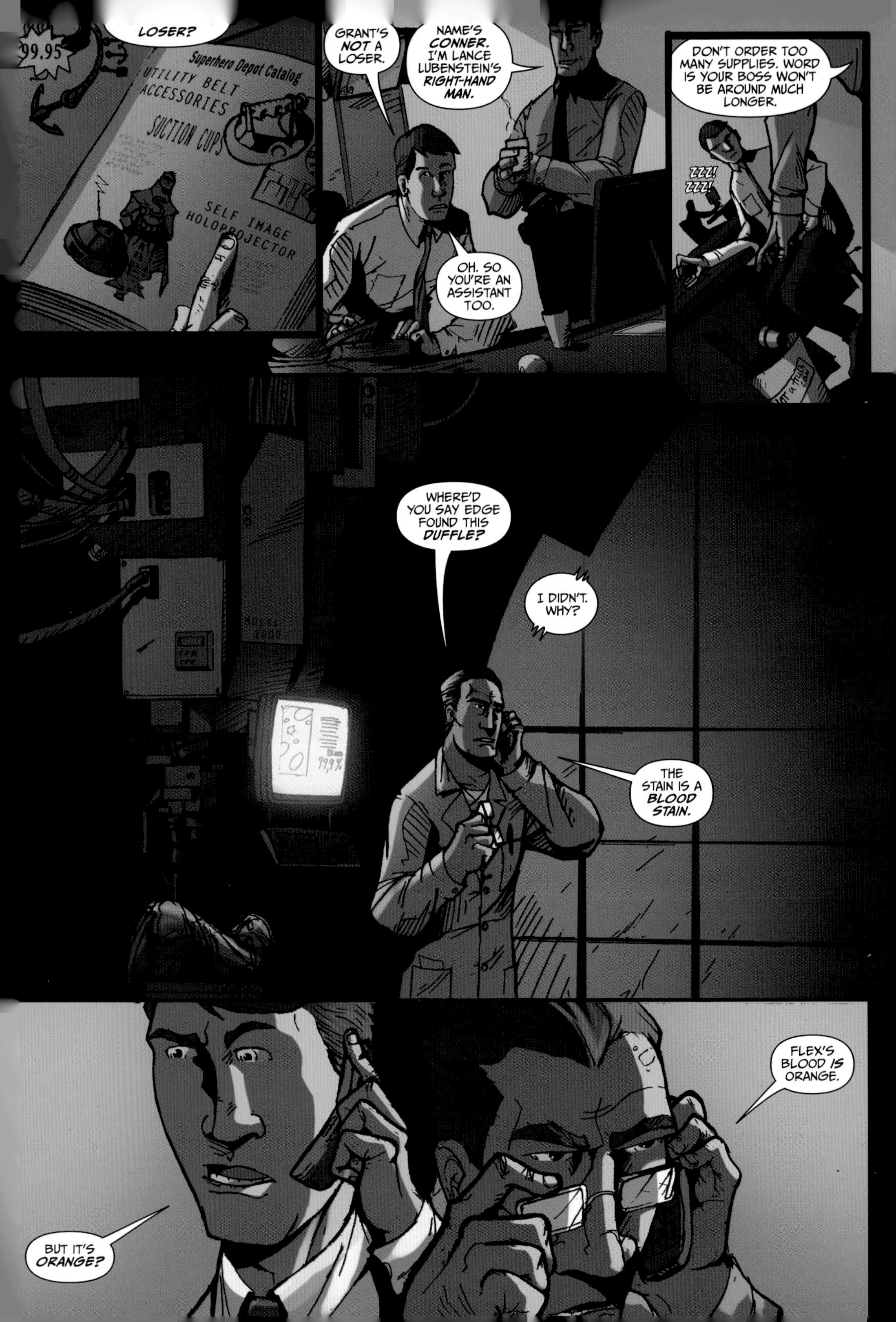

LOSER?
99.95
Superhero Depot Catalog
UTILITY BELT ACCESSORIES
SUCTION CUPS
SELF IMAGE HOLOPROJECTOR
GRANT'S NOT A LOSER.
NAME'S CONNER. I'M LANCE LUBENSTEIN'S RIGHT-HAND MAN.
OH. SO YOU'RE AN ASSISTANT TOO.
DON'T ORDER TOO MANY SUPPLIES. WORD IS YOUR BOSS WON'T BE AROUND MUCH LONGER.
ZZZ! ZZZ!
WHERE'D YOU SAY EDGE FOUND THIS DUFFLE?
I DIDN'T. WHY?
MULTI 2000
Blood 99.9%
THE STAIN IS A BLOOD STAIN.
BUT IT'S ORANGE?
FLEX'S BLOOD IS ORANGE.

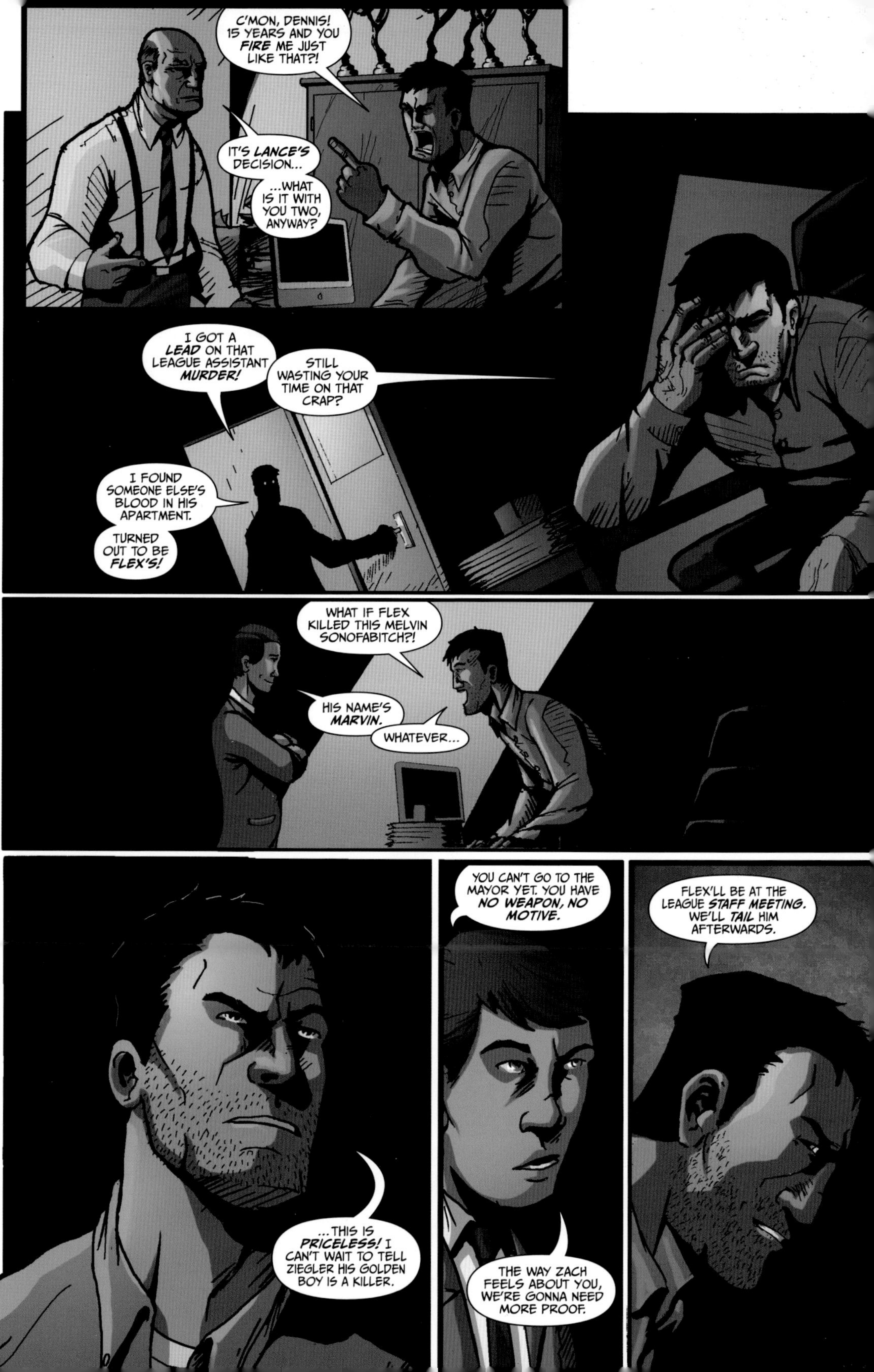
C'MON, DENNIS! 15 YEARS AND YOU FIRE ME JUST LIKE THAT?!
IT'S LANCE'S DECISION...
...WHAT IS IT WITH YOU TWO, ANYWAY?
I GOT A LEAD ON THAT LEAGUE ASSISTANT MURDER!
STILL WASTING YOUR TIME ON THAT CRAP?
I FOUND SOMEONE ELSE'S BLOOD IN HIS APARTMENT.
TURNED OUT TO BE FLEX'S!
WHAT IF FLEX KILLED THIS MELVIN SONOFABITCH?!
HIS NAME'S MARVIN.
WHATEVER...
...THIS IS PRICELESS! I CAN'T WAIT TO TELL ZIEGLER HIS GOLDEN BOY IS A KILLER.
YOU CAN'T GO TO THE MAYOR YET. YOU HAVE NO WEAPON, NO MOTIVE.
THE WAY ZACH FEELS ABOUT YOU, WE'RE GONNA NEED MORE PROOF.
FLEX'LL BE AT THE LEAGUE STAFF MEETING. WE'LL TAIL HIM AFTERWARDS.

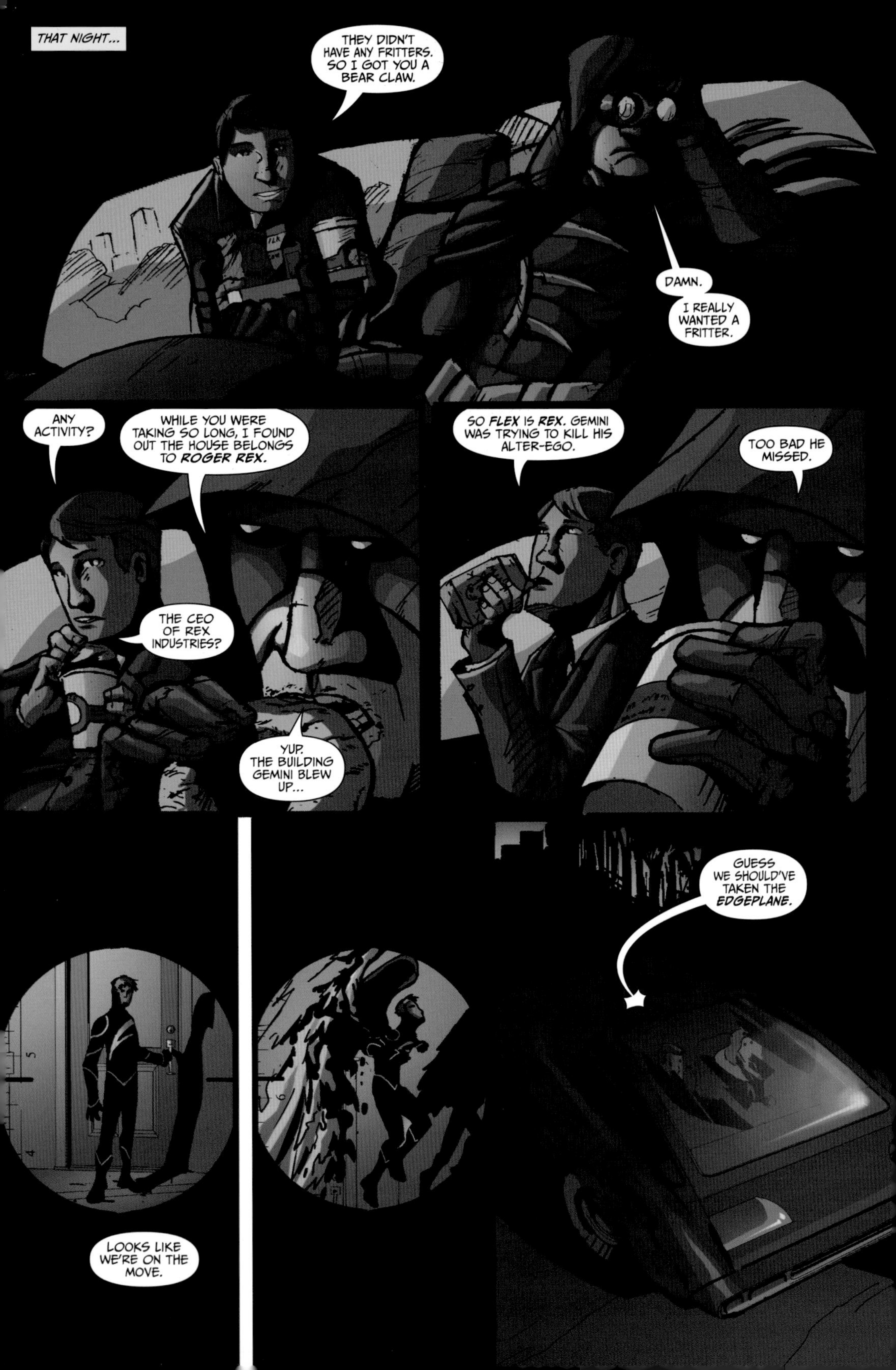
THAT NIGHT...
THEY DIDN'T HAVE ANY FRITTERS. SO I GOT YOU A BEAR CLAW.
DAMN.
I REALLY WANTED A FRITTER.
ANY ACTIVITY?
WHILE YOU WERE TAKING SO LONG, I FOUND OUT THE HOUSE BELONGS TO ROGER REX.
THE CEO OF REX INDUSTRIES?
YUP. THE BUILDING GEMINI BLEW UP...
SO FLEX IS REX. GEMINI WAS TRYING TO KILL HIS ALTER-EGO.
TOO BAD HE MISSED.
LOOKS LIKE WE'RE ON THE MOVE.
GUESS WE SHOULD'VE TAKEN THE EDGEPLANE.

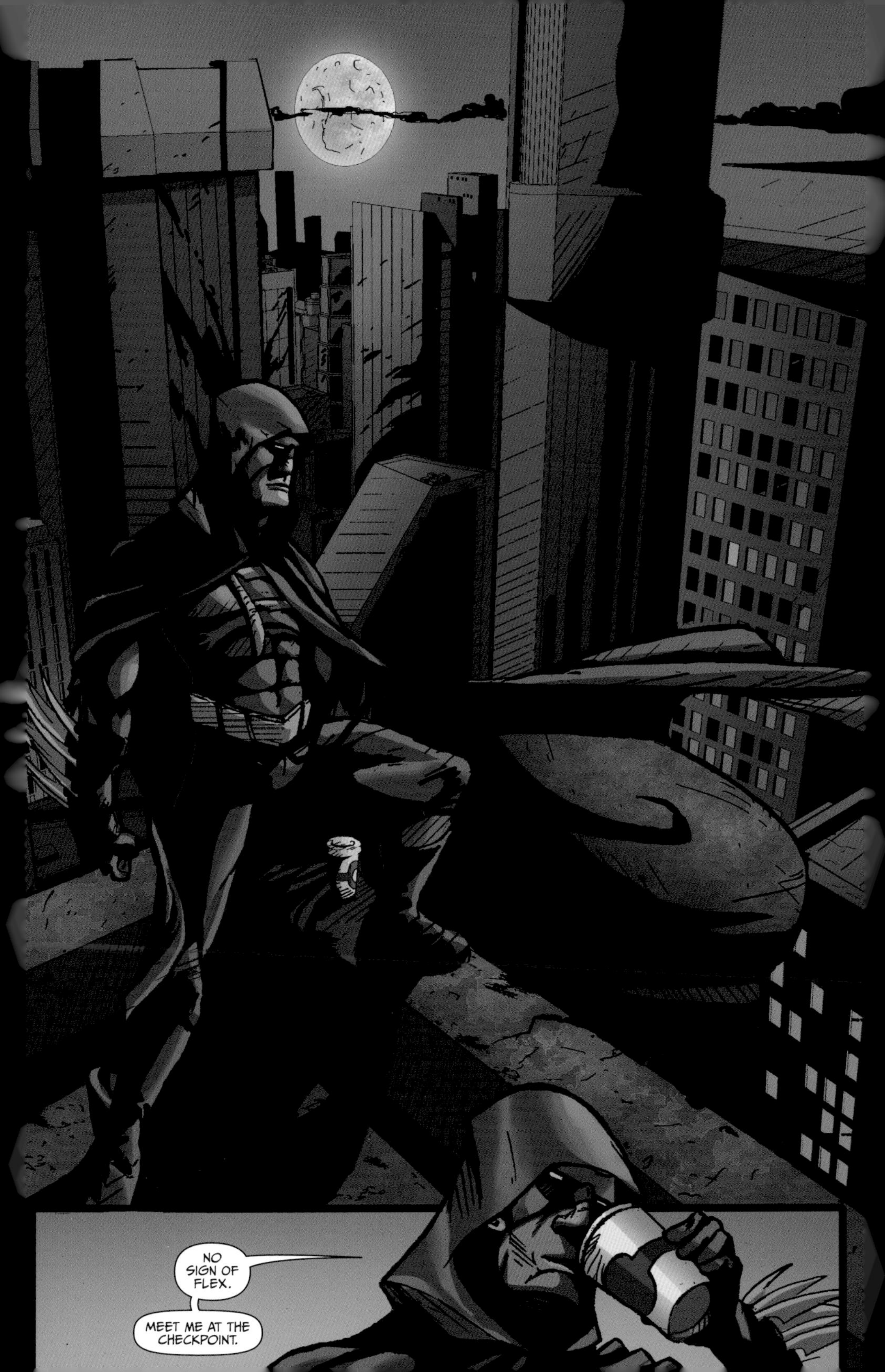

NO SIGN OF FLEX.
MEET ME AT THE CHECKPOINT.

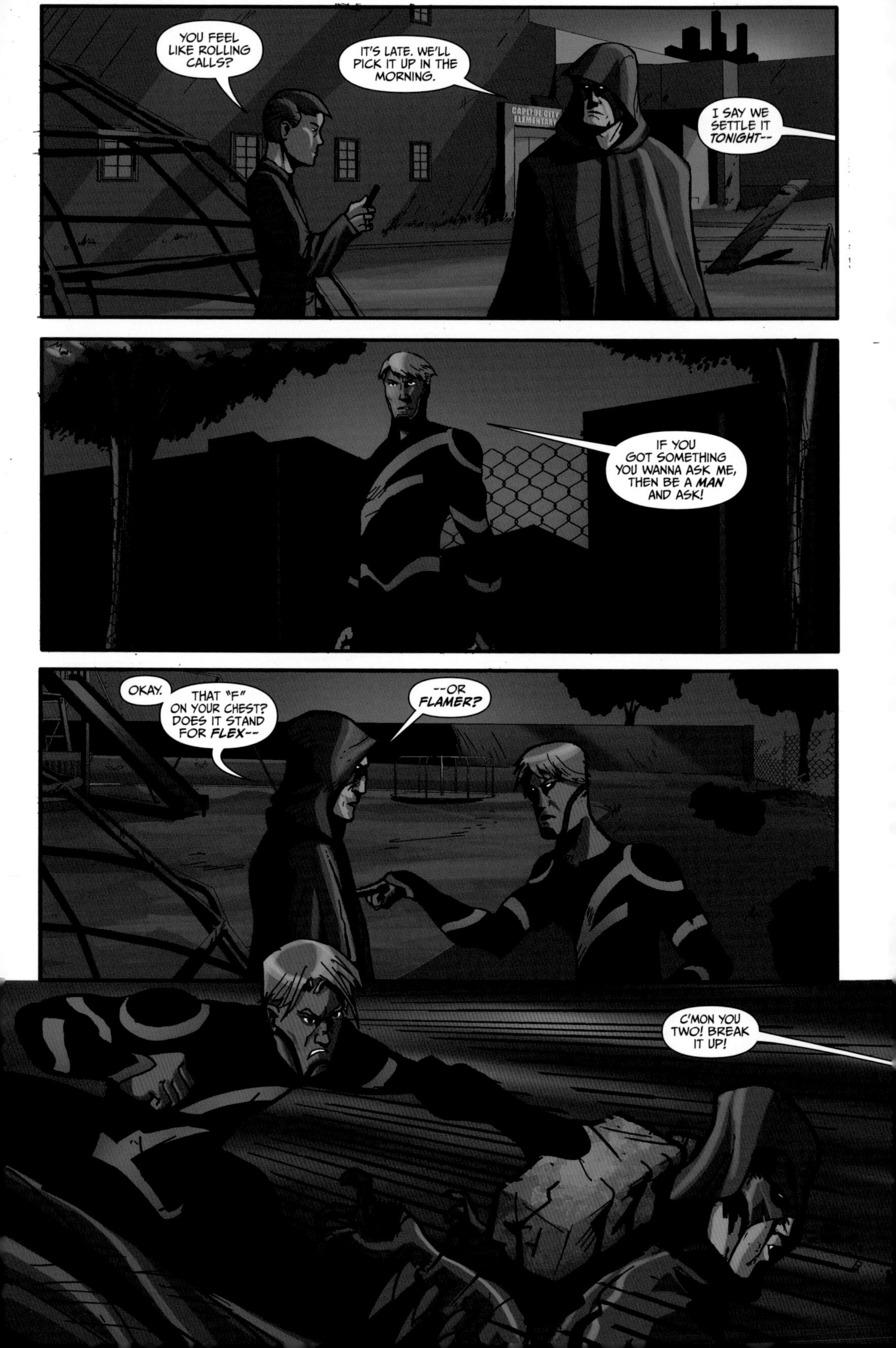
YOU FEEL LIKE ROLLING CALLS?
IT'S LATE. WE'LL PICK IT UP IN THE MORNING.
CAPITOL CITY ELEMENTARY
I SAY WE SETTLE IT *TONIGHT*--
IF YOU GOT SOMETHING YOU WANNA ASK ME, THEN BE A *MAN* AND ASK!
OKAY.
THAT "F" ON YOUR CHEST? DOES IT STAND FOR *FLEX*--
--OR *FLAMER?*
C'MON YOU TWO! BREAK IT UP!

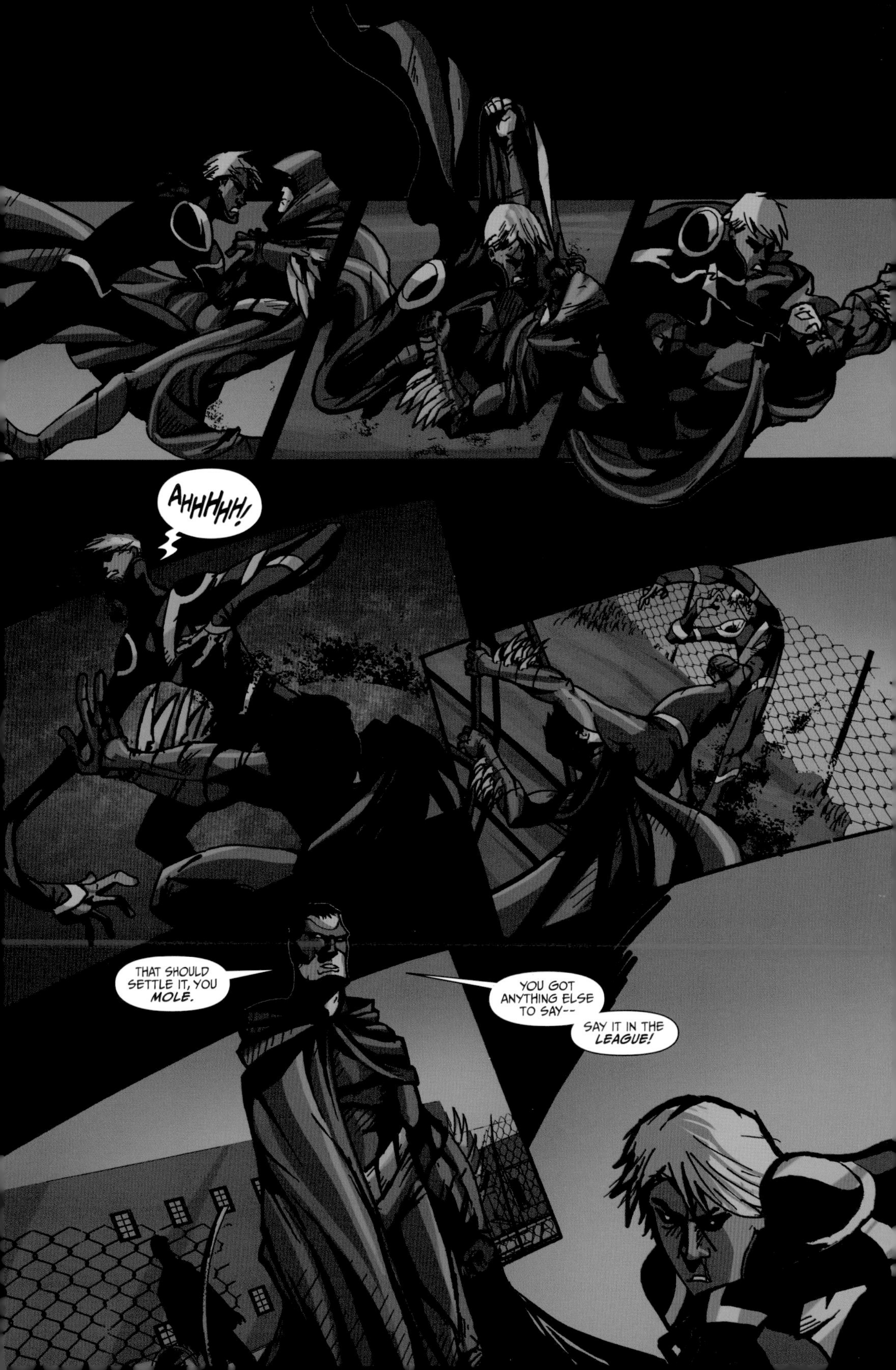

AHHHHH!
THAT SHOULD SETTLE IT, YOU MOLE.
YOU GOT ANYTHING ELSE TO SAY--
SAY IT IN THE LEAGUE!

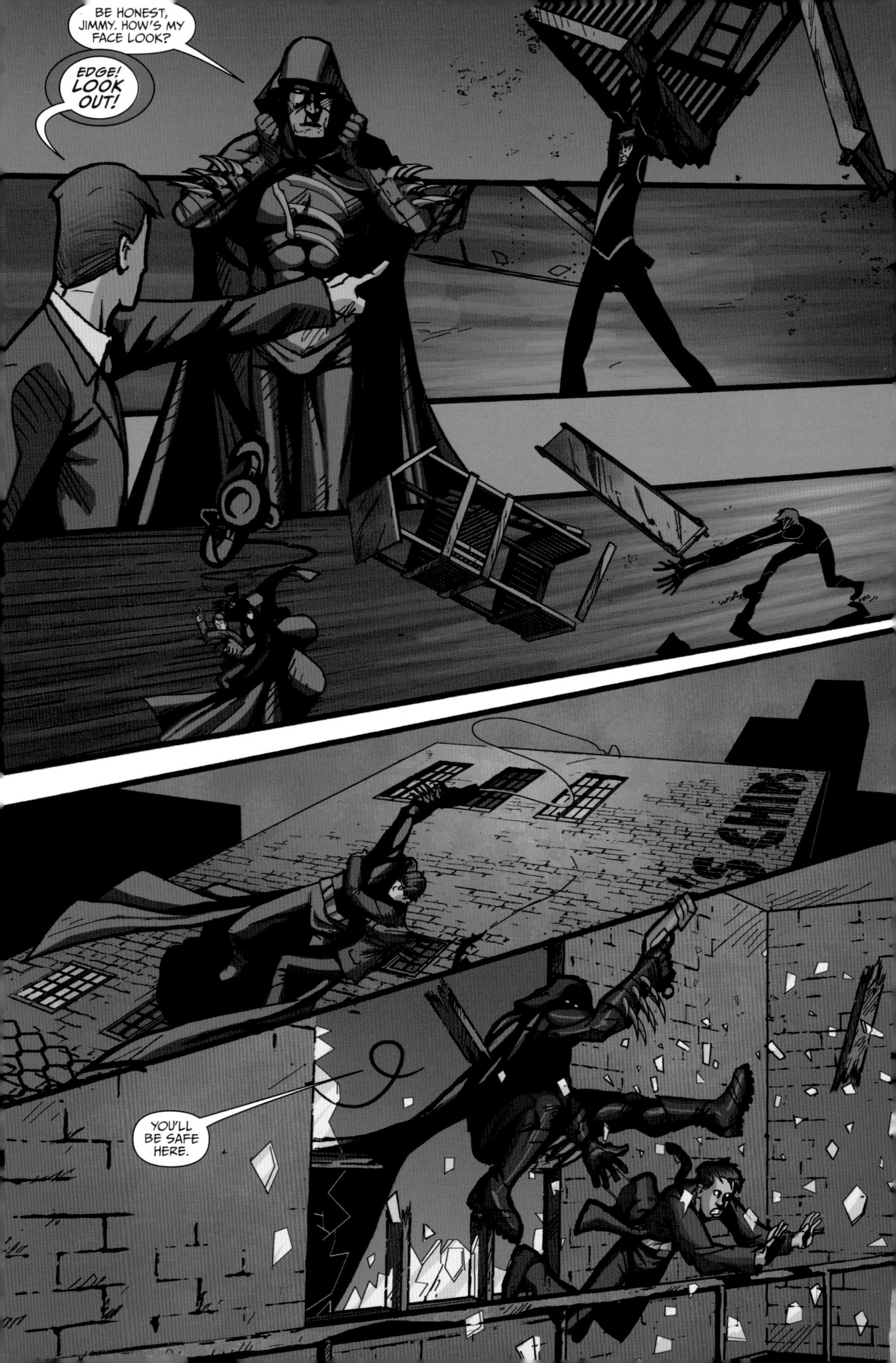

BE HONEST, JIMMY. HOW'S MY FACE LOOK?
EDGE! LOOK OUT!
YOU'LL BE SAFE HERE.

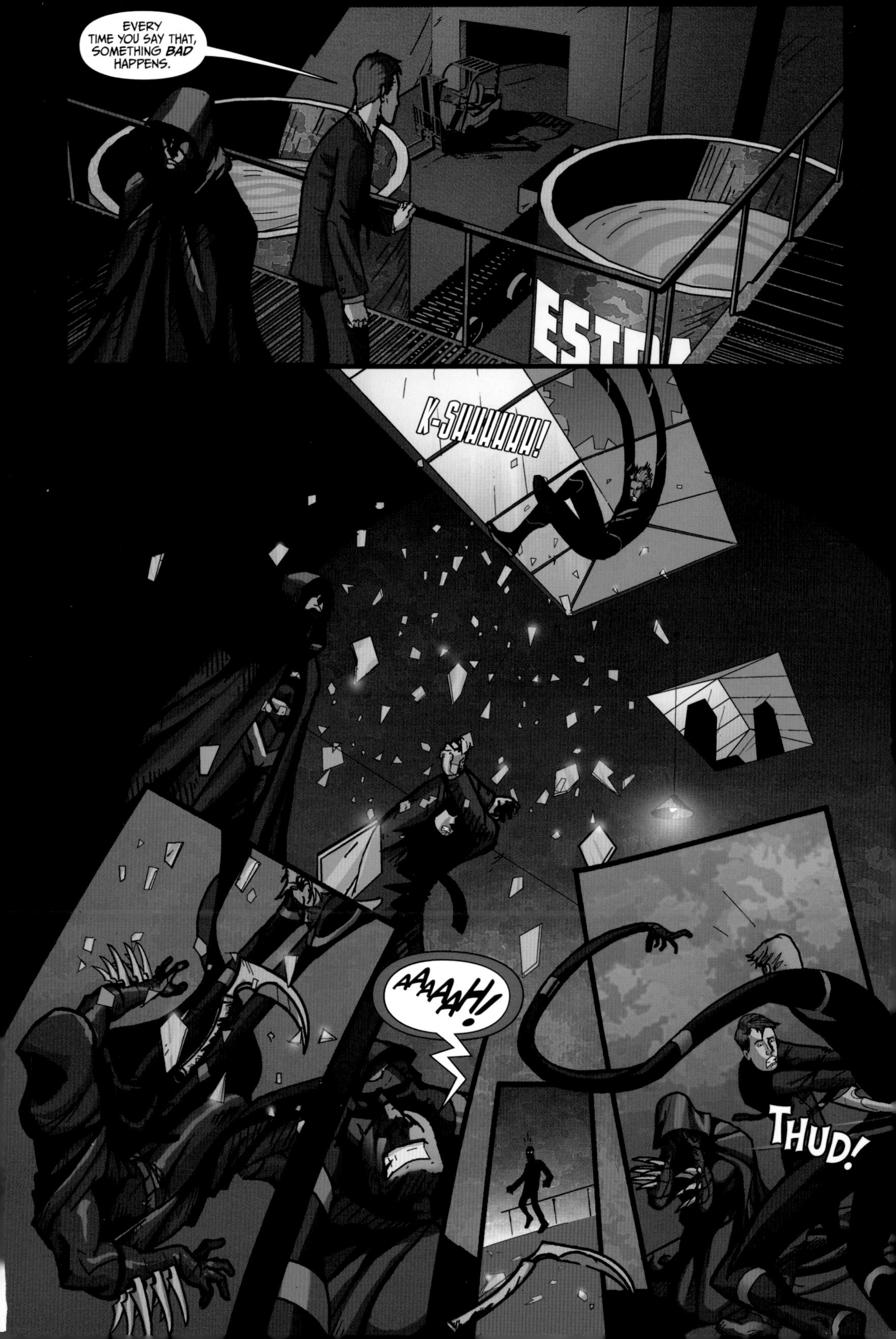
EVERY TIME YOU SAY THAT, SOMETHING *BAD* HAPPENS.
K-SHHHHHH!
AAAAAH!
THUD!

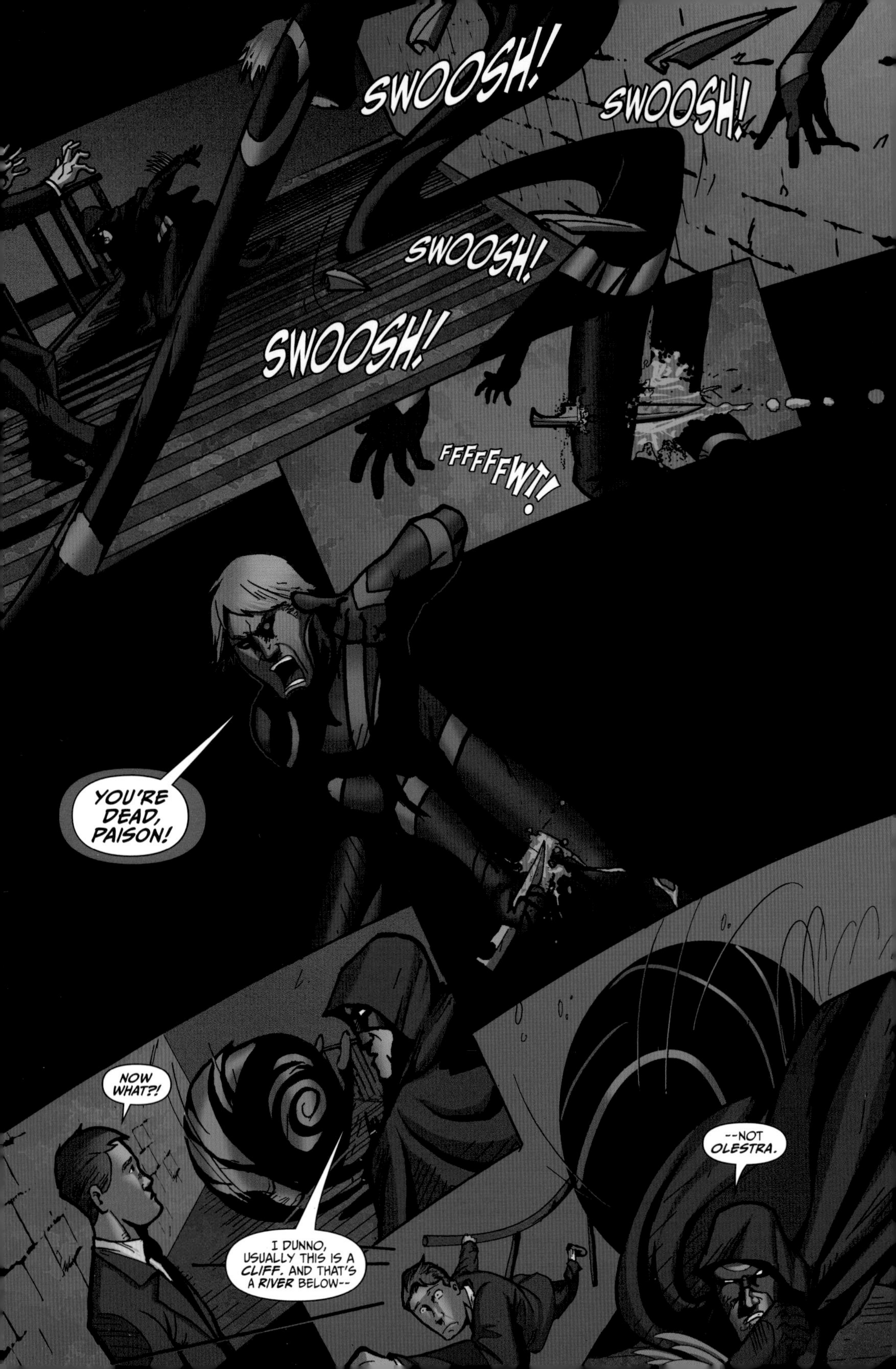
SWOOSH!
SWOOSH!
SWOOSH!
SWOOSH!
FFFFFFWT!!
YOU'RE DEAD, PAISON!
NOW WHAT?!
I DUNNO, USUALLY THIS IS A CLIFF. AND THAT'S A RIVER BELOW--
--NOT OLESTRA.

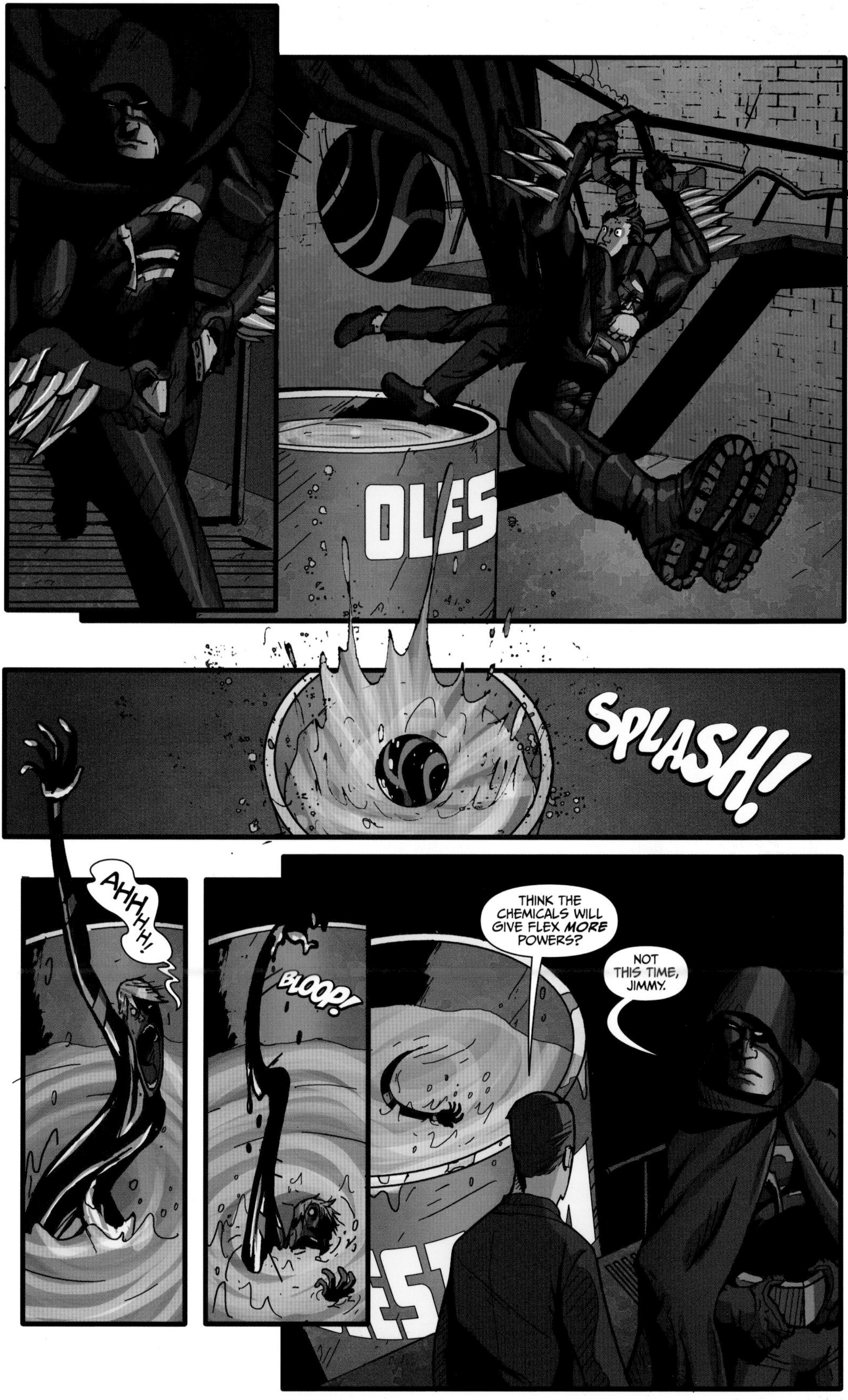
OLES
SPLASH!
AHHHH!
BLOOP!
THINK THE CHEMICALS WILL GIVE FLEX *MORE* POWERS?
NOT THIS TIME, JIMMY.

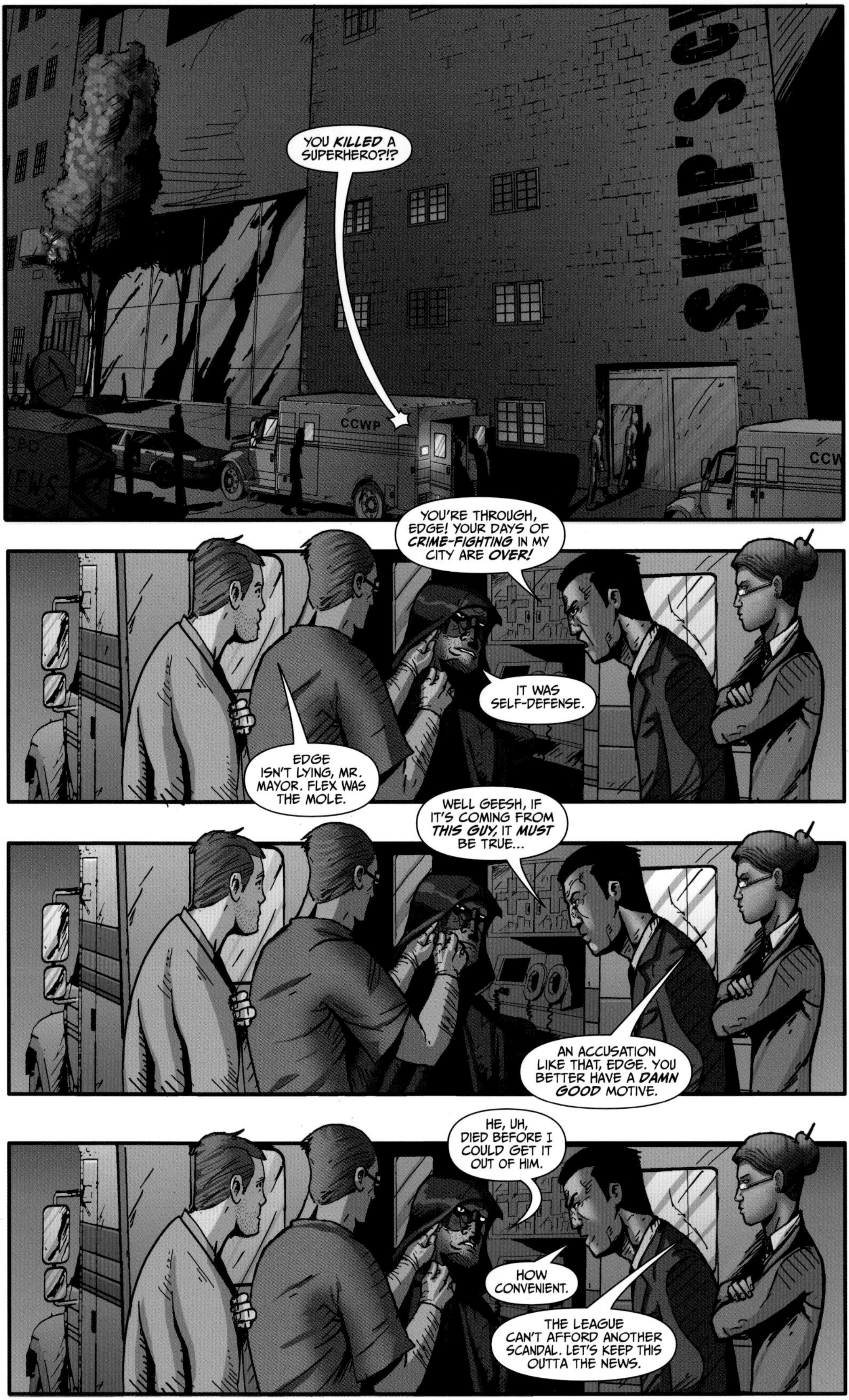
SKIP'S
YOU *KILLED* A SUPERHERO?!?
CCWP
YOU'RE THROUGH, EDGE! YOUR DAYS OF *CRIME-FIGHTING* IN MY CITY ARE *OVER!*
IT WAS SELF-DEFENSE.
EDGE ISN'T LYING, MR. MAYOR. FLEX WAS THE MOLE.
WELL GEESH, IF IT'S COMING FROM *THIS GUY,* IT *MUST* BE TRUE...
AN ACCUSATION LIKE THAT, EDGE. YOU BETTER HAVE A *DAMN GOOD* MOTIVE.
HE, UH, DIED BEFORE I COULD GET IT OUT OF HIM.
HOW CONVENIENT.
THE LEAGUE CAN'T AFFORD ANOTHER SCANDAL. LET'S KEEP THIS OUTTA THE NEWS.

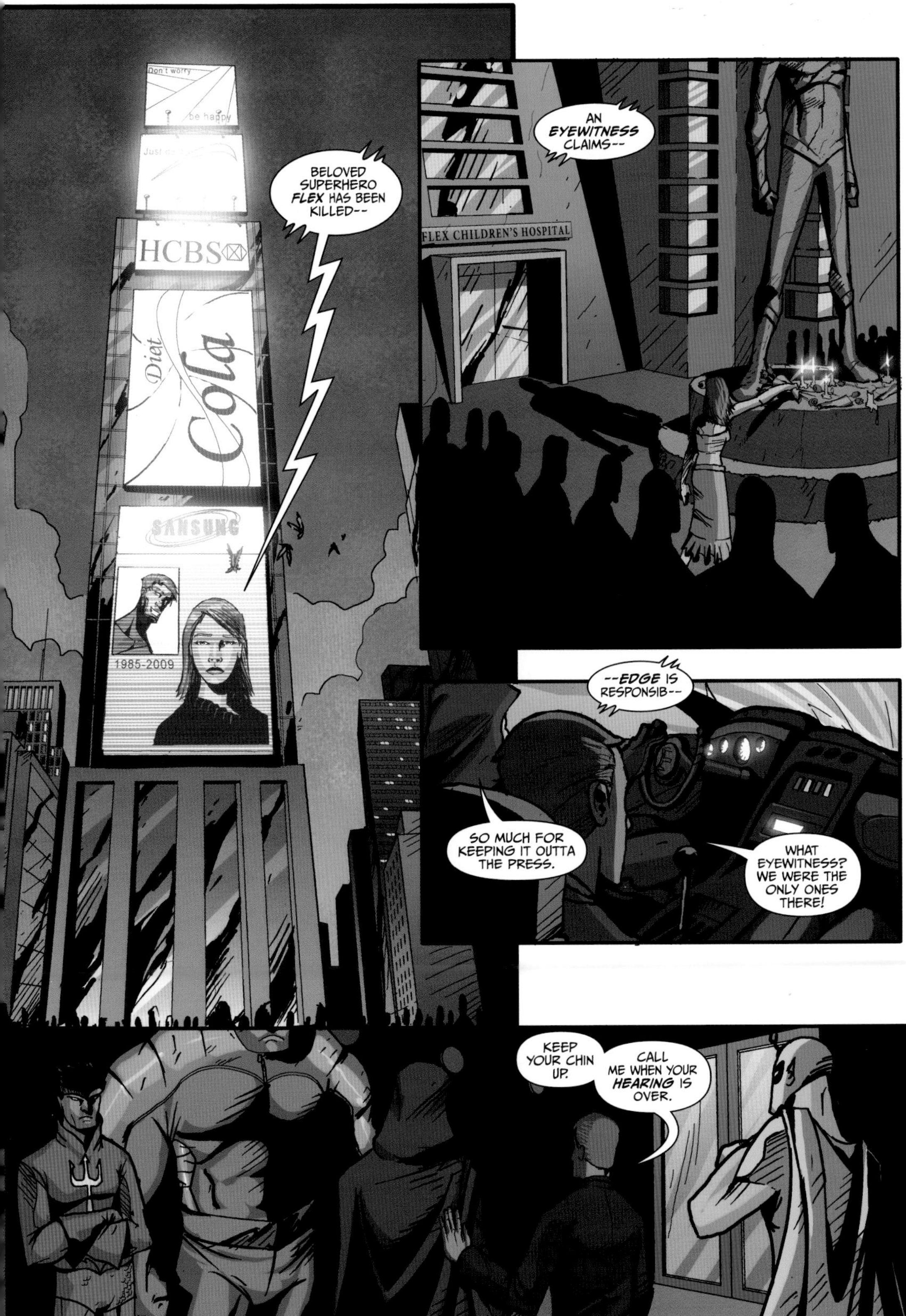

Don't worry
be happy
HCBS
Diet
Cola
SAMSUNG
1985-2009
BELOVED SUPERHERO FLEX HAS BEEN KILLED--
FLEX CHILDREN'S HOSPITAL
AN EYEWITNESS CLAIMS--
--EDGE IS RESPONSIB--
SO MUCH FOR KEEPING IT OUTTA THE PRESS.
WHAT EYEWITNESS? WE WERE THE ONLY ONES THERE!
KEEP YOUR CHIN UP.
CALL ME WHEN YOUR HEARING IS OVER.

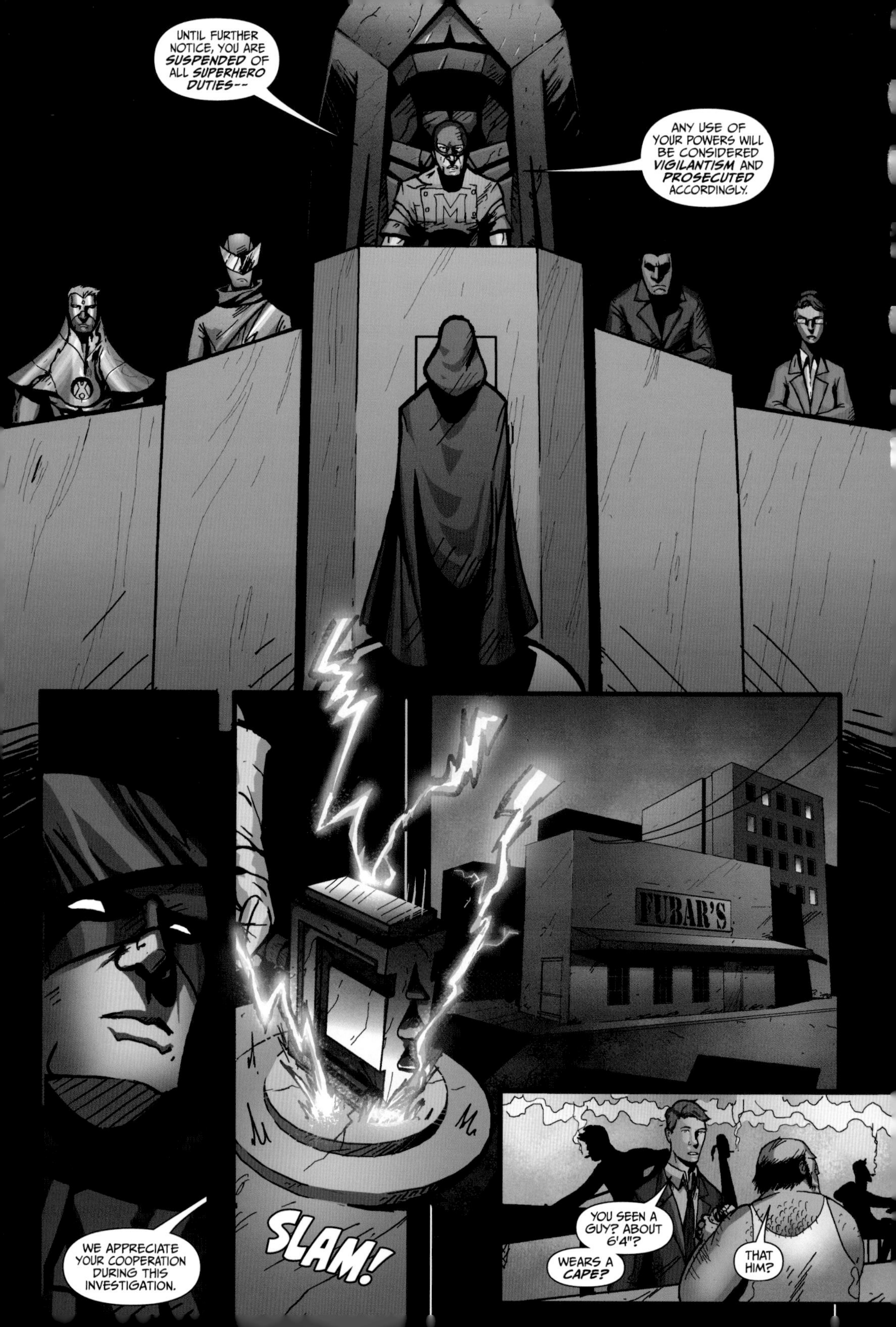
UNTIL FURTHER NOTICE, YOU ARE SUSPENDED OF ALL SUPERHERO DUTIES--
ANY USE OF YOUR POWERS WILL BE CONSIDERED VIGILANTISM AND PROSECUTED ACCORDINGLY.
FUBAR'S
WE APPRECIATE YOUR COOPERATION DURING THIS INVESTIGATION.
SLAM!
YOU SEEN A GUY? ABOUT 6'4"?
WEARS A CAPE?
THAT HIM?

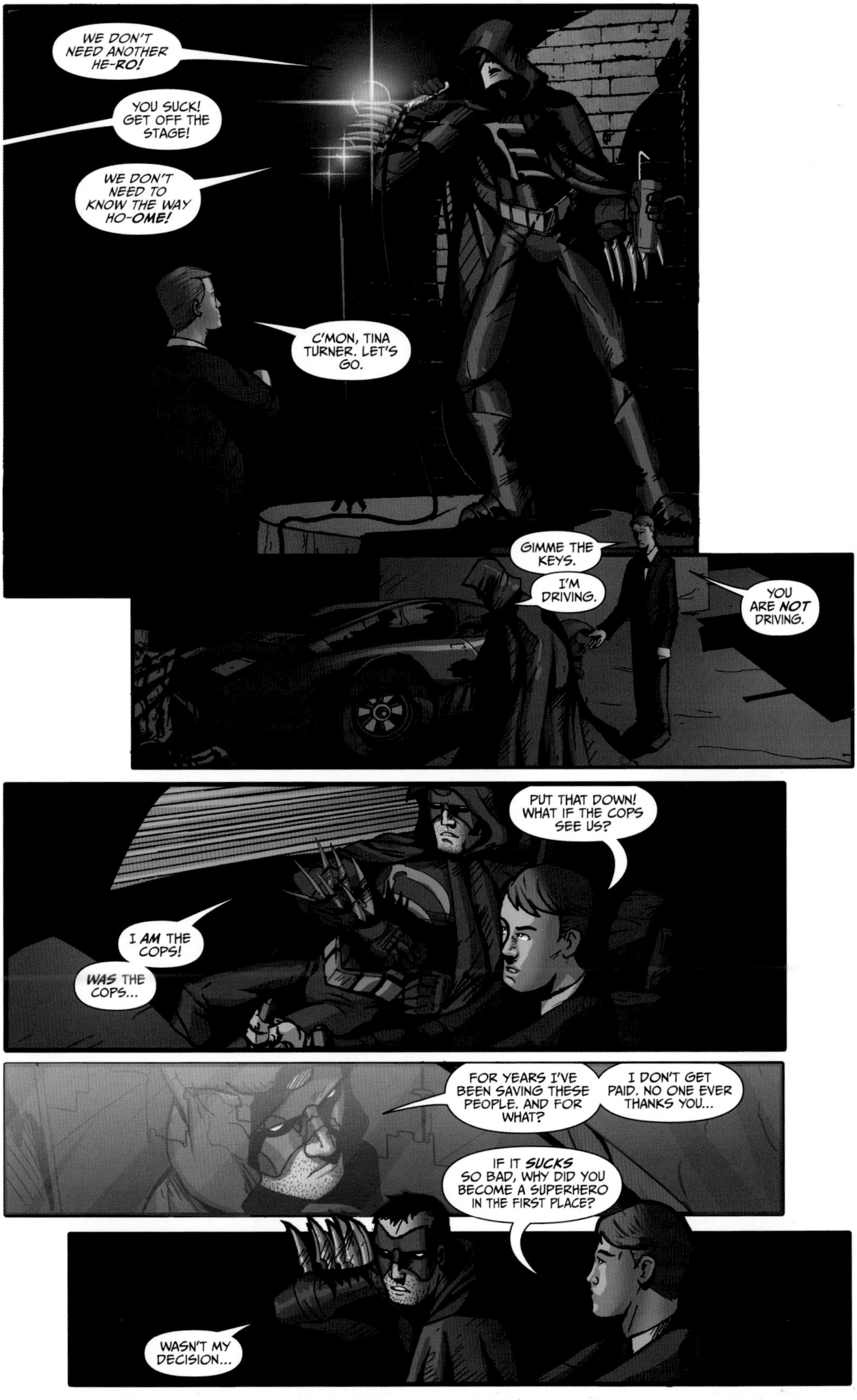
WE DON'T NEED ANOTHER HE-RO!
YOU SUCK! GET OFF THE STAGE!
WE DON'T NEED TO KNOW THE WAY HO-OME!
C'MON, TINA TURNER. LET'S GO.
GIMME THE KEYS.
I'M DRIVING.
YOU ARE NOT DRIVING.
PUT THAT DOWN! WHAT IF THE COPS SEE US?
I AM THE COPS!
WAS THE COPS...
FOR YEARS I'VE BEEN SAVING THESE PEOPLE. AND FOR WHAT?
I DON'T GET PAID. NO ONE EVER THANKS YOU...
IF IT SUCKS SO BAD, WHY DID YOU BECOME A SUPERHERO IN THE FIRST PLACE?
WASN'T MY DECISION...

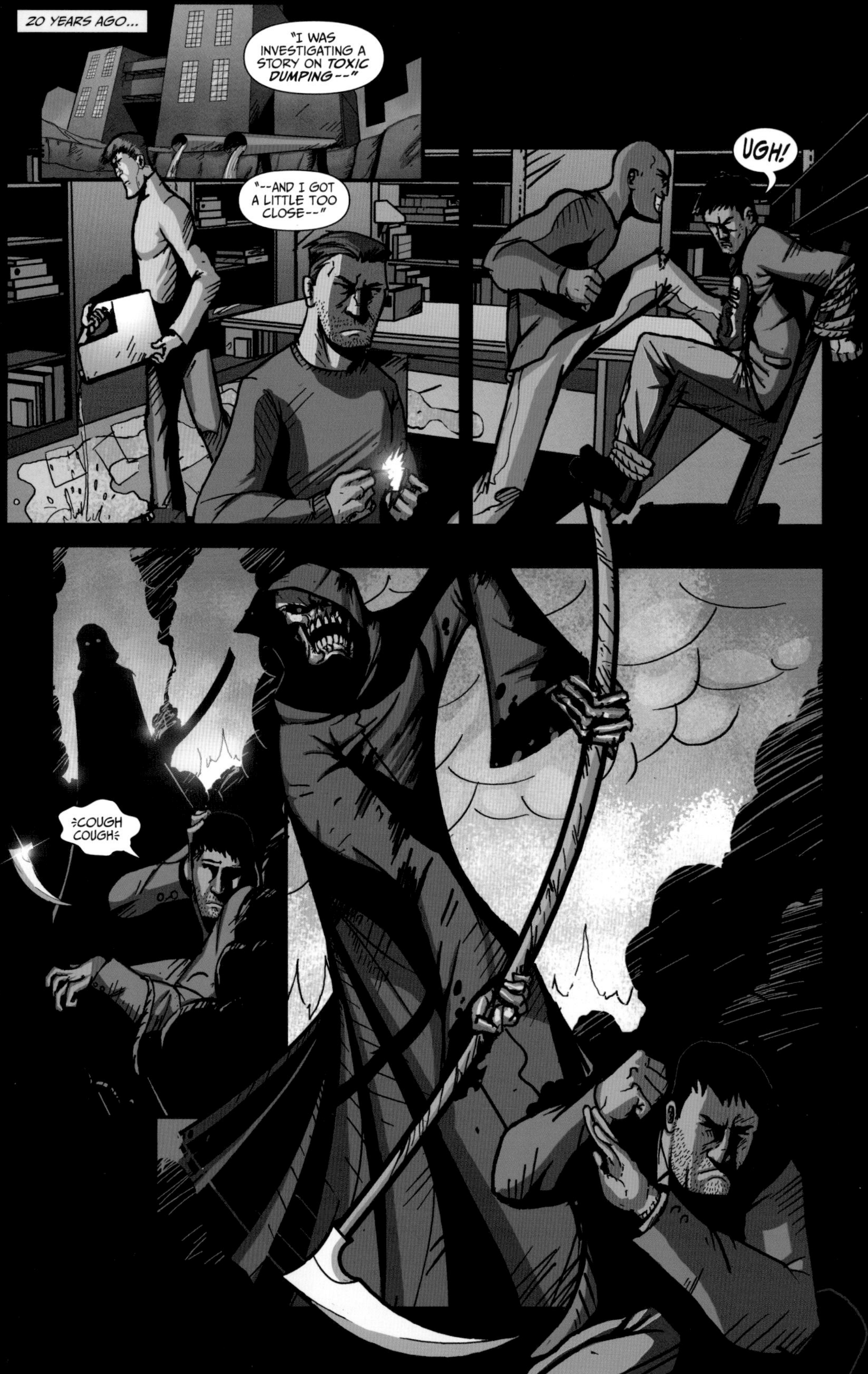
20 YEARS AGO...
"I WAS INVESTIGATING A STORY ON TOXIC DUMPING--"
"--AND I GOT A LITTLE TOO CLOSE--"
UGH!
COUGH COUGH

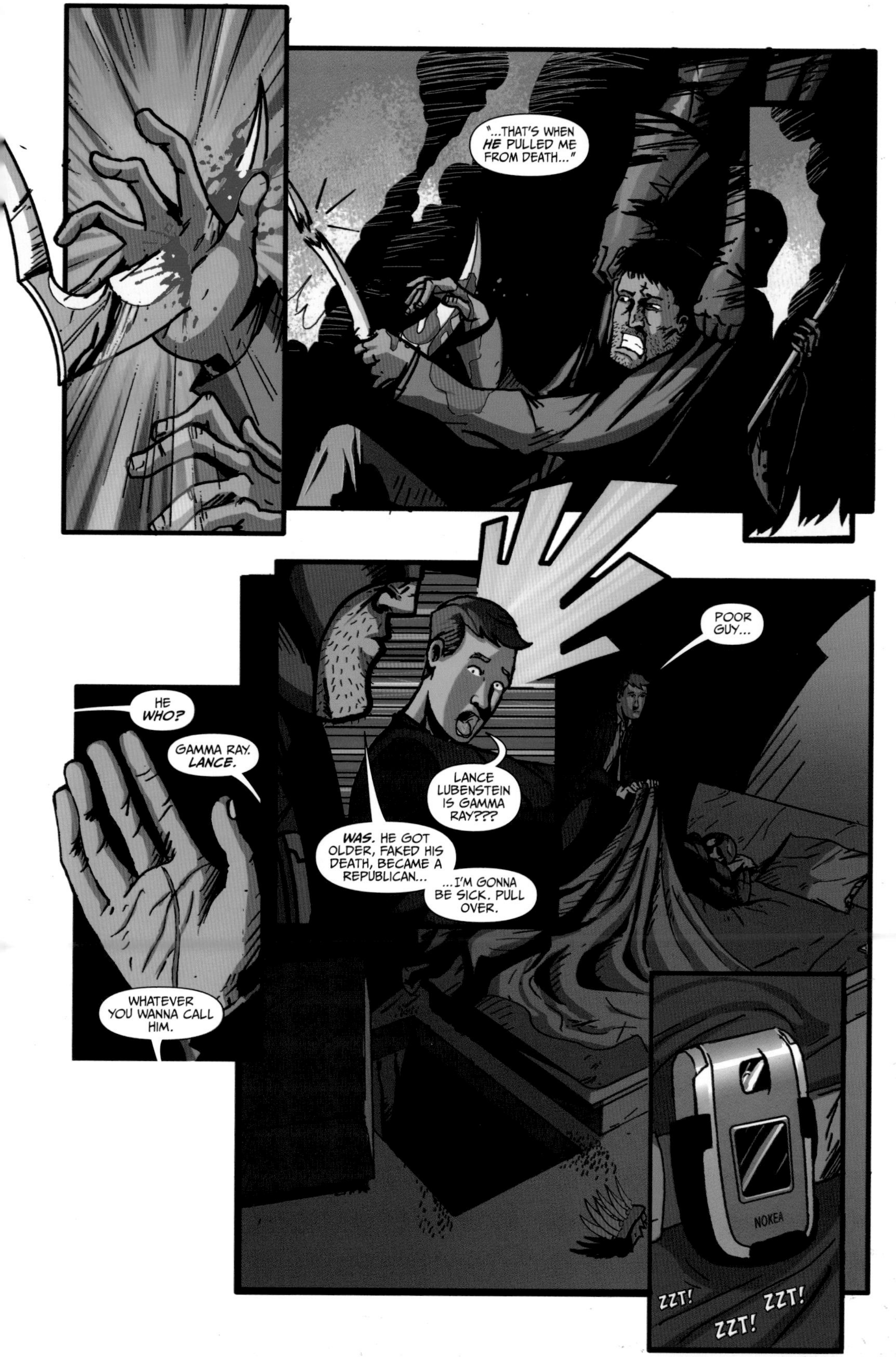
"...THAT'S WHEN HE PULLED ME FROM DEATH..."
POOR GUY...
HE WHO?
GAMMA RAY. LANCE.
LANCE LUBENSTEIN IS GAMMA RAY???
WAS. HE GOT OLDER, FAKED HIS DEATH, BECAME A REPUBLICAN...
...I'M GONNA BE SICK. PULL OVER.
WHATEVER YOU WANNA CALL HIM.
NOKEA
ZZT!
ZZT!
ZZT!

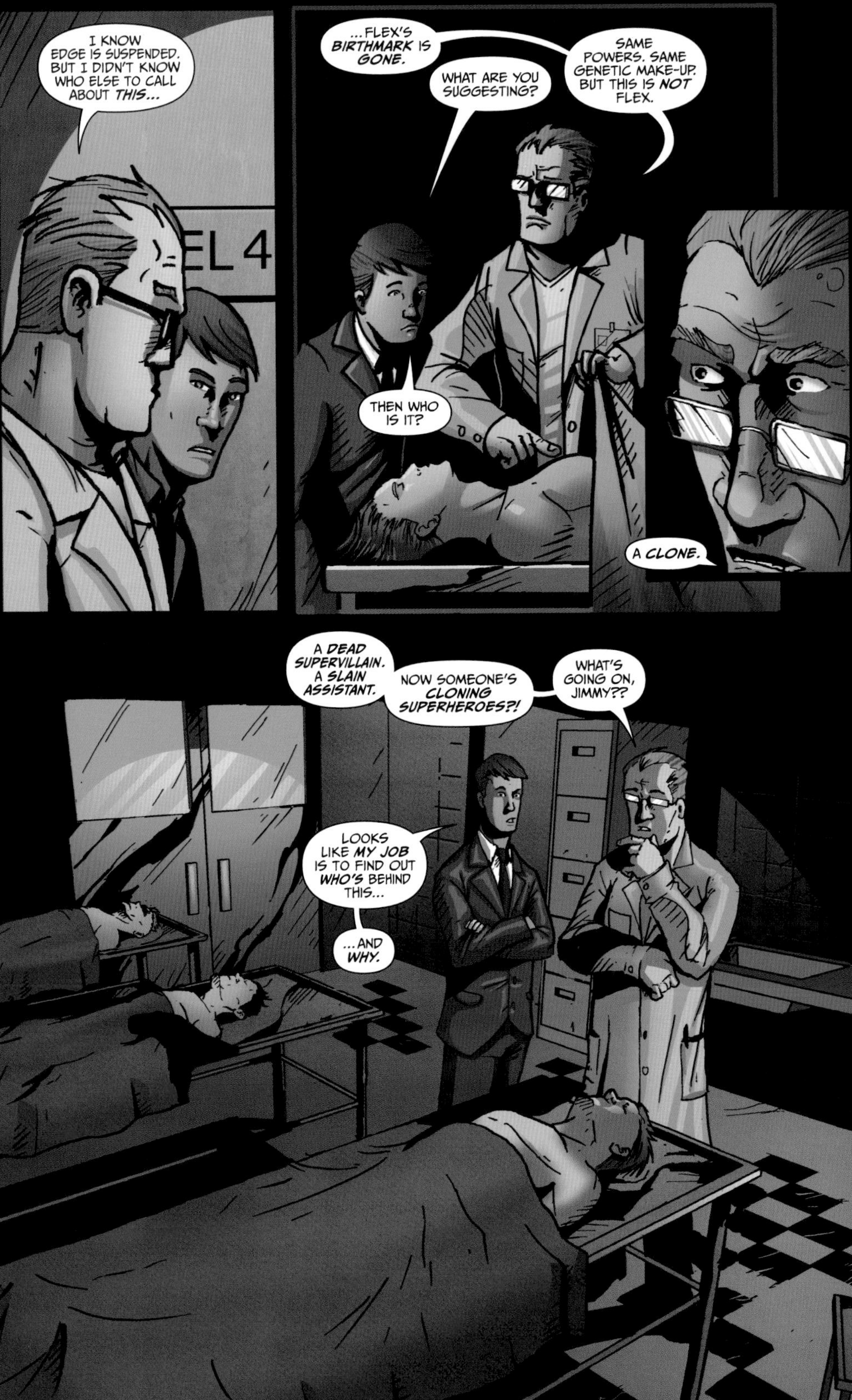
I KNOW EDGE IS SUSPENDED. BUT I DIDN'T KNOW WHO ELSE TO CALL ABOUT *THIS*...
EL 4
...FLEX'S *BIRTHMARK* IS *GONE.*
SAME POWERS. SAME GENETIC MAKE-UP. BUT THIS IS *NOT* FLEX.
WHAT ARE YOU SUGGESTING?
THEN WHO IS IT?
A *CLONE.*
A *DEAD SUPERVILLAIN.* A *SLAIN ASSISTANT.*
NOW SOMEONE'S *CLONING SUPERHEROES?!*
WHAT'S GOING ON, JIMMY??
LOOKS LIKE *MY JOB* IS TO FIND OUT *WHO'S* BEHIND THIS...
...AND *WHY.*

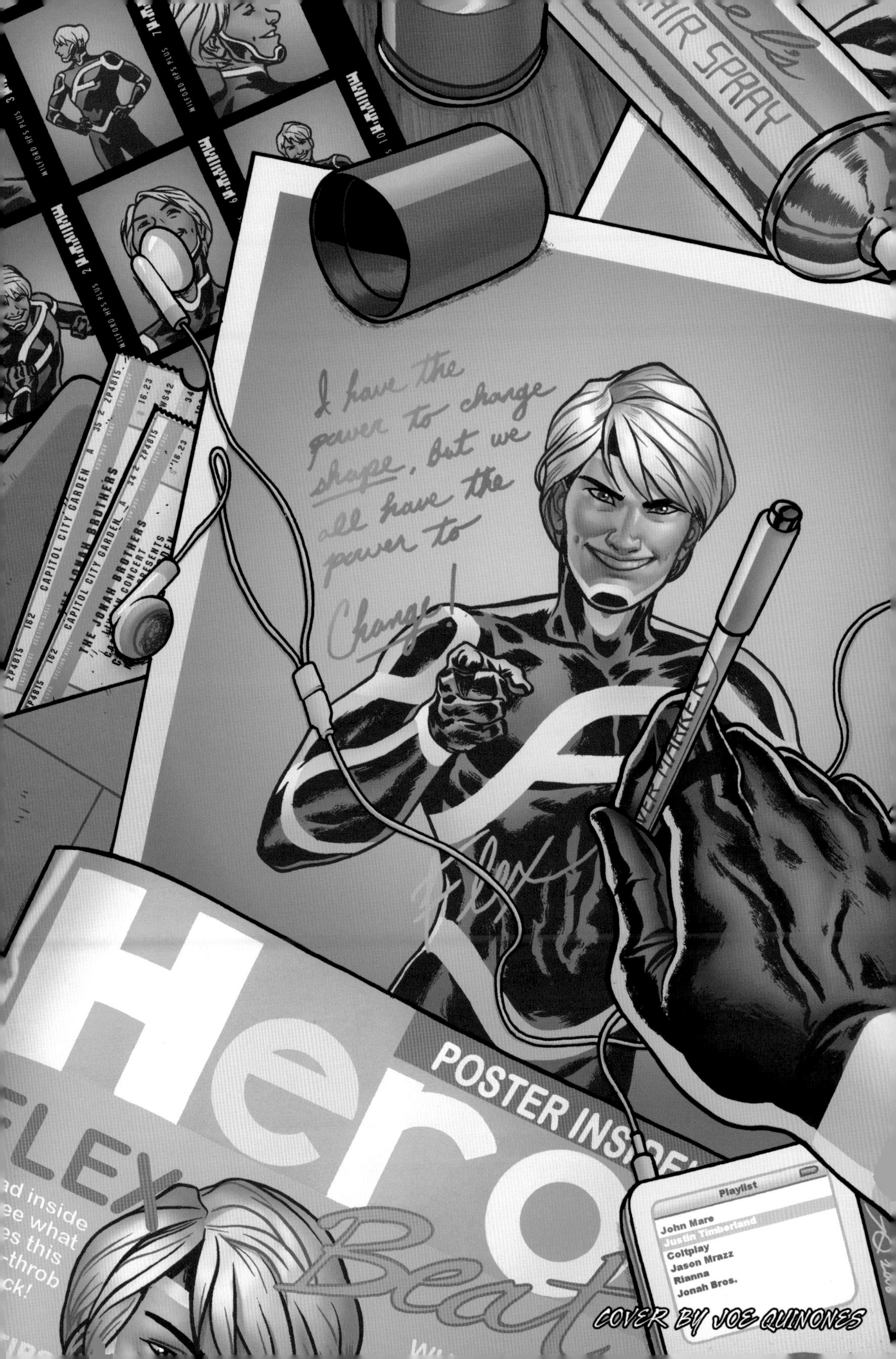

AIR SPRAY
MILFORD HPS PLUS
CAPITOL CITY GARDEN
THE JONAH BROTHERS
I have the power to change shape, but we all have the power to Change!
POSTER INSIDE
Hero
FLEX
Beat
Playlist
John Mare
Justin Timberland
Coltplay
Jason Mrazz
Rianna
Jonah Bros.
COVER BY JOE QUINONES

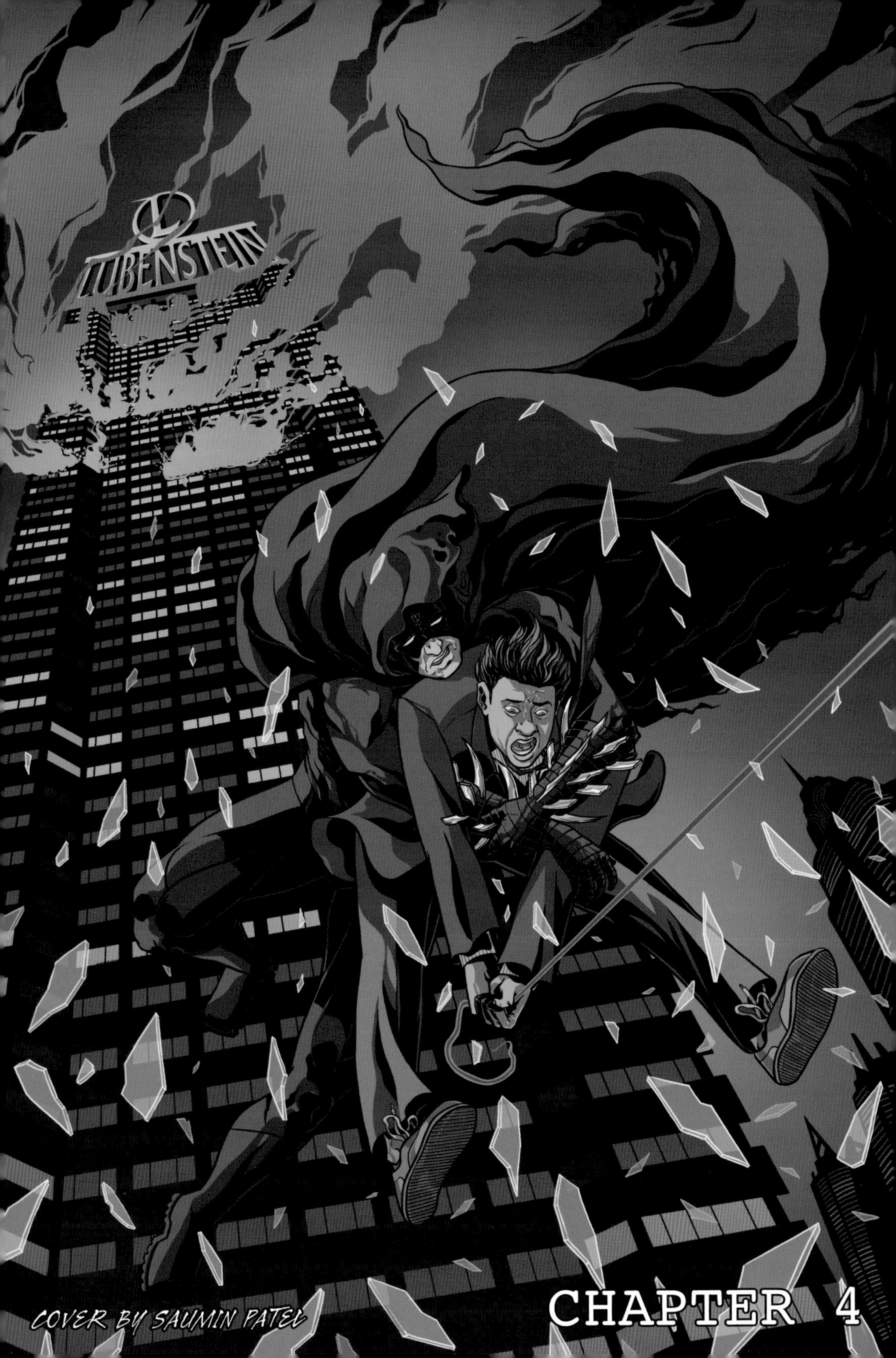
LUBENSTEIN

COVER BY SAUMIN PATEL

CHAPTER 4

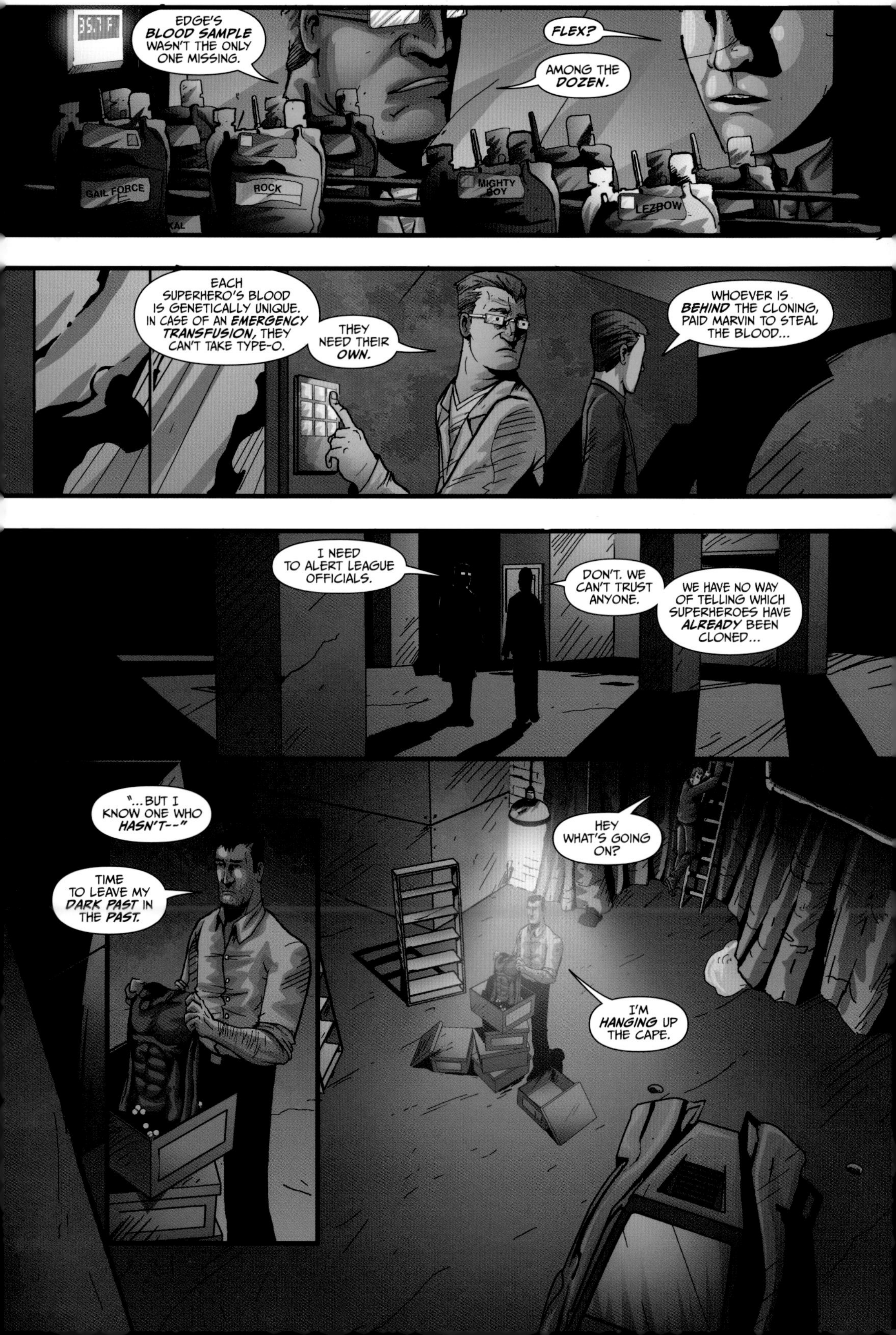
35.7 F
EDGE'S BLOOD SAMPLE WASN'T THE ONLY ONE MISSING.
FLEX?
AMONG THE DOZEN.
GAIL FORCE
ROCK
MIGHTY BOY
LEZBOW
EACH SUPERHERO'S BLOOD IS GENETICALLY UNIQUE. IN CASE OF AN EMERGENCY TRANSFUSION, THEY CAN'T TAKE TYPE-O.
THEY NEED THEIR OWN.
WHOEVER IS BEHIND THE CLONING, PAID MARVIN TO STEAL THE BLOOD...
I NEED TO ALERT LEAGUE OFFICIALS.
DON'T. WE CAN'T TRUST ANYONE.
WE HAVE NO WAY OF TELLING WHICH SUPERHEROES HAVE ALREADY BEEN CLONED...
"...BUT I KNOW ONE WHO HASN'T--"
TIME TO LEAVE MY DARK PAST IN THE PAST.
HEY WHAT'S GOING ON?
I'M HANGING UP THE CAPE.

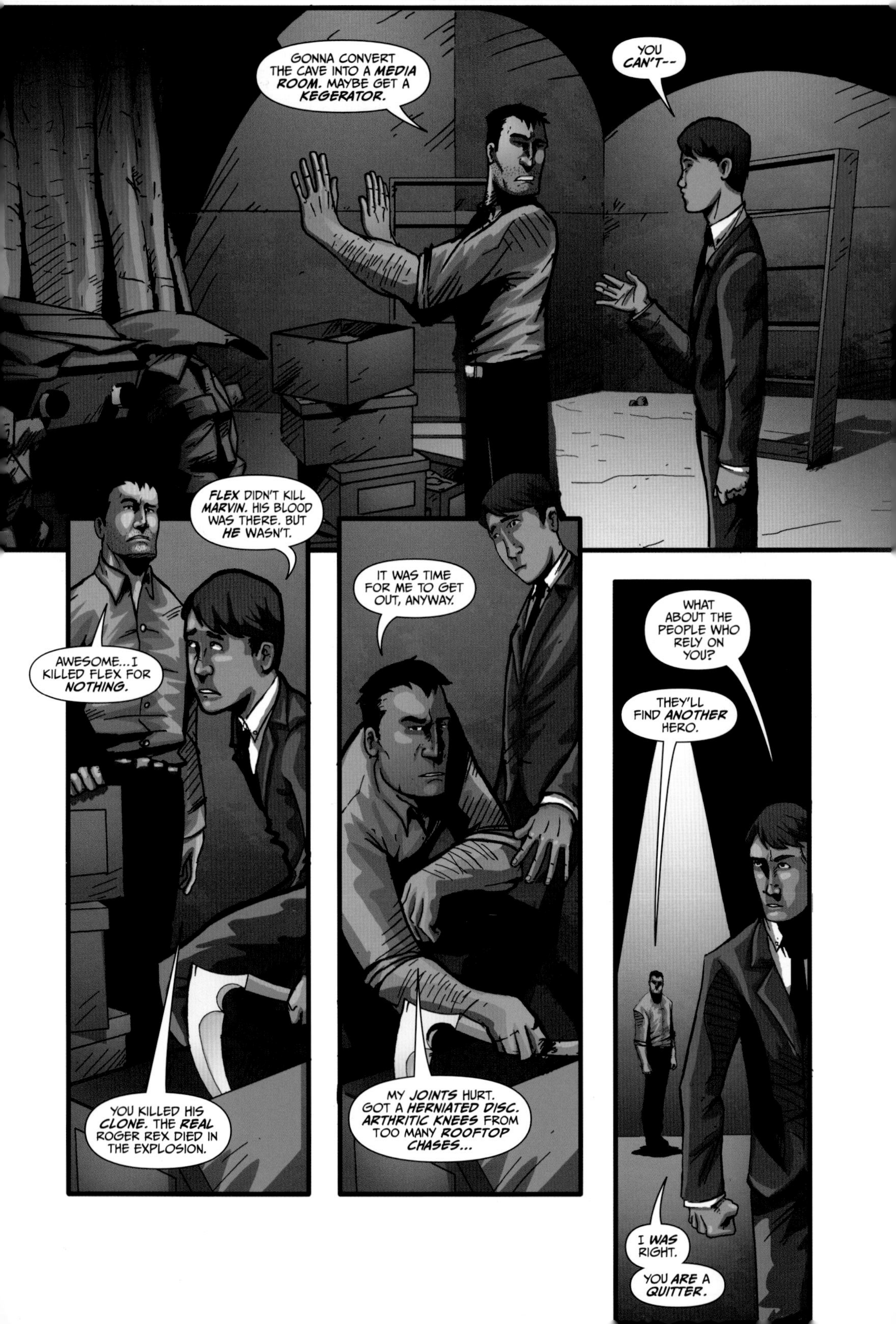
GONNA CONVERT THE CAVE INTO A MEDIA ROOM. MAYBE GET A KEGERATOR.
YOU CAN'T--
FLEX DIDN'T KILL MARVIN. HIS BLOOD WAS THERE. BUT HE WASN'T.
AWESOME...I KILLED FLEX FOR NOTHING.
YOU KILLED HIS CLONE. THE REAL ROGER REX DIED IN THE EXPLOSION.
IT WAS TIME FOR ME TO GET OUT, ANYWAY.
MY JOINTS HURT. GOT A HERNIATED DISC. ARTHRITIC KNEES FROM TOO MANY ROOFTOP CHASES...
WHAT ABOUT THE PEOPLE WHO RELY ON YOU?
THEY'LL FIND ANOTHER HERO.
I WAS RIGHT.
YOU ARE A QUITTER.

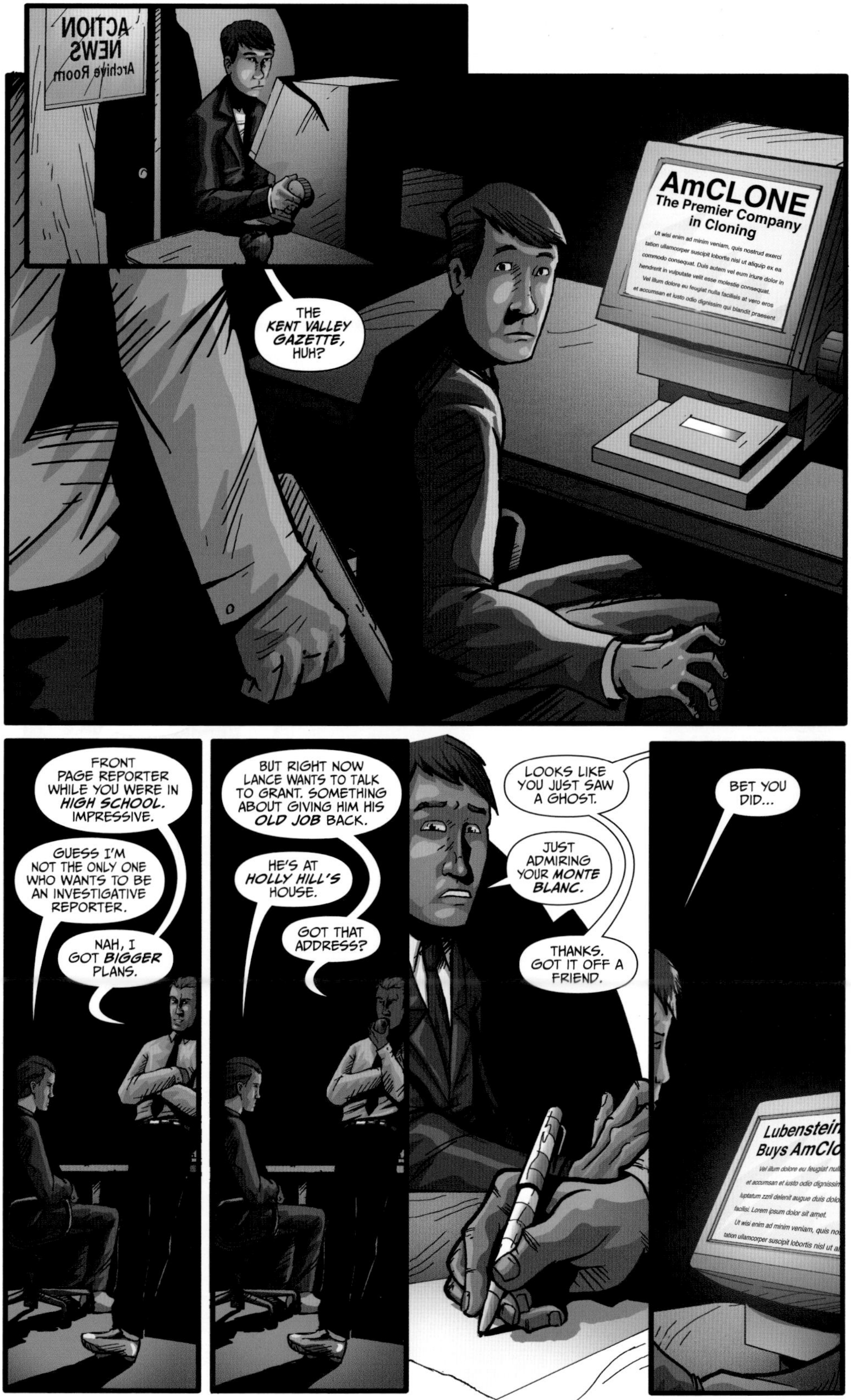

ACTION NEWS Archive Room
AmCLONE
The Premier Company in Cloning
Ut wisi enim ad minim veniam, quis nostrud exerci tation ullamcorper suscipit lobortis nisl ut aliquip ex ea commodo consequat. Duis autem vel eum iriure dolor in hendrerit in vulputate velit esse molestie consequat. Vel illum dolore eu feugiat nulla facilisis at vero eros et accumsan et iusto odio dignissim qui blandit praesent
THE *KENT VALLEY GAZETTE,* HUH?
FRONT PAGE REPORTER WHILE YOU WERE IN *HIGH SCHOOL.* IMPRESSIVE.
GUESS I'M NOT THE ONLY ONE WHO WANTS TO BE AN INVESTIGATIVE REPORTER.
NAH, I GOT *BIGGER* PLANS.
BUT RIGHT NOW LANCE WANTS TO TALK TO GRANT. SOMETHING ABOUT GIVING HIM HIS *OLD JOB* BACK.
HE'S AT *HOLLY HILL'S* HOUSE.
GOT THAT ADDRESS?
LOOKS LIKE YOU JUST SAW A GHOST.
JUST ADMIRING YOUR *MONTE BLANC.*
THANKS. GOT IT OFF A FRIEND.
BET YOU DID...
Lubenstein
Buys AmClo

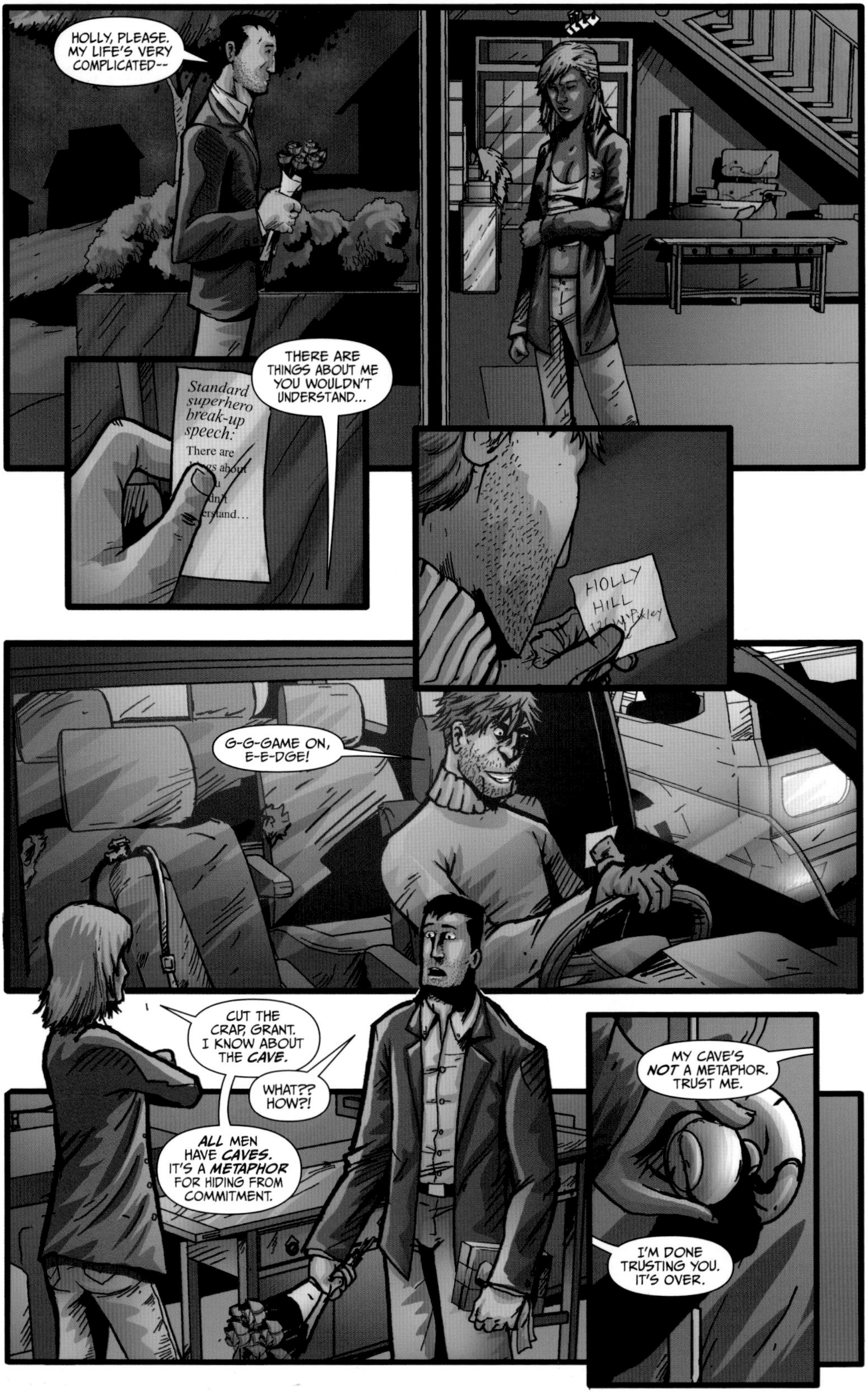
HOLLY, PLEASE. MY LIFE'S VERY COMPLICATED--
Standard superhero break-up speech:
There are
THERE ARE THINGS ABOUT ME YOU WOULDN'T UNDERSTAND...
HOLLY HILL
G-G-GAME ON, E-E-DGE!
CUT THE CRAP, GRANT. I KNOW ABOUT THE *CAVE.*
WHAT?? HOW?!
ALL MEN HAVE ***CAVES.*** IT'S A ***METAPHOR*** FOR HIDING FROM COMMITMENT.
MY CAVE'S ***NOT*** A METAPHOR. TRUST ME.
I'M DONE TRUSTING YOU. IT'S OVER.

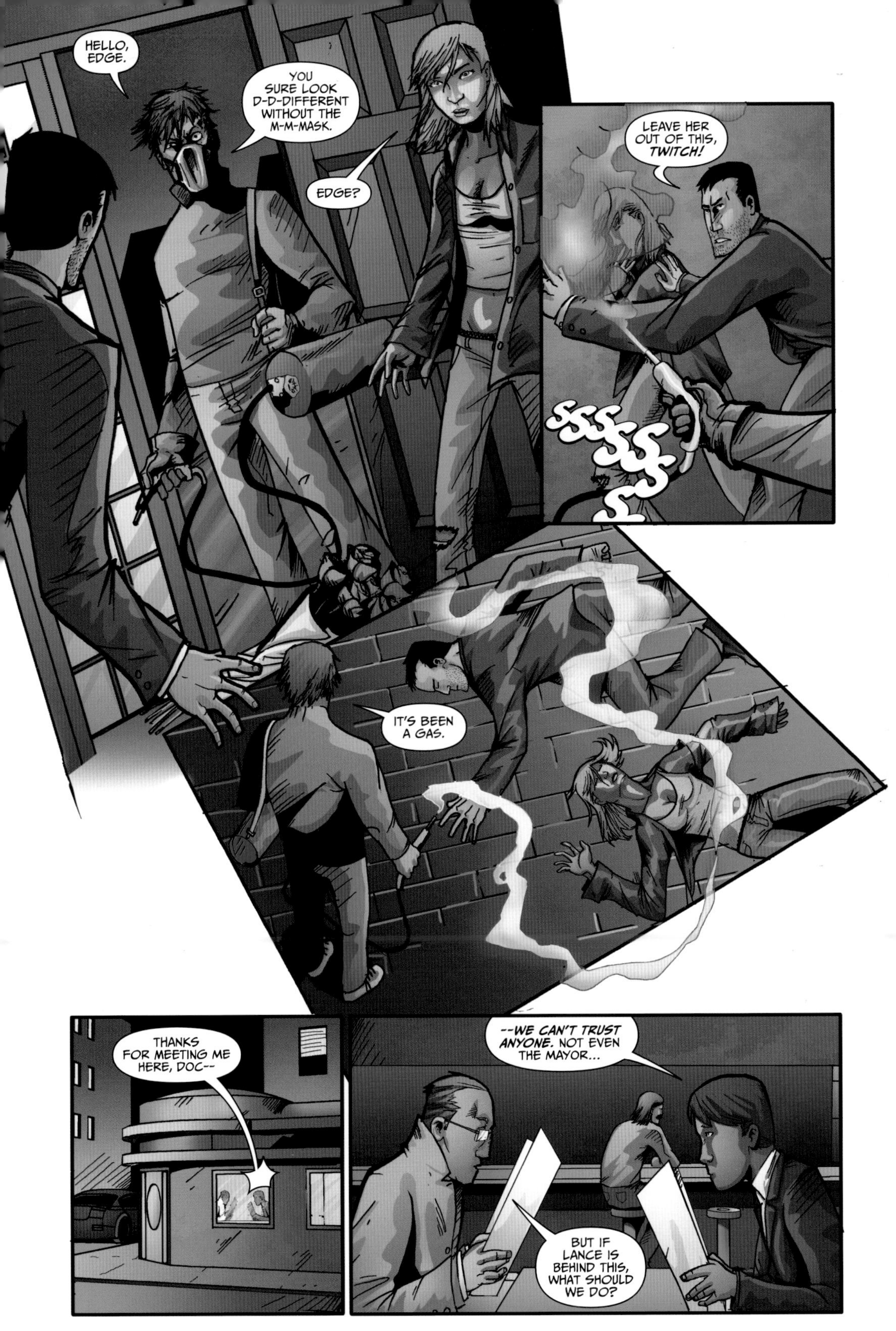
HELLO, EDGE.
YOU SURE LOOK D-D-DIFFERENT WITHOUT THE M-M-MASK.
EDGE?
LEAVE HER OUT OF THIS, *TWITCH!*
SSSSSSS
IT'S BEEN A GAS.
THANKS FOR MEETING ME HERE, DOC--
--*WE CAN'T TRUST ANYONE.* NOT EVEN THE MAYOR...
BUT IF LANCE IS BEHIND THIS, WHAT SHOULD WE DO?

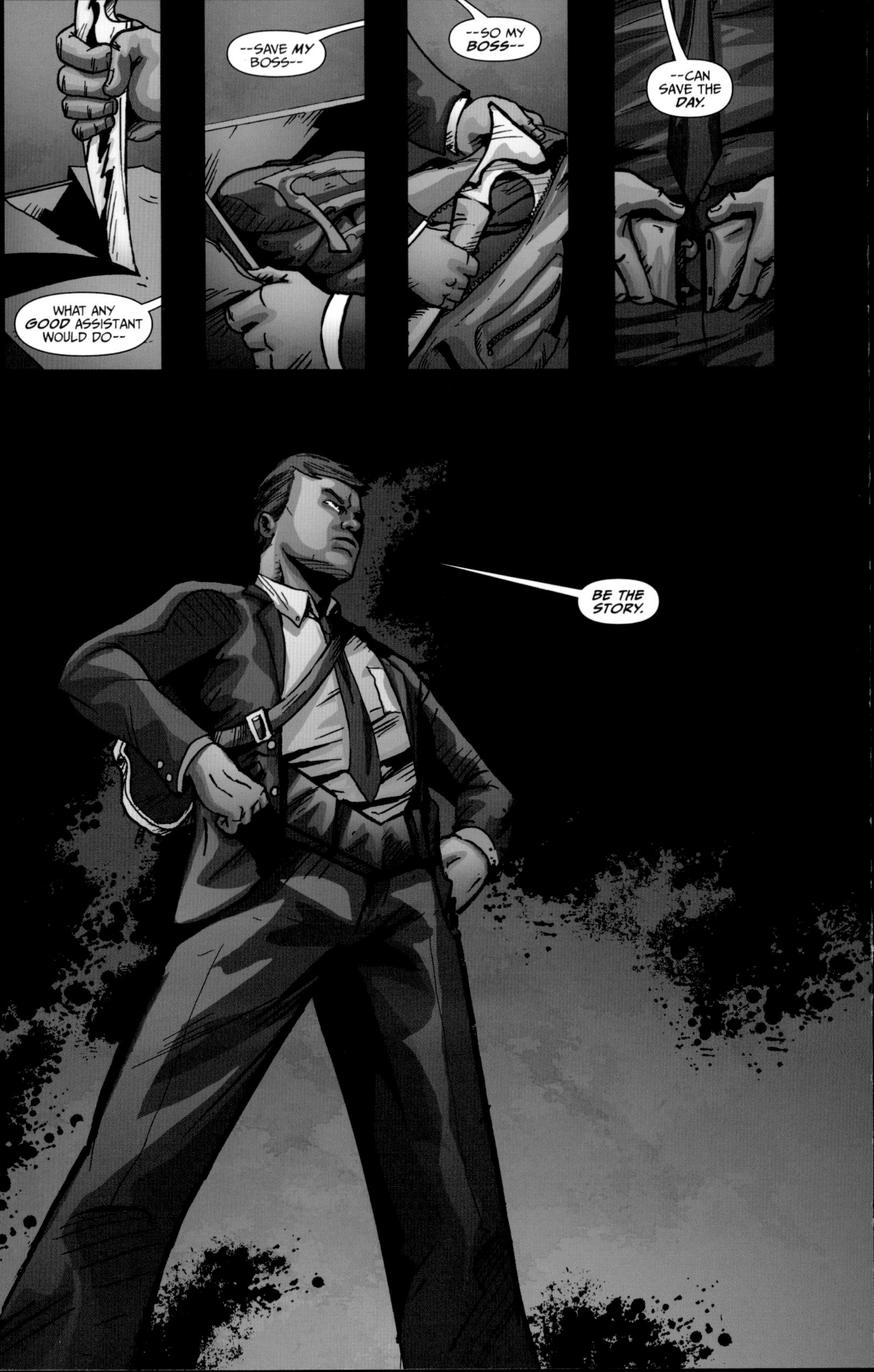
WHAT ANY GOOD ASSISTANT WOULD DO--
--SAVE MY BOSS--
--SO MY BOSS--
--CAN SAVE THE DAY.
BE THE STORY.

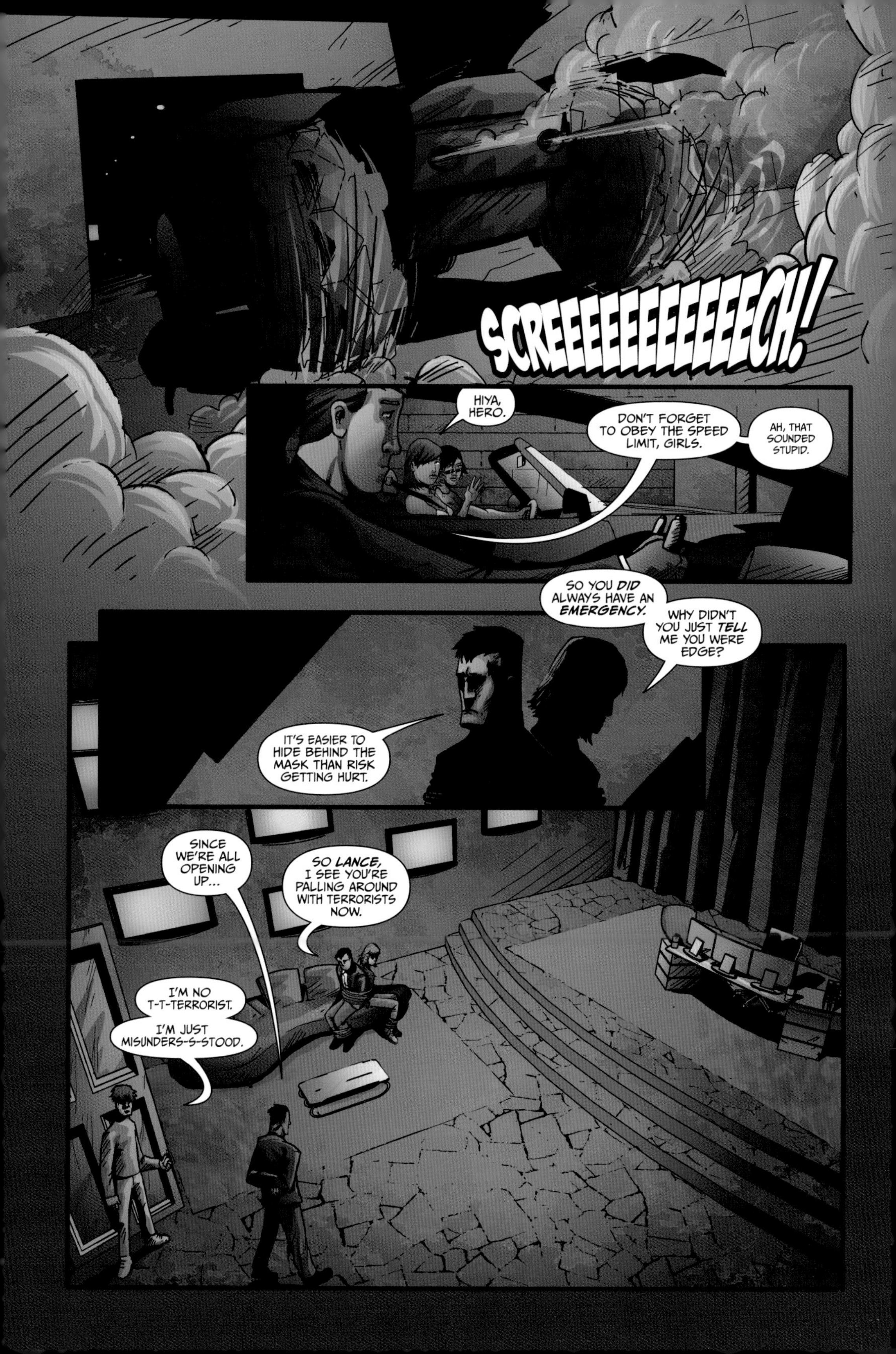
SCREEEEEEEEEEEECH!
HIYA, HERO.
DON'T FORGET TO OBEY THE SPEED LIMIT, GIRLS.
AH, THAT SOUNDED STUPID.
SO YOU DID ALWAYS HAVE AN EMERGENCY.
WHY DIDN'T YOU JUST TELL ME YOU WERE EDGE?
IT'S EASIER TO HIDE BEHIND THE MASK THAN RISK GETTING HURT.
SINCE WE'RE ALL OPENING UP...
SO LANCE, I SEE YOU'RE PALLING AROUND WITH TERRORISTS NOW.
I'M NO T-T-TERRORIST.
I'M JUST MISUNDERS-S-STOOD.

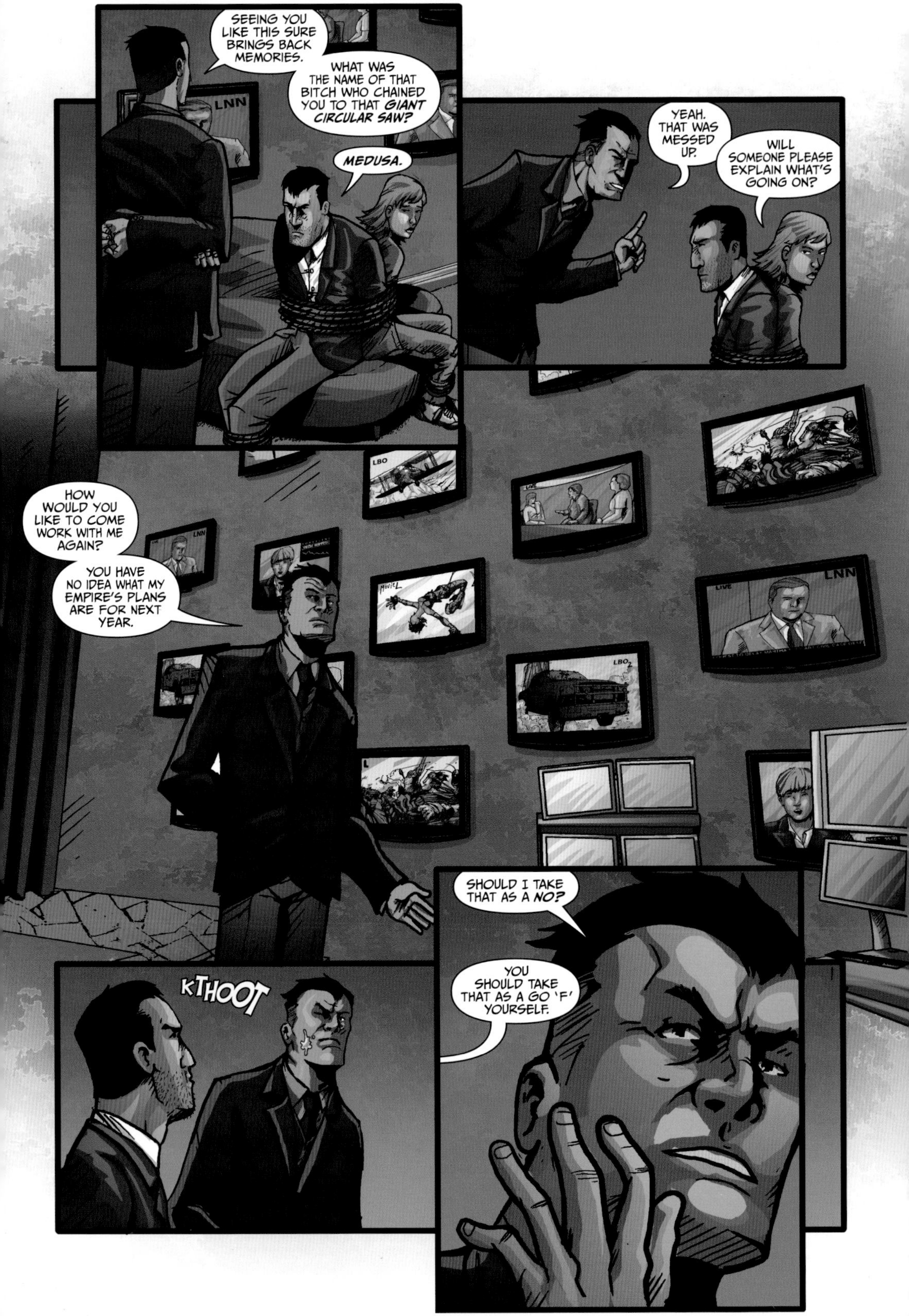
SEEING YOU LIKE THIS SURE BRINGS BACK MEMORIES.
WHAT WAS THE NAME OF THAT BITCH WHO CHAINED YOU TO THAT GIANT CIRCULAR SAW?
MEDUSA.
YEAH. THAT WAS MESSED UP.
WILL SOMEONE PLEASE EXPLAIN WHAT'S GOING ON?
HOW WOULD YOU LIKE TO COME WORK WITH ME AGAIN?
YOU HAVE NO IDEA WHAT MY EMPIRE'S PLANS ARE FOR NEXT YEAR.
LNN
LBO
LIVE
SHOULD I TAKE THAT AS A NO?
YOU SHOULD TAKE THAT AS A GO 'F' YOURSELF.
KTHOOT

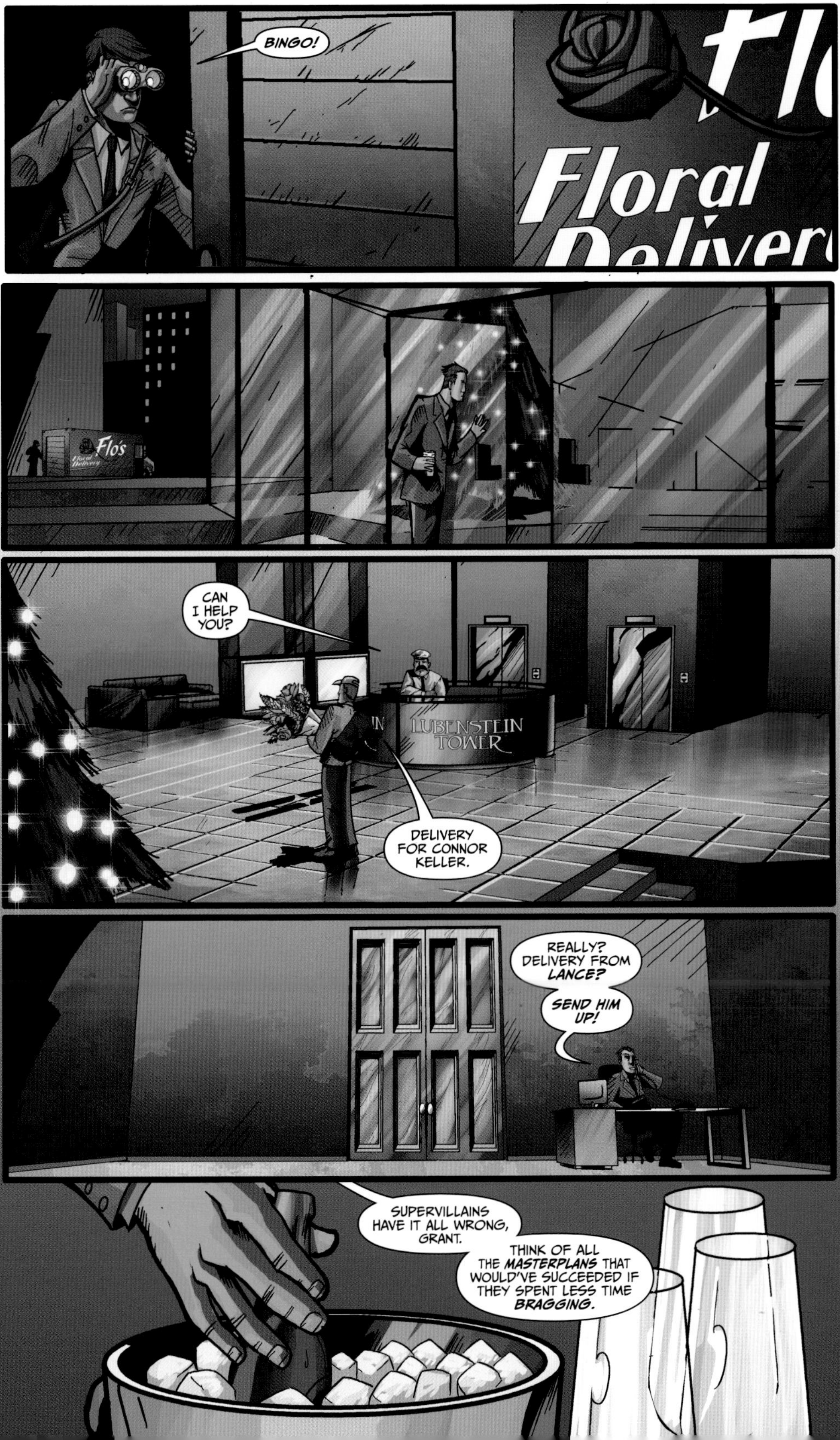
BINGO!
Floral Delivery
Flo's Floral Delivery
CAN I HELP YOU?
LUBENSTEIN TOWER
DELIVERY FOR CONNOR KELLER.
REALLY? DELIVERY FROM LANCE?
SEND HIM UP!
SUPERVILLAINS HAVE IT ALL WRONG, GRANT.
THINK OF ALL THE MASTERPLANS THAT WOULD'VE SUCCEEDED IF THEY SPENT LESS TIME BRAGGING.

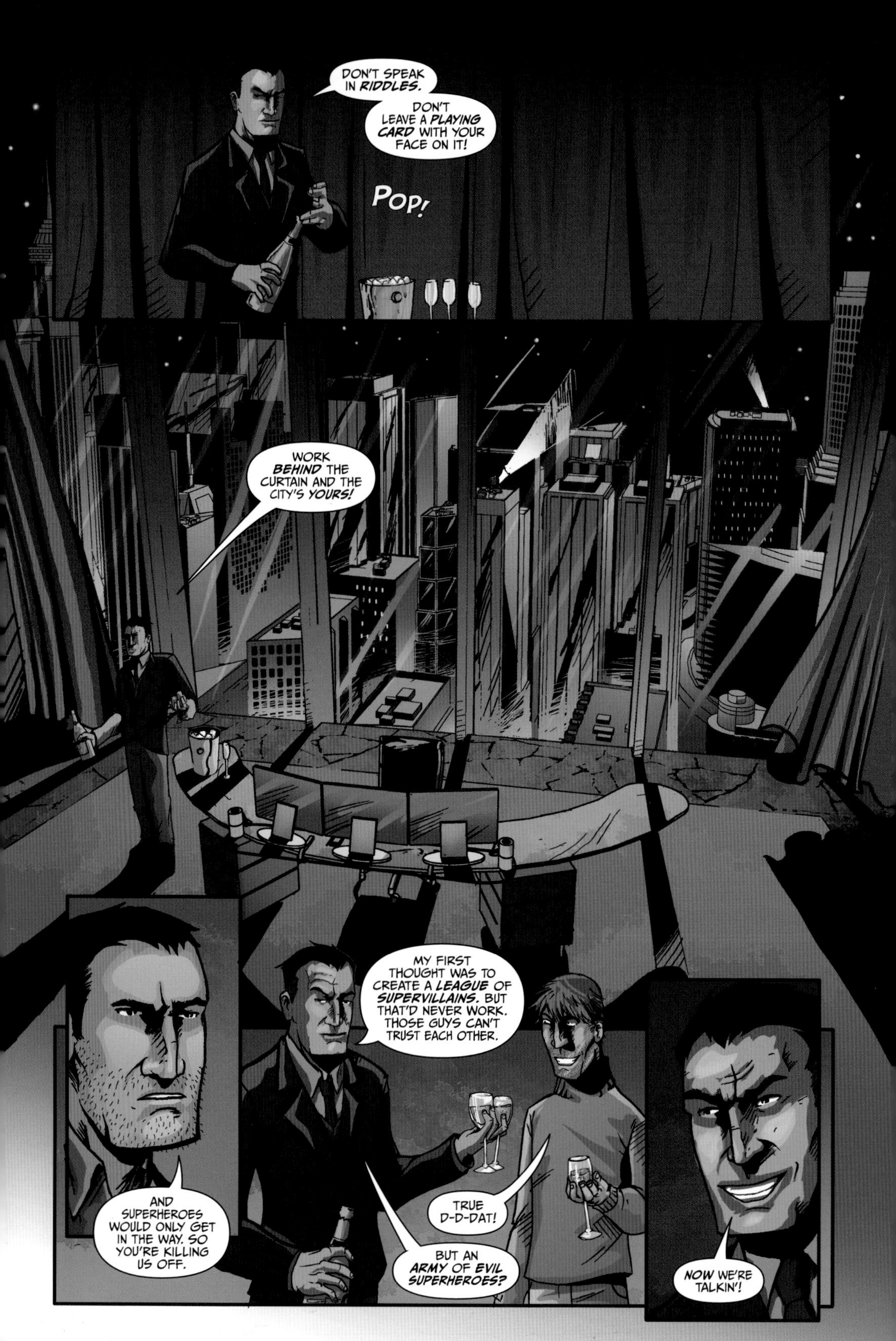
DON'T SPEAK IN *RIDDLES.*
DON'T LEAVE A *PLAYING CARD* WITH YOUR FACE ON IT!
POP!
WORK *BEHIND* THE CURTAIN AND THE CITY'S *YOURS!*
MY FIRST THOUGHT WAS TO CREATE A *LEAGUE* OF *SUPERVILLAINS.* BUT THAT'D NEVER WORK. THOSE GUYS CAN'T TRUST EACH OTHER.
AND SUPERHEROES WOULD ONLY GET IN THE WAY. SO YOU'RE KILLING US OFF.
TRUE D-D-DAT!
BUT AN *ARMY* OF *EVIL SUPERHEROES?*
NOW WE'RE TALKIN'!

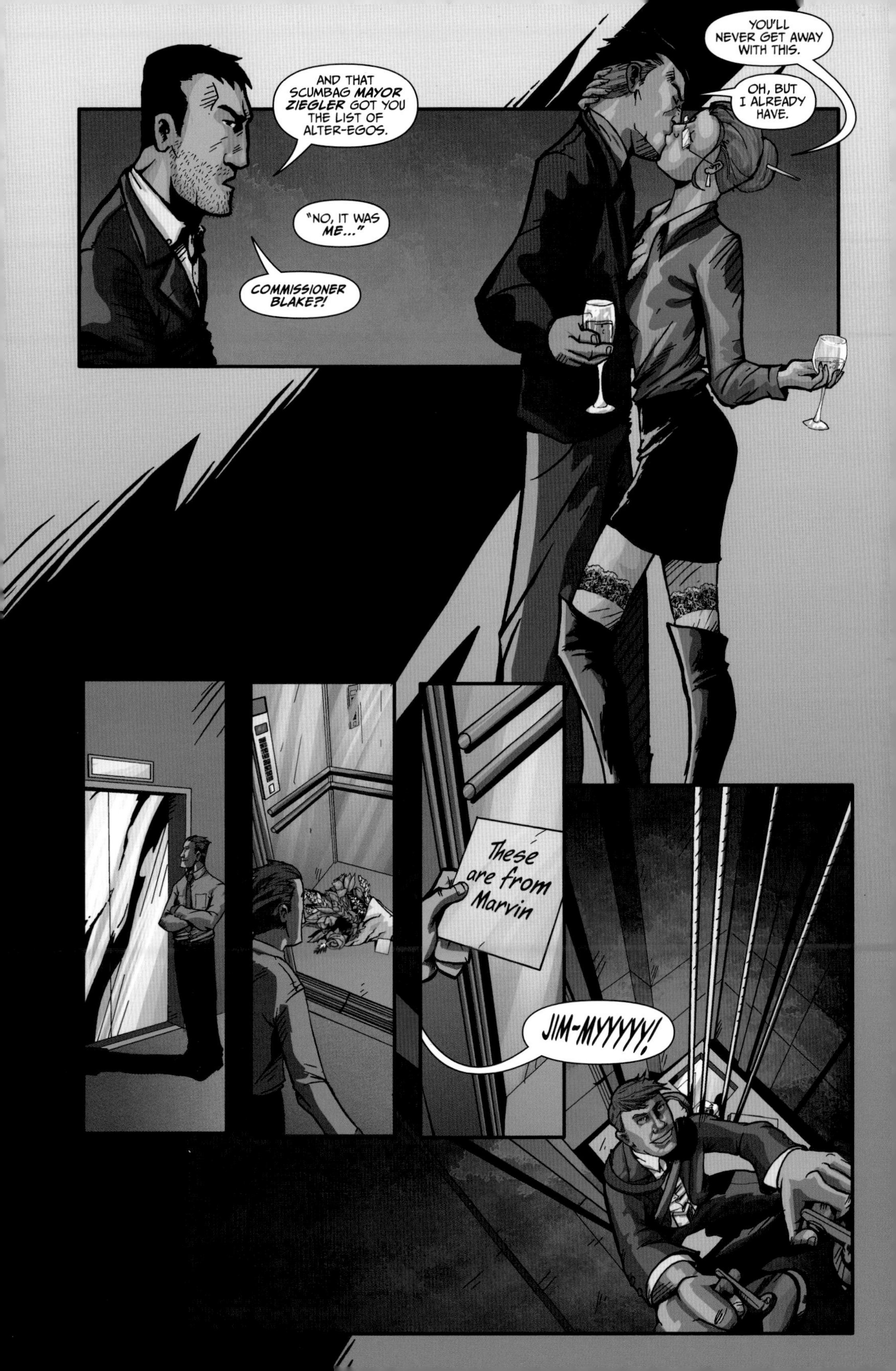

AND THAT SCUMBAG MAYOR ZIEGLER GOT YOU THE LIST OF ALTER-EGOS.
"NO, IT WAS ME..."
COMMISSIONER BLAKE?!
YOU'LL NEVER GET AWAY WITH THIS.
OH, BUT I ALREADY HAVE.
These are from Marvin
JIM-MYYYYY!

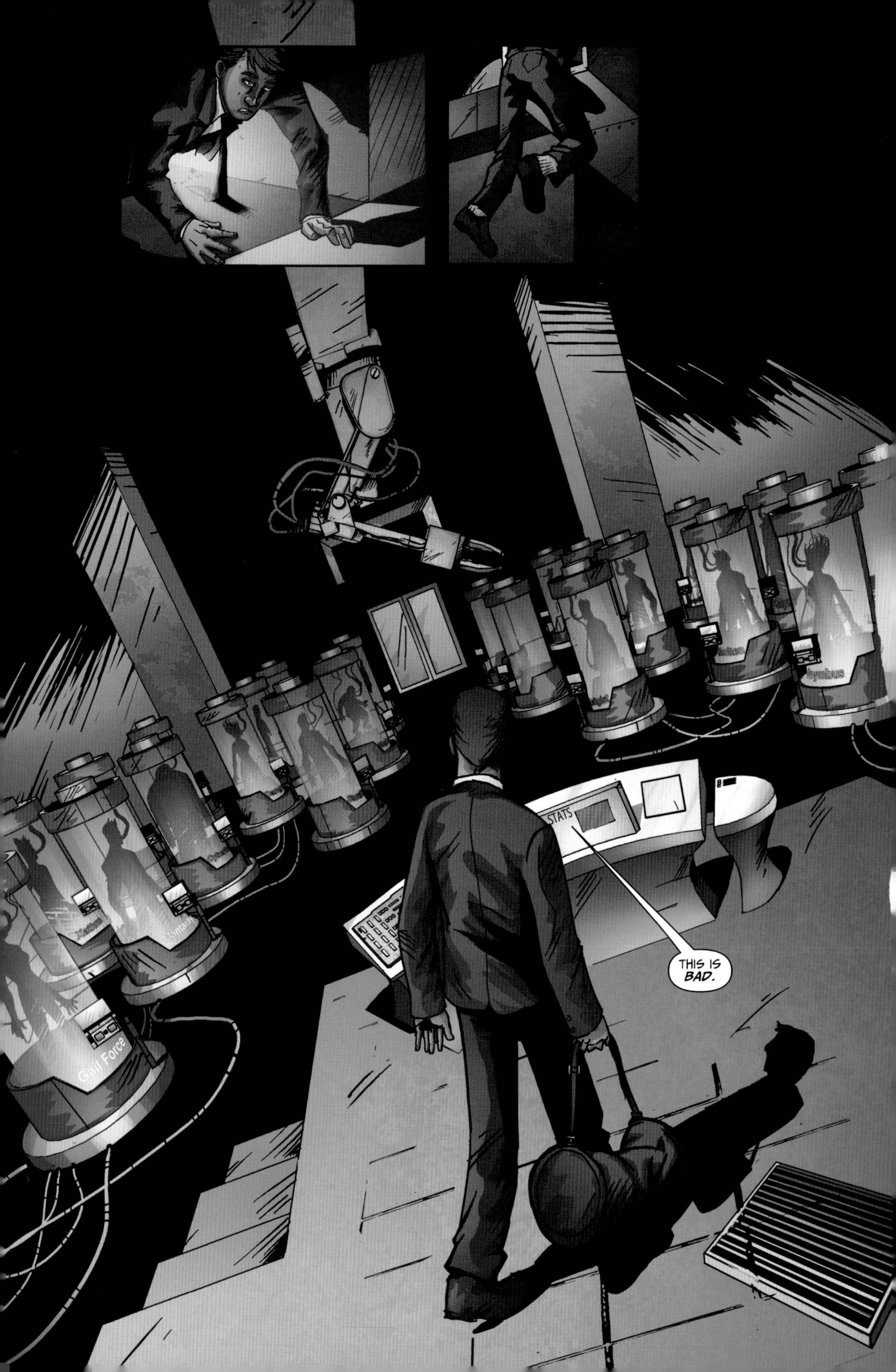
STATS
Gail Force
THIS IS *BAD.*

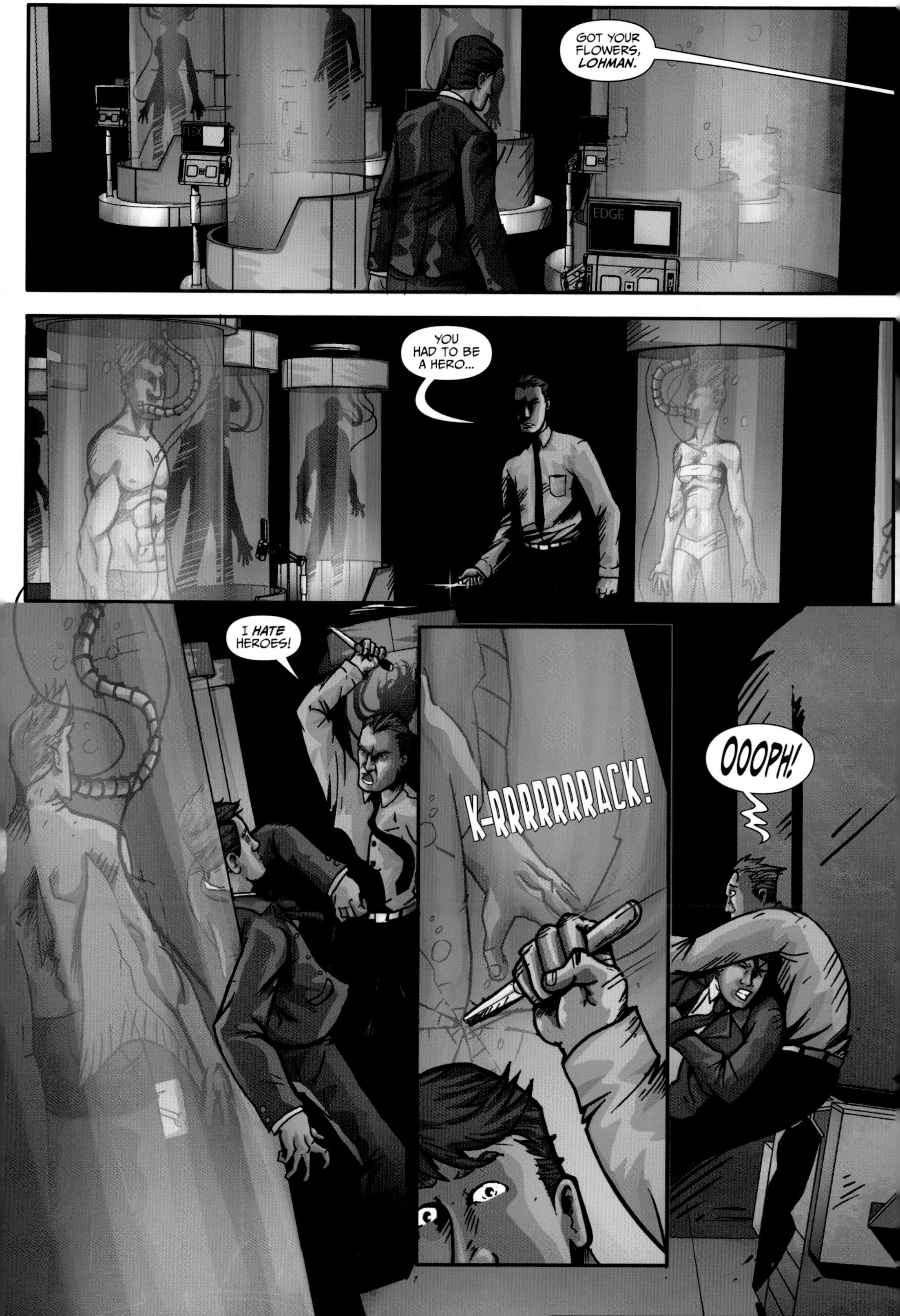

GOT YOUR FLOWERS, LOHMAN.
FLEX
EDGE
YOU HAD TO BE A HERO...
I HATE HEROES!
K-RRRRRRRACK!
OOOPH!

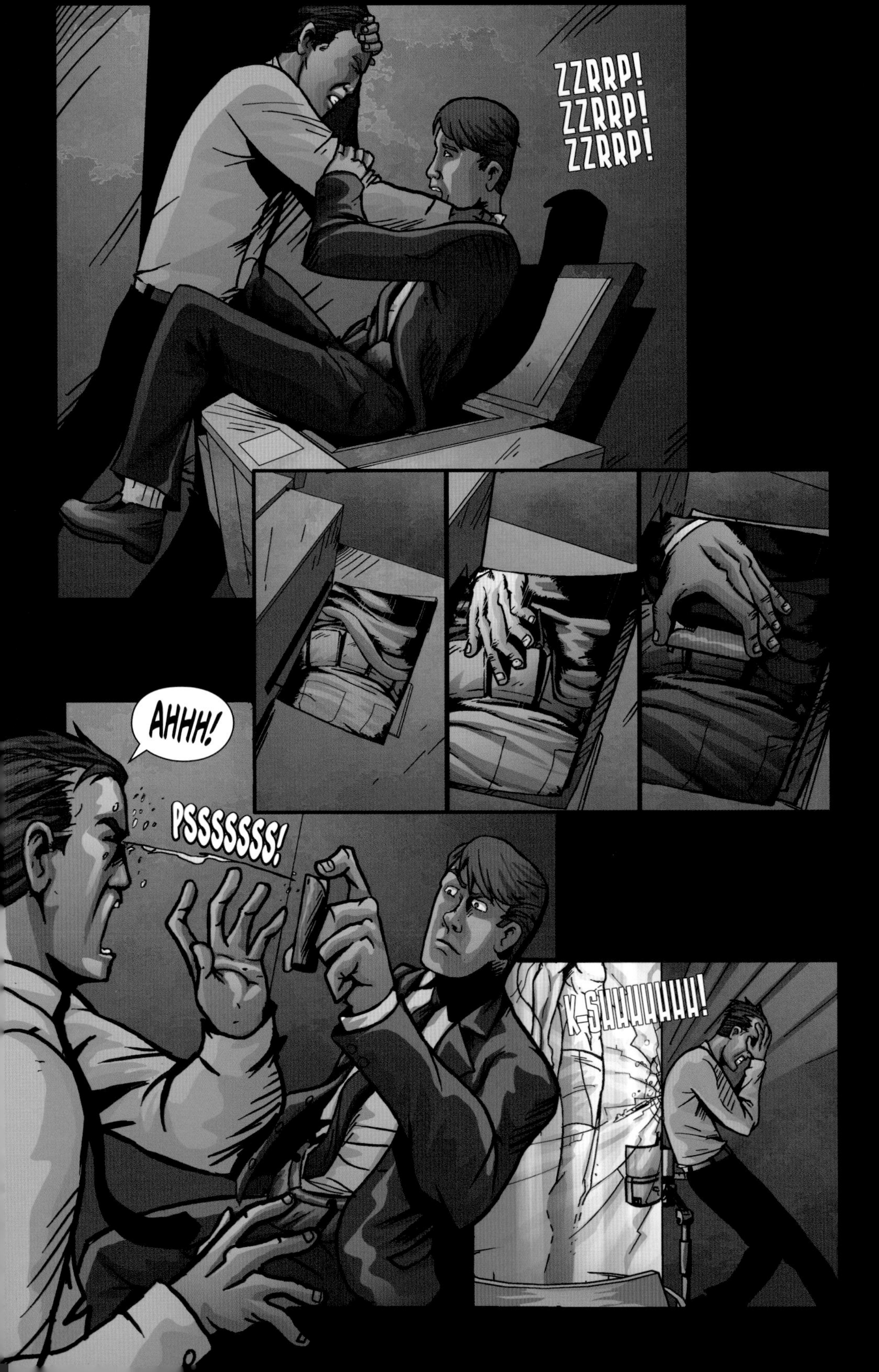
ZZRRP!
ZZRRP!
ZZRRP!
AHHH!
PSSSSSSS!
K-SHHHHHHH!

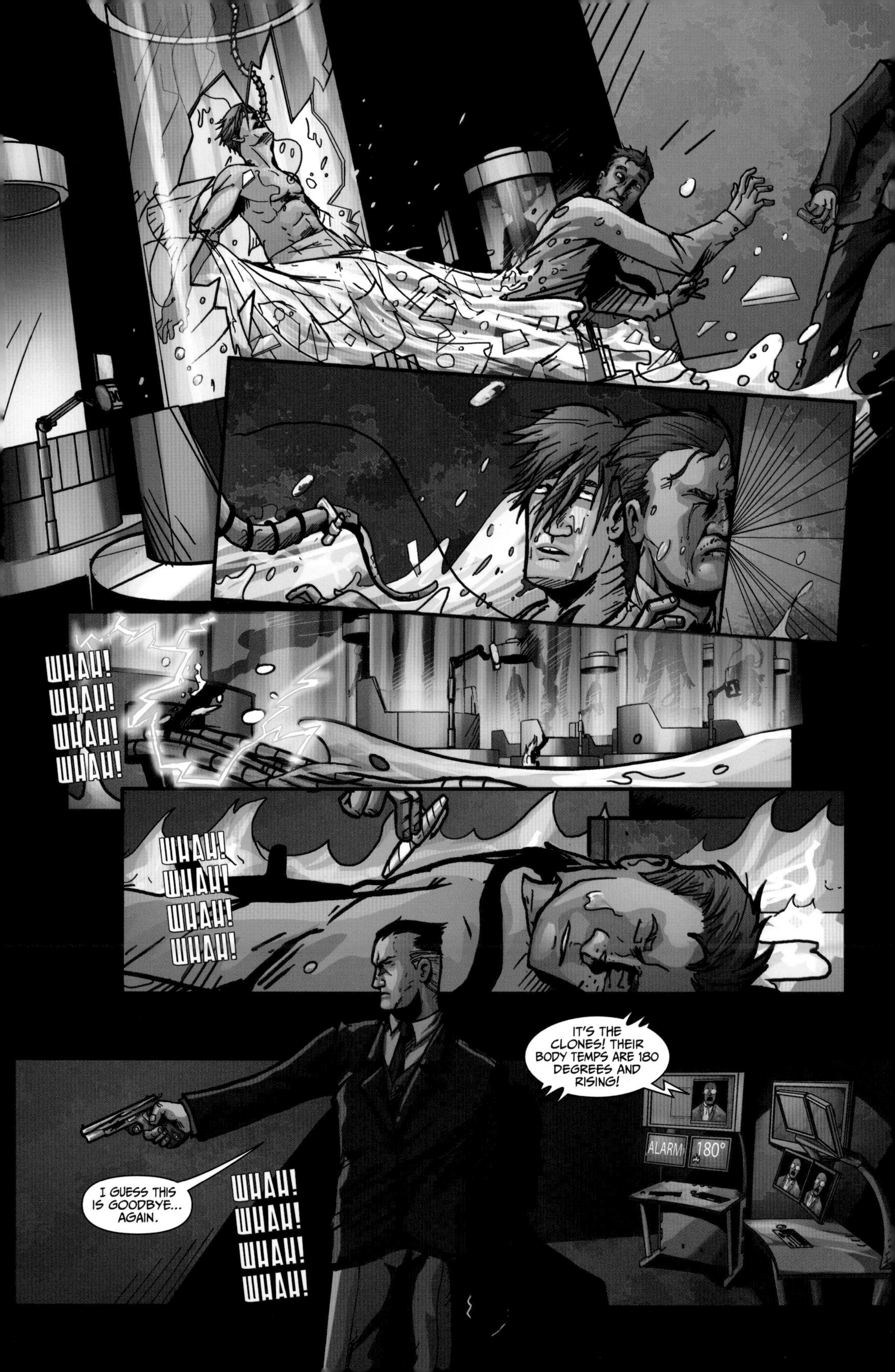
WHAH!
WHAH!
WHAH!
WHAH!
WHAH!
WHAH!
WHAH!
WHAH!
IT'S THE CLONES! THEIR BODY TEMPS ARE 180 DEGREES AND RISING!
ALARM
180°
I GUESS THIS IS GOODBYE... AGAIN.
WHAH!
WHAH!
WHAH!
WHAH!

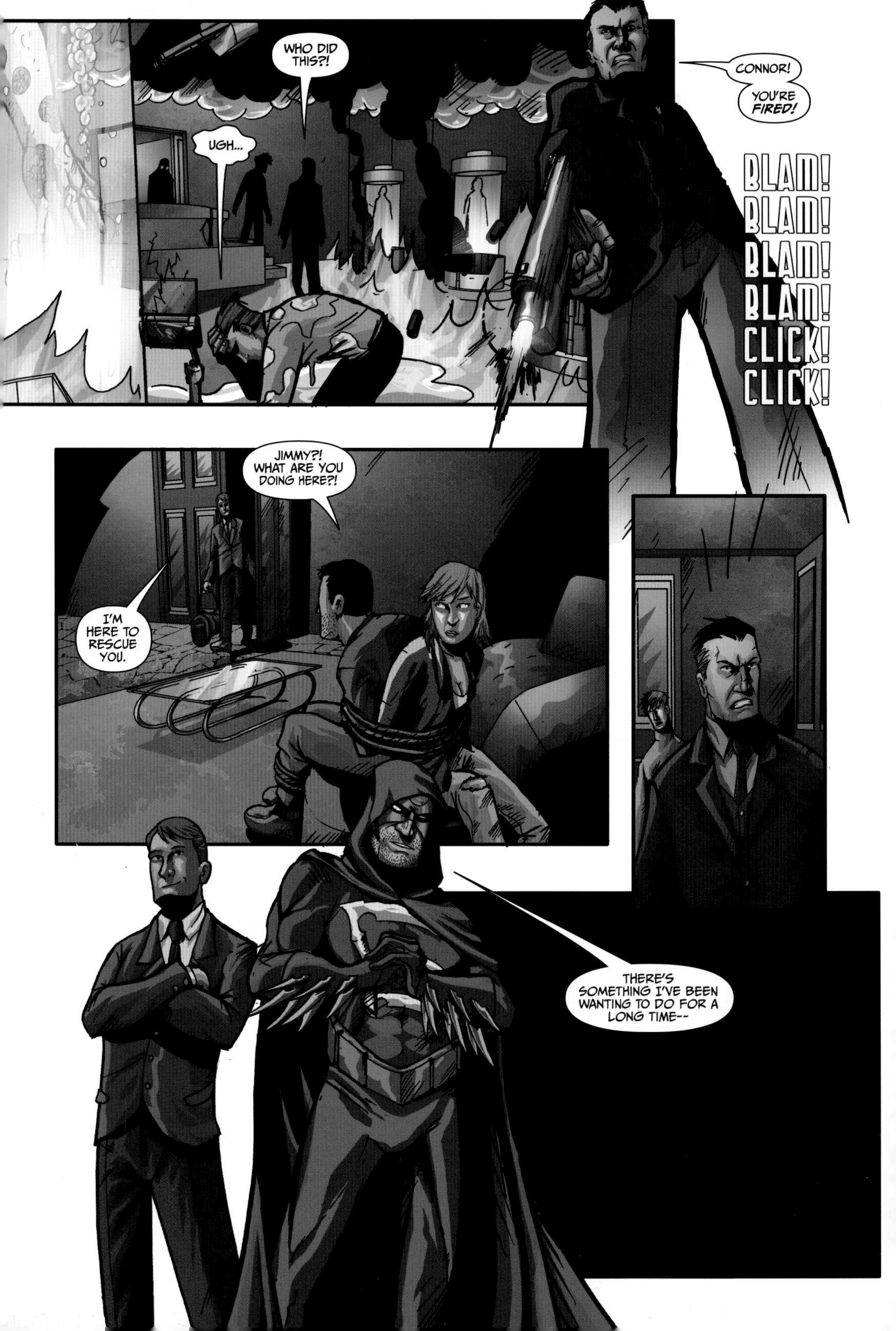
UGH...
WHO DID THIS?!
CONNOR!
YOU'RE FIRED!
BLAM!
BLAM!
BLAM!
BLAM!
CLICK!
CLICK!
JIMMY?! WHAT ARE YOU DOING HERE?!
I'M HERE TO RESCUE YOU.
THERE'S SOMETHING I'VE BEEN WANTING TO DO FOR A LONG TIME--

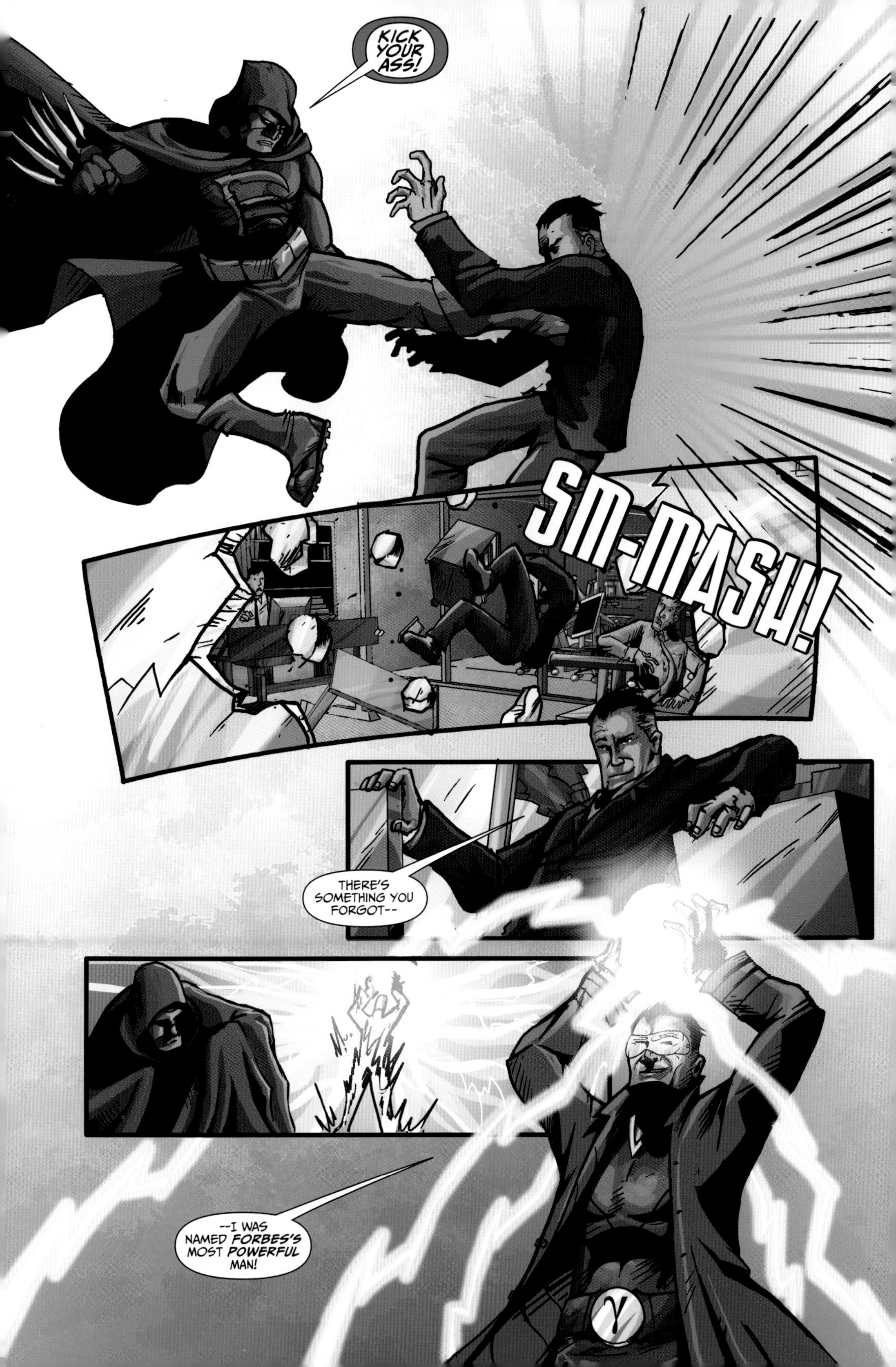
KICK YOUR ASS!
SM-MASH!
THERE'S SOMETHING YOU FORGOT--
--I WAS NAMED FORBES'S MOST POWERFUL MAN!

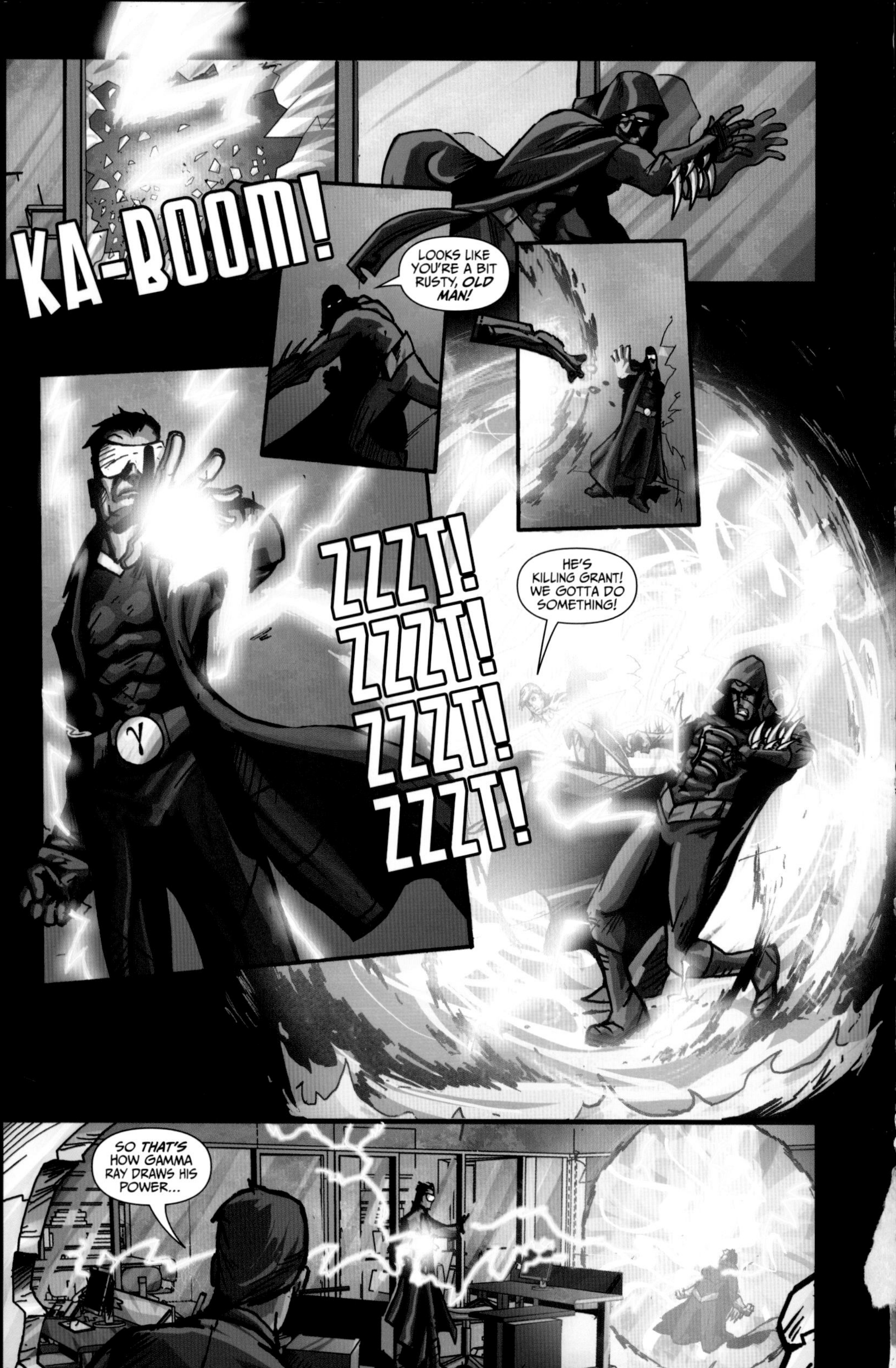
KA-BOOM!
LOOKS LIKE YOU'RE A BIT RUSTY, *OLD MAN!*
ZZZZT! ZZZZT! ZZZZT! ZZZZT!
HE'S KILLING GRANT! WE GOTTA DO SOMETHING!
SO *THAT'S* HOW GAMMA RAY DRAWS HIS POWER...

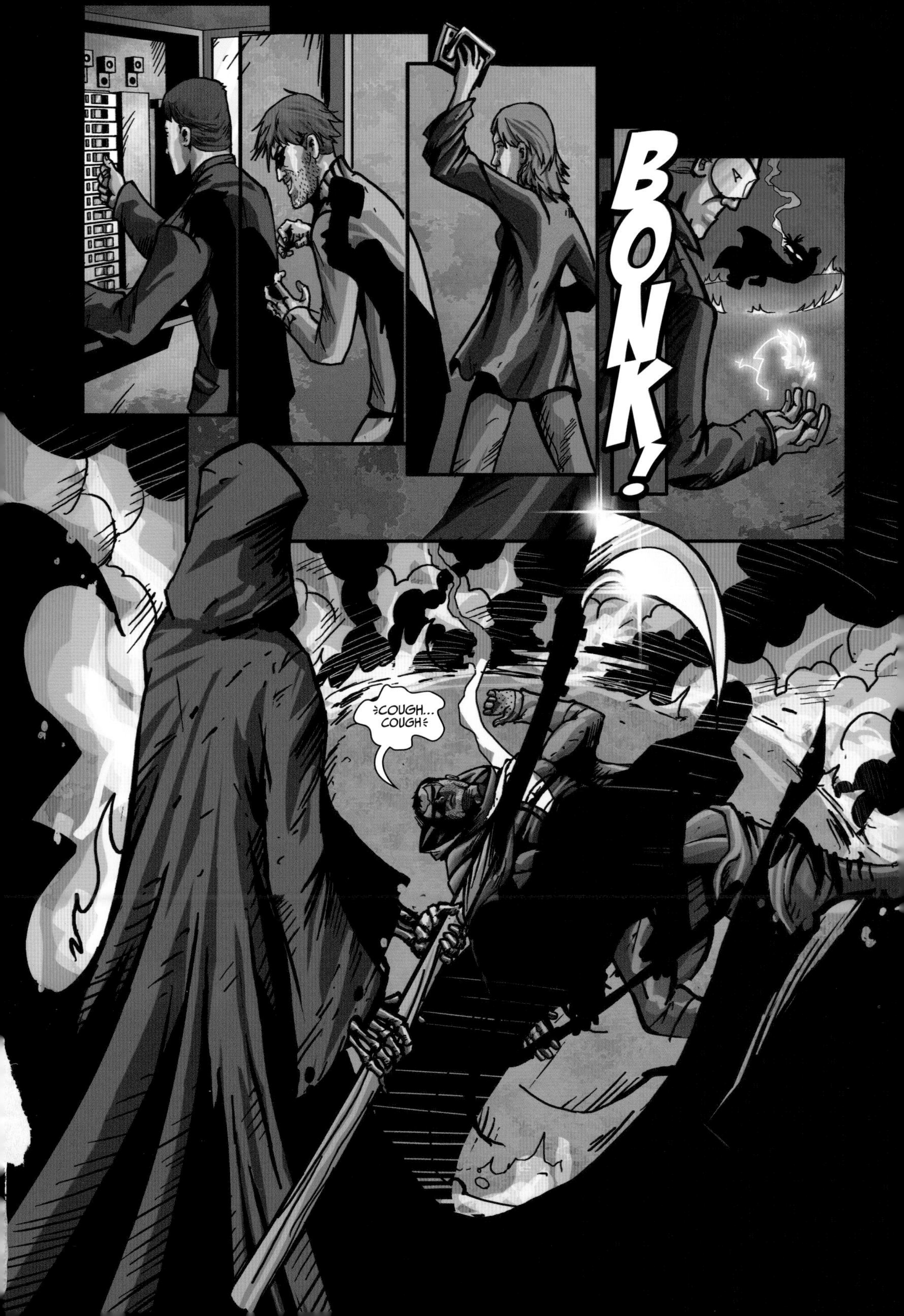
BONK!
COUGH... COUGH

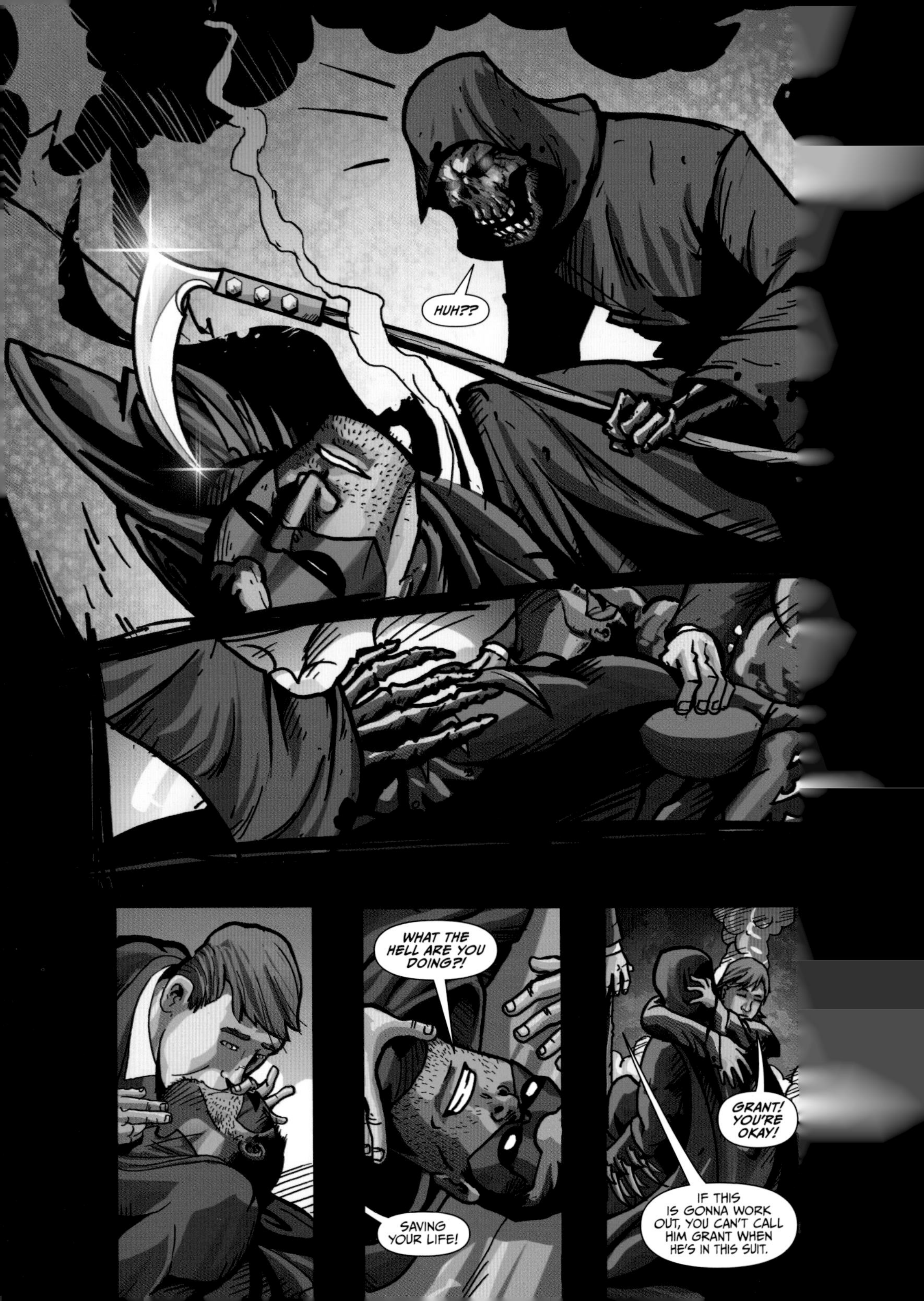
HUH??
WHAT THE HELL ARE YOU DOING?!
SAVING YOUR LIFE!
GRANT! YOU'RE OKAY!
IF THIS IS GONNA WORK OUT, YOU CAN'T CALL HIM GRANT WHEN HE'S IN THIS SUIT.

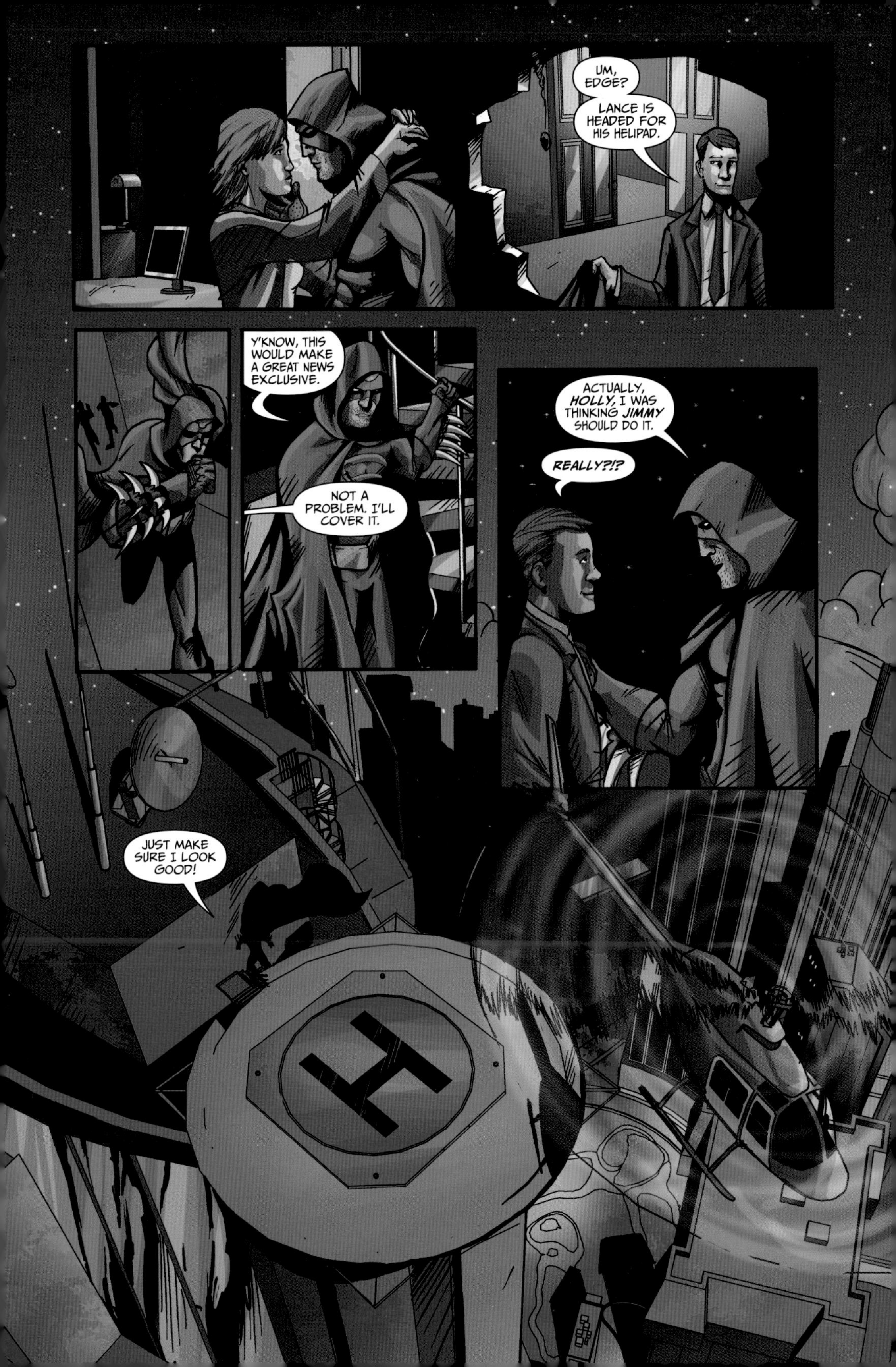
UM, EDGE?
LANCE IS HEADED FOR HIS HELIPAD.
Y'KNOW, THIS WOULD MAKE A GREAT NEWS EXCLUSIVE.
NOT A PROBLEM. I'LL COVER IT.
ACTUALLY, HOLLY, I WAS THINKING JIMMY SHOULD DO IT.
REALLY?!?
JUST MAKE SURE I LOOK GOOD!

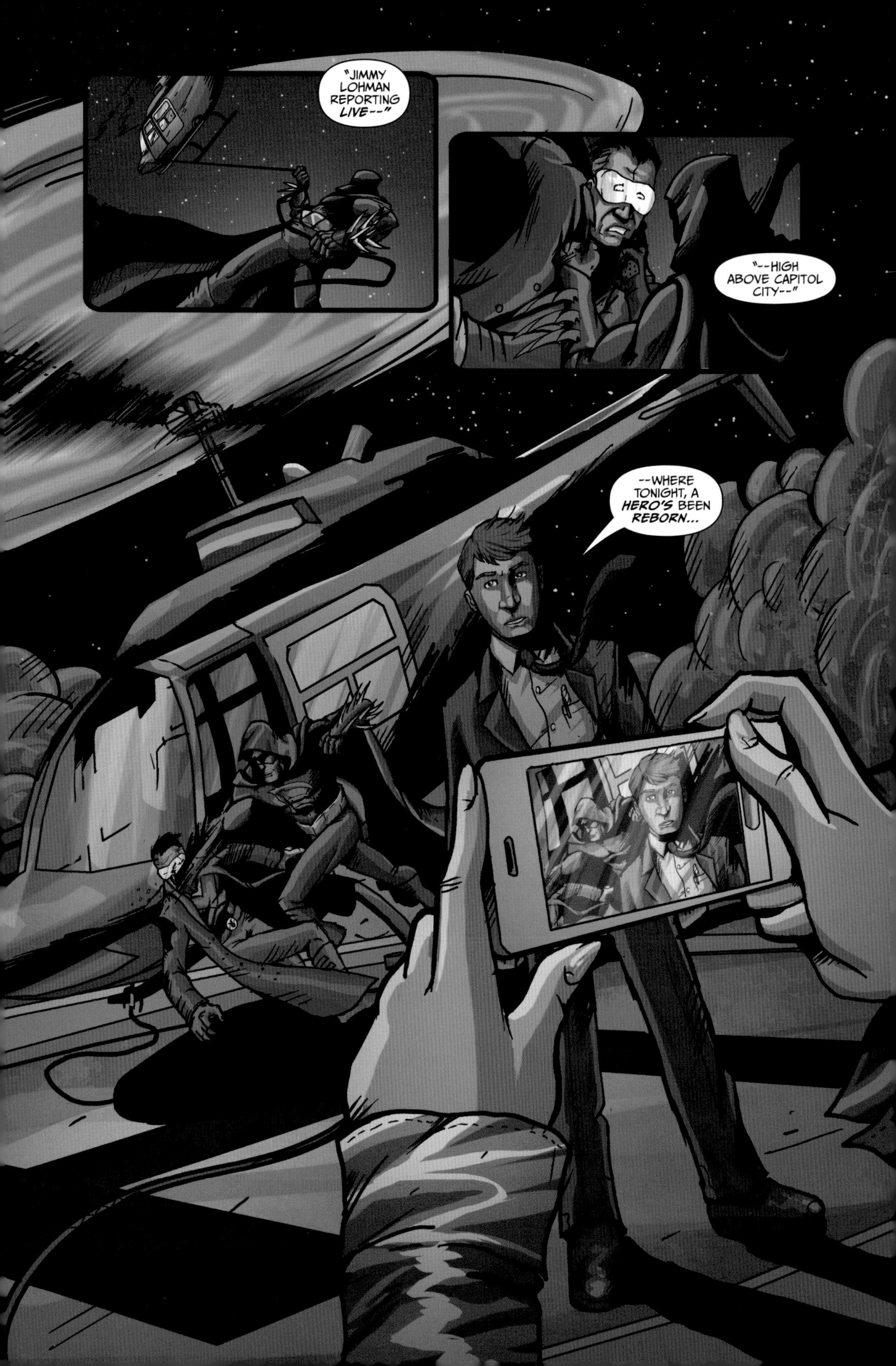
"JIMMY LOHMAN REPORTING *LIVE*--"
"--HIGH ABOVE CAPITOL CITY--"
--WHERE TONIGHT, A *HERO'S* BEEN *REBORN*...

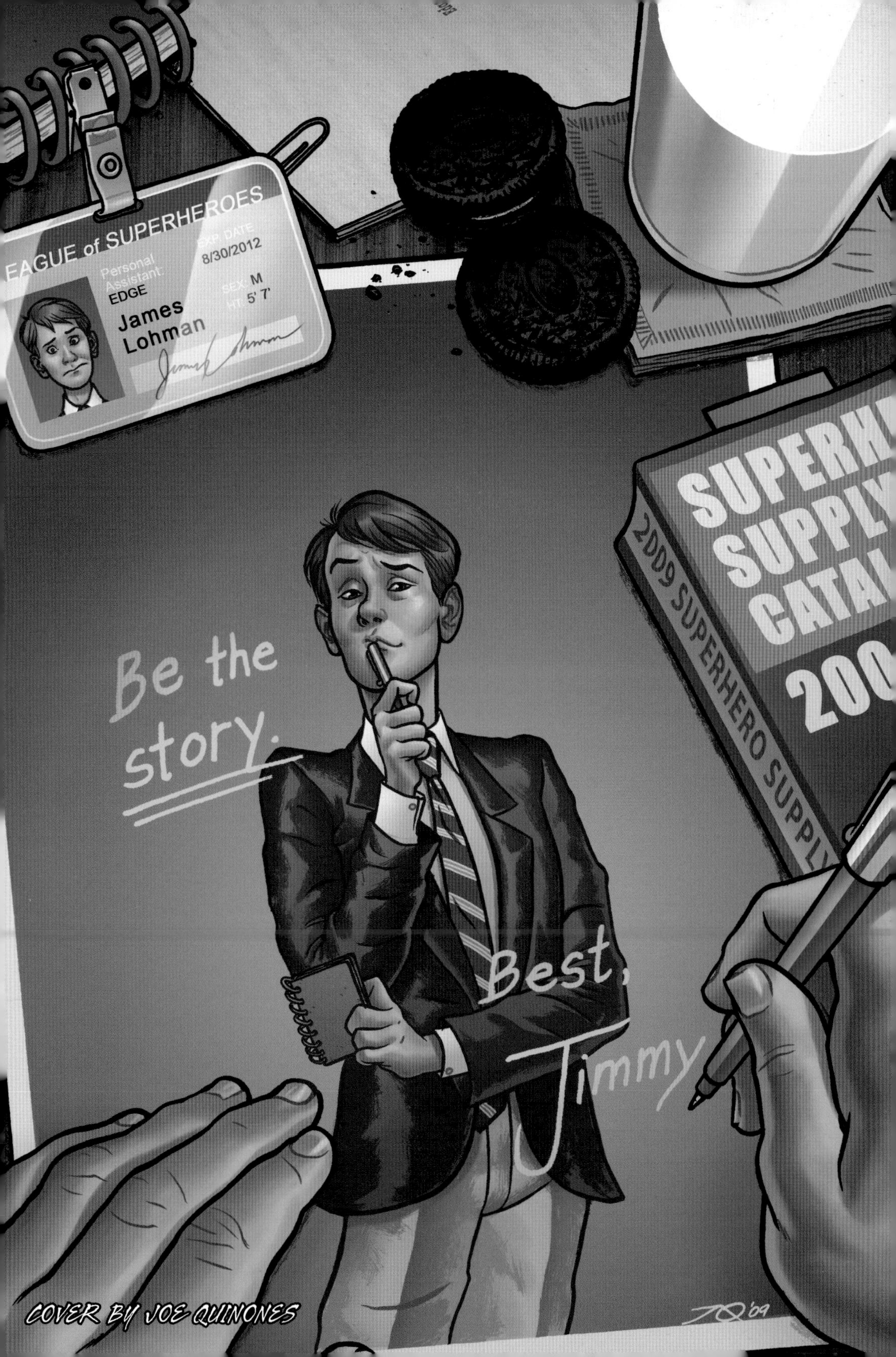
EAGUE of SUPERHEROES
Personal Assistant:
EDGE
James Lohman
EXP. DATE 8/30/2012
SEX: M
HT: 5' 7'
SUPERH
SUPPLY
CATAL
200
2009 SUPERHERO SUPPLY
Be the story.
Best,
Jimmy
COVER BY JOE QUINONES
JQ '09

CHARACTER DESIGNS BY CALEB CLEVELAND

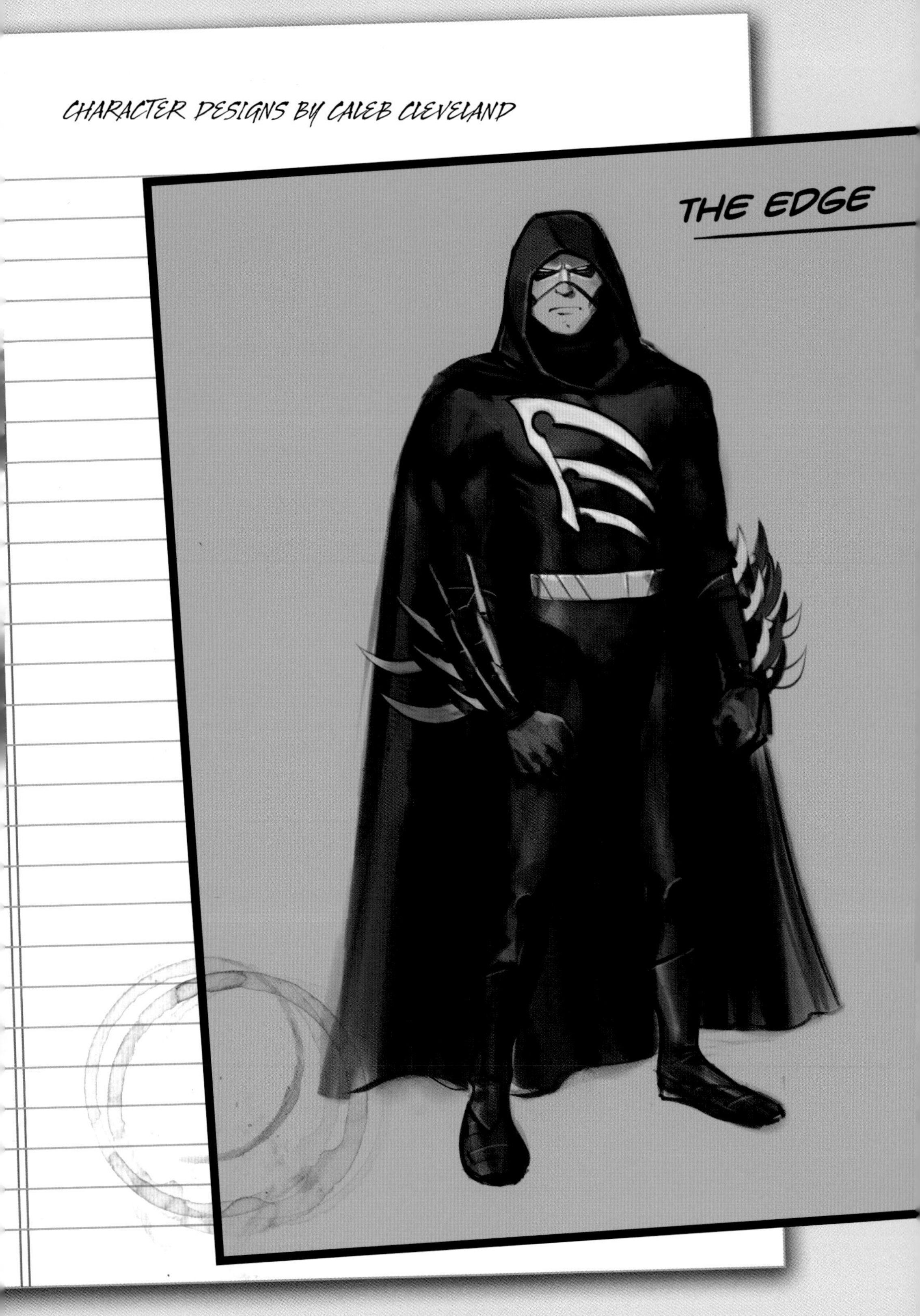
THE EDGE

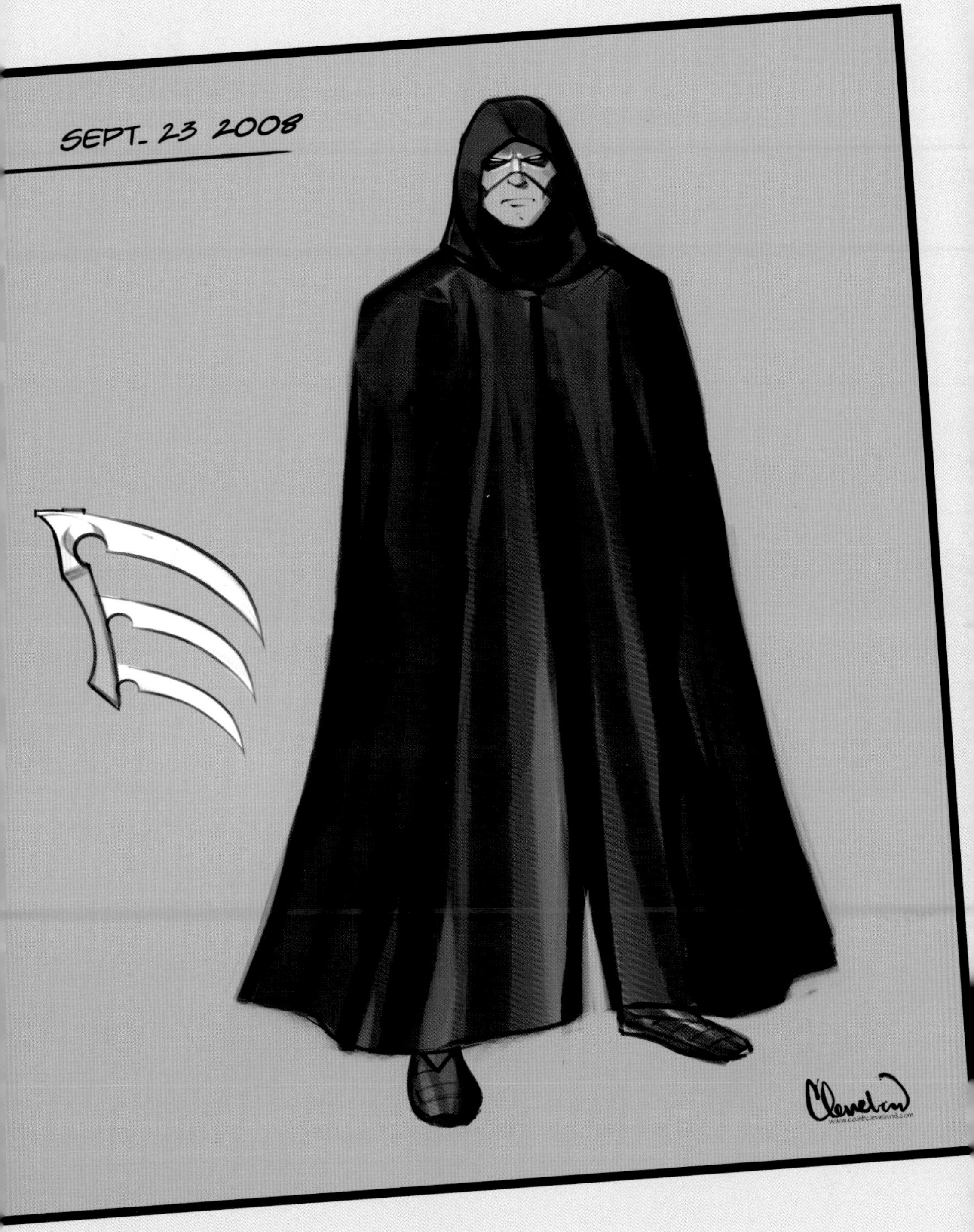
SEPT. 23 2008
Cleveland
www.colecleveland.com

FLEX

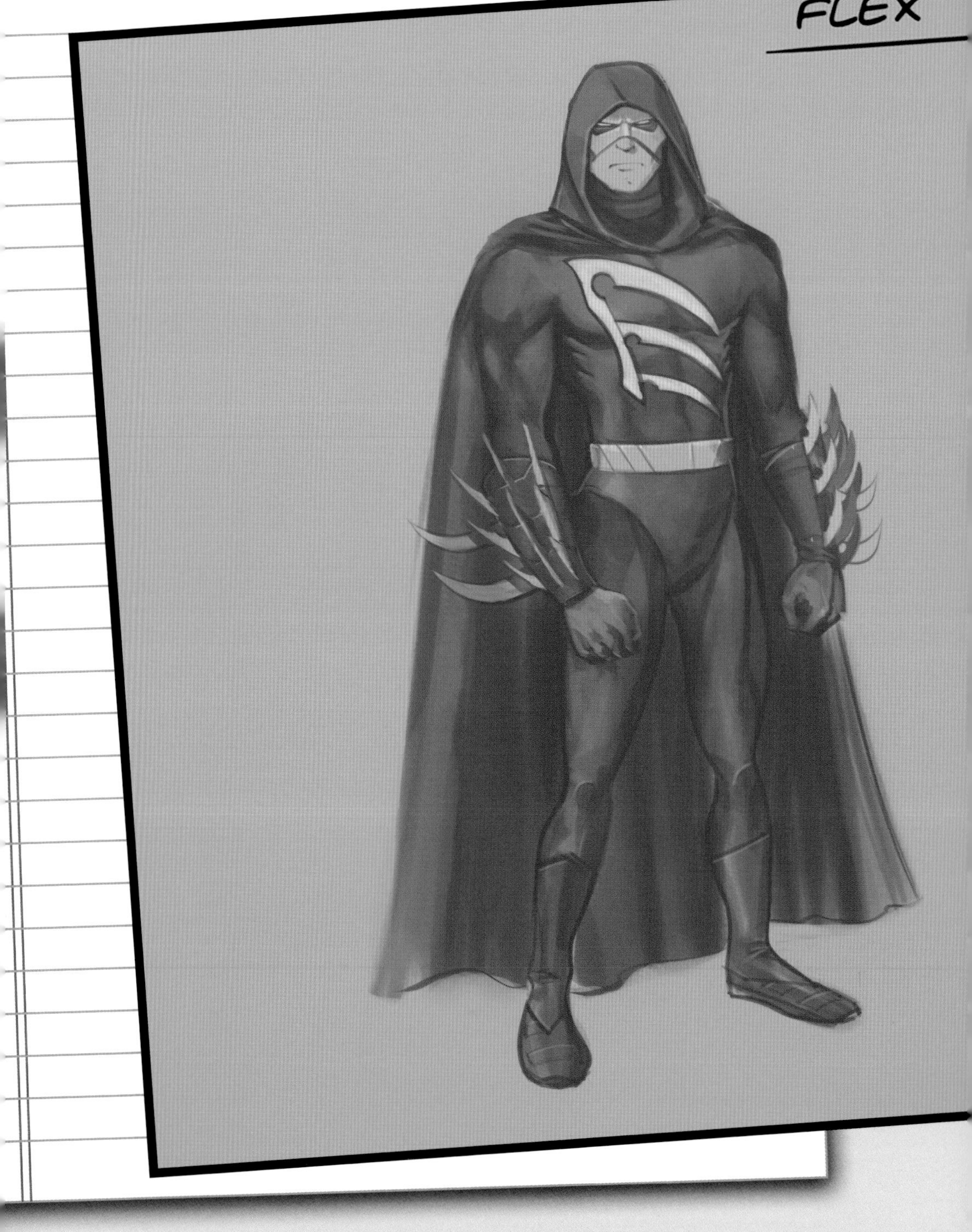

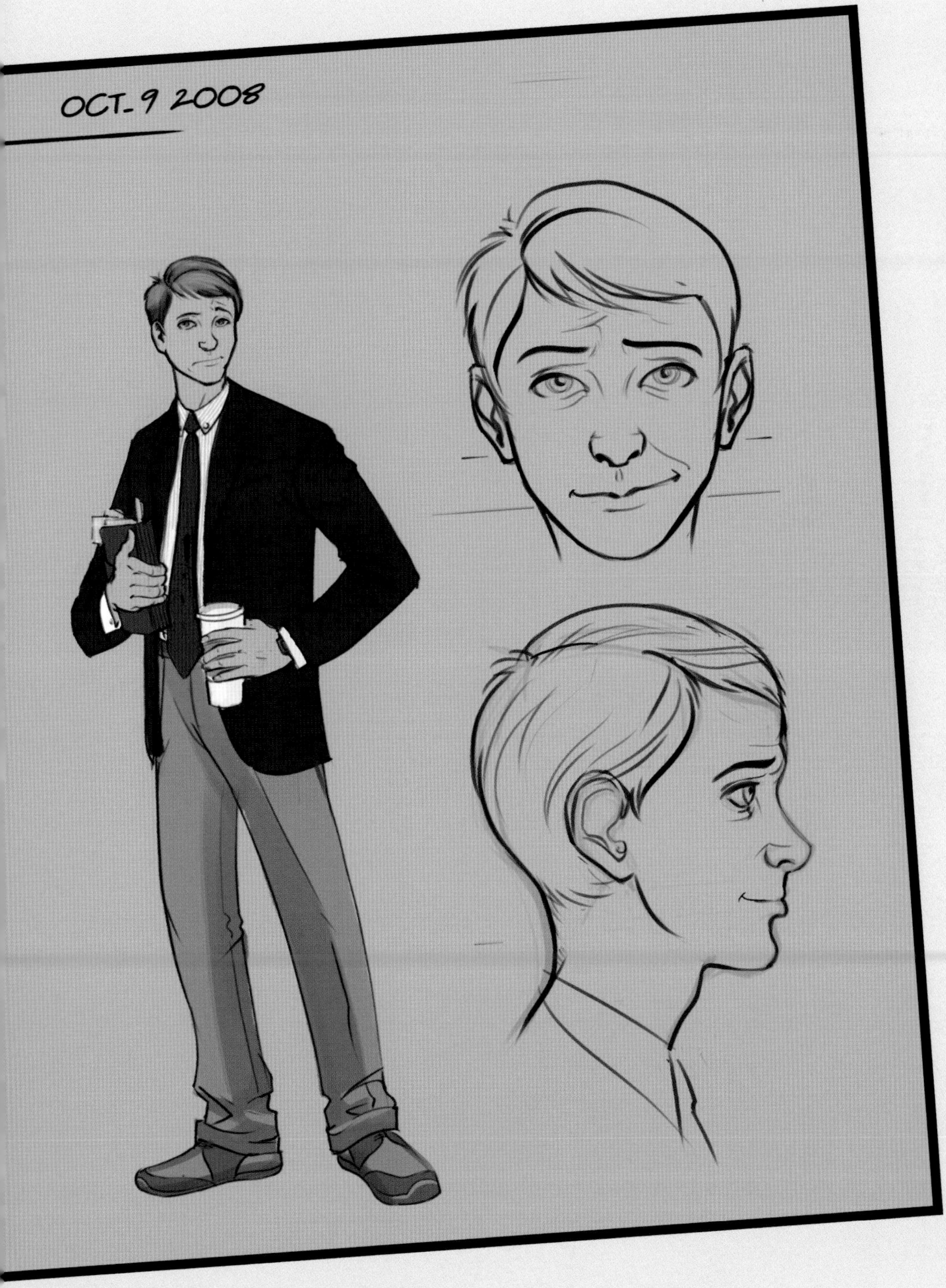
OCT. 9 2008

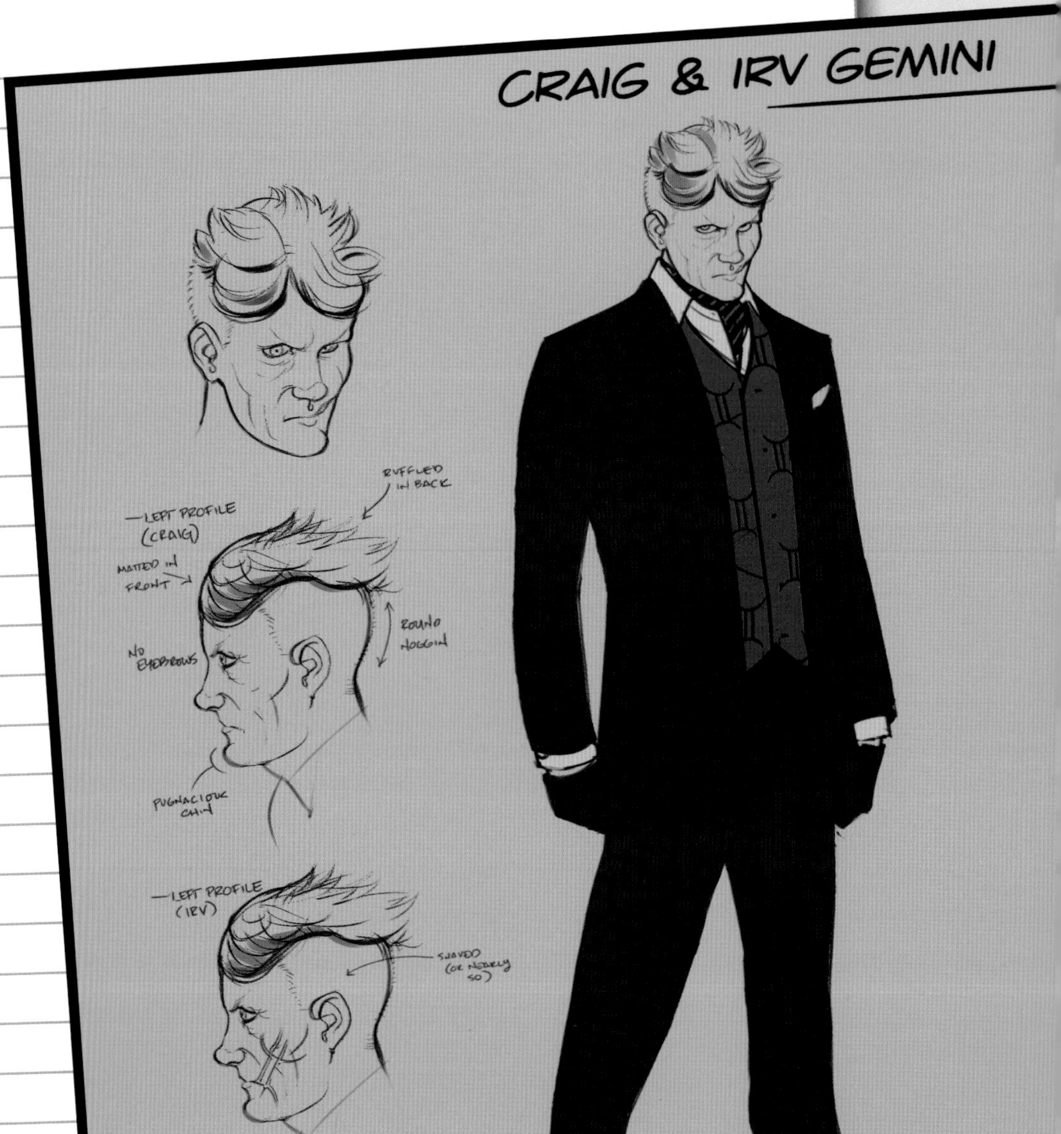
CRAIG & IRV GEMINI
RUFFLED IN BACK
—LEFT PROFILE (CRAIG)
MATTED IN FRONT
ROUND NOGGIN
NO EYEBROWS
PUGNACIOUS CHIN
—LEFT PROFILE (IRV)
SHAVED (OR NEARLY SO)

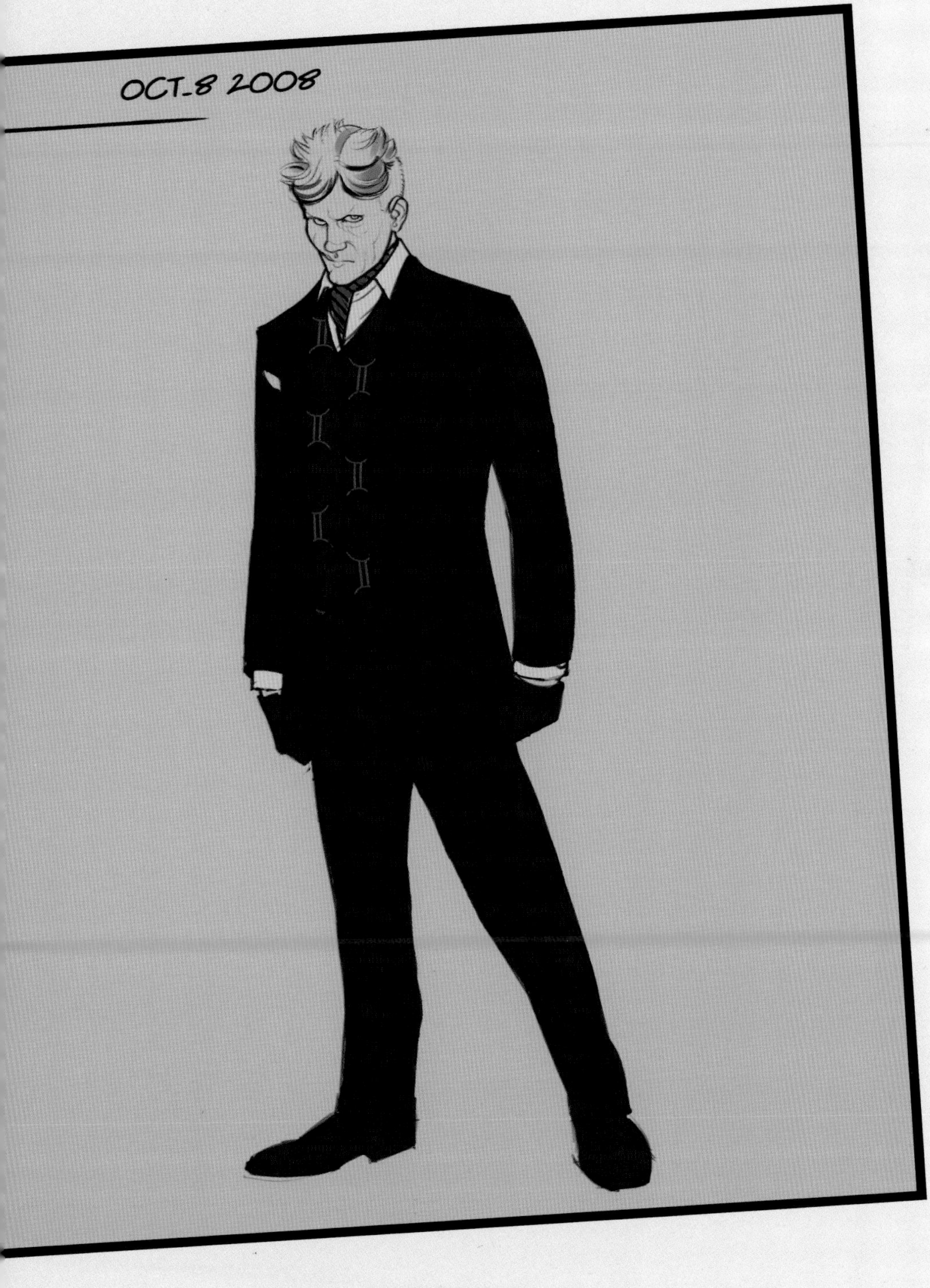
OCT_8 2008

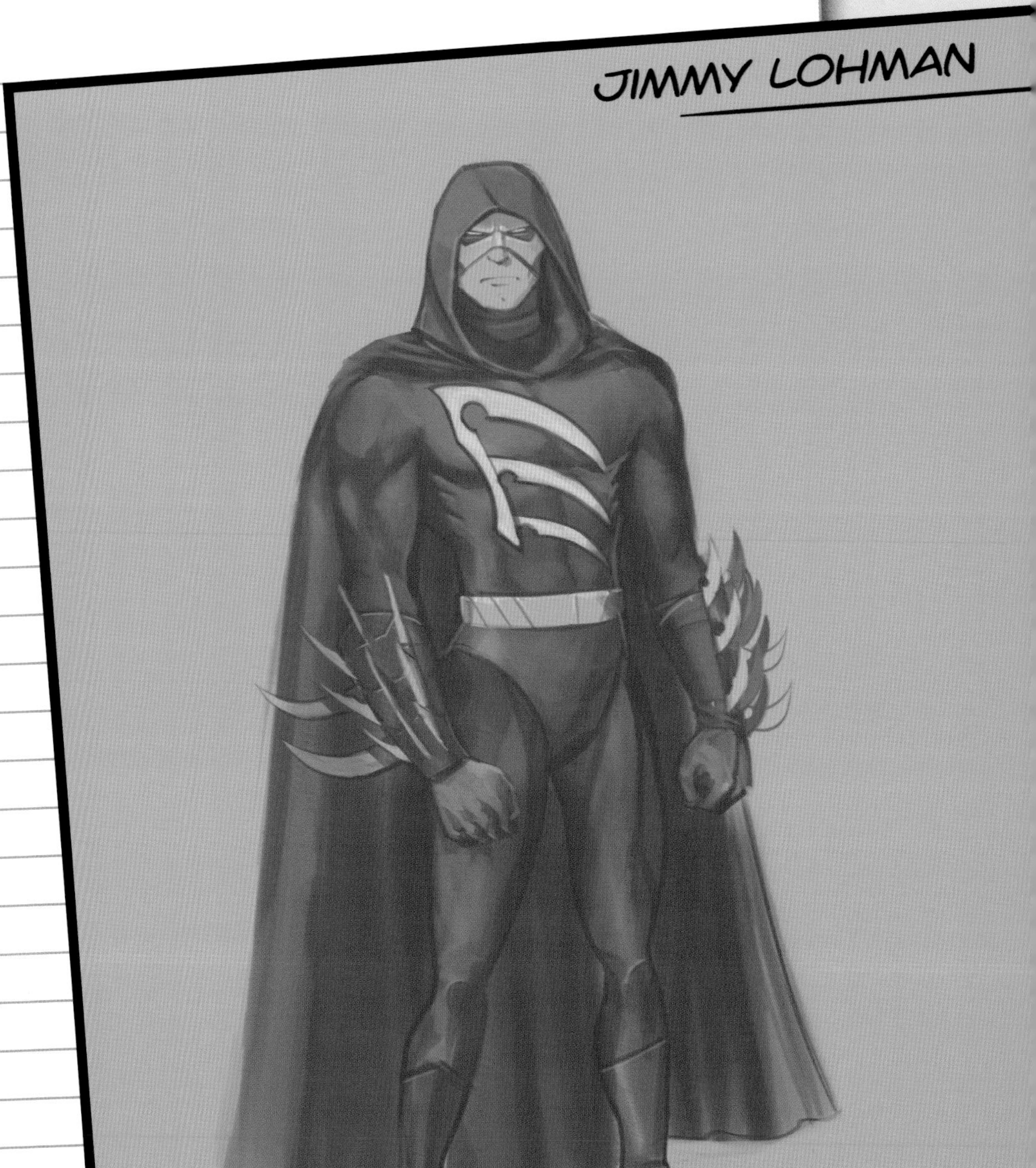
JIMMY LOHMAN

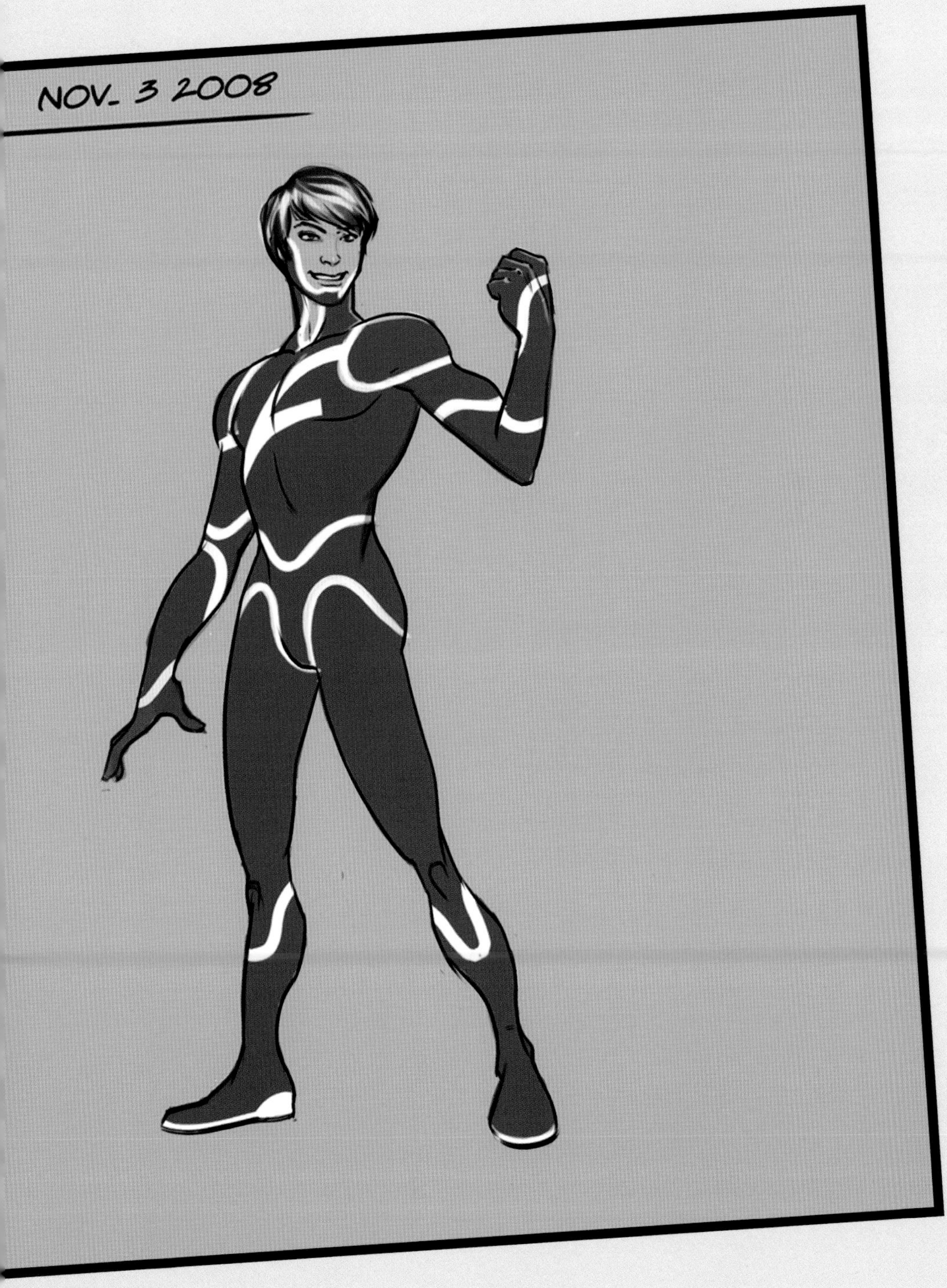
NOV. 3 2008

Currently on CAPED...

In hopes of furthering **CAPED**'s farcical and witty style, editor Ian Brill devised a plan to make the inside front covers (IFC's) of every issue of **CAPED** look as if they were from the front page of a blog, also called **CAPED**. In the **CAPED** world some superheroes were like celebrities, that is to say spoiled and media-hungry. So wouldn't there be, in turn, a blog dedicated not to celebrity-gossip but to the gossip of the long underwear crowd?

Each IFC was meant to not only include the credits for each issue, but explain whom the characters were, as well as establish a tone for this book. To replicate the up-to-the-minute feel of new media, they didn't say "previously on..." but instead declared "currently on **CAPED**." They even came with typos and mistakes built into them, to make them feel like true blog posts (editor Brill is hoping, *hoping*, people believe that!).

Designer Jose Macasocol, Jr. put in an amazing job creating these every month, especially considering that each e-mail from Brill was the electronic equivalent of a note written on a barroom napkin.

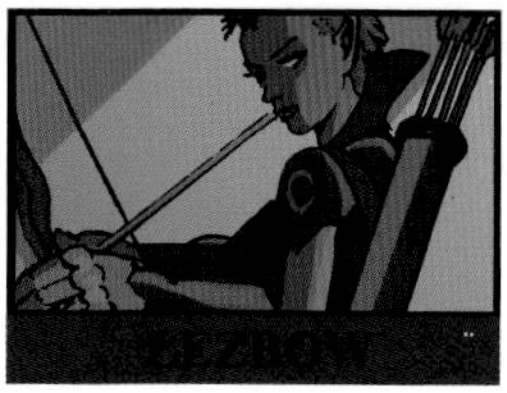

SET FOR "L WORD" CAMEO

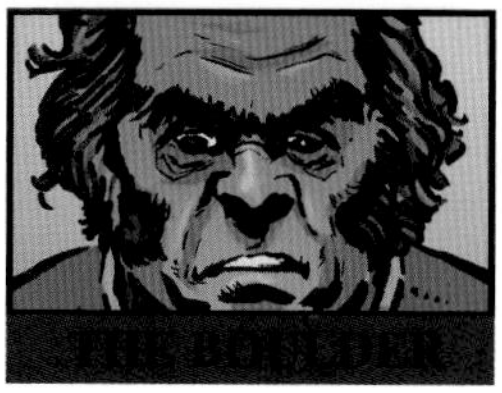

MET WITH STEPHEN HAWKING ON FRIDAY

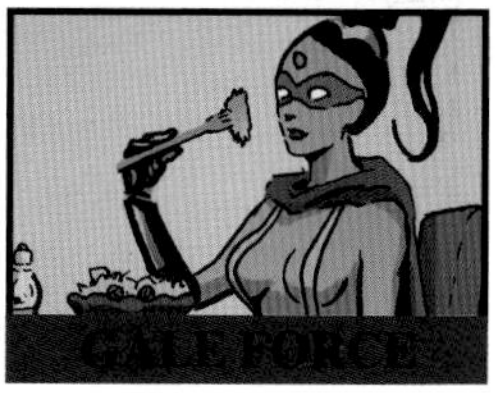

STARRING IN NEW BODY DYSMORPHIC DISORDER PSA

CURRENTLY ON CAPED...

CAPED TEAM

STORY
Josh Lobis and Darin Moiselle

ART
Yair Herrera

COLORS
Renato Faccini

LETTERS
Johnny Lowe

EDITS
Ian Brill

COVERS
Saumin Patel
Joe Quinones

SPECIAL THANKS
Caleb Cleveland
Jose Macasocol, Jr.

BOOM STAFF:

FOUNDERS
Andrew Cosby
Ross Richie

EDITOR-IN-CHIEF
Mark Waid

VICE PRESIDENT NEW BUSINESS
Adam Fortier

MARKETING & SALES DIRECTOR
Chip Mosher

MANAGING EDITOR
Matt Gagnon

DESIGNER
Ed Dukeshire

SUBSCRIBE TO Caped

New: Breaking news and daily top stories via email
476 Subscribers

CHARACTERS

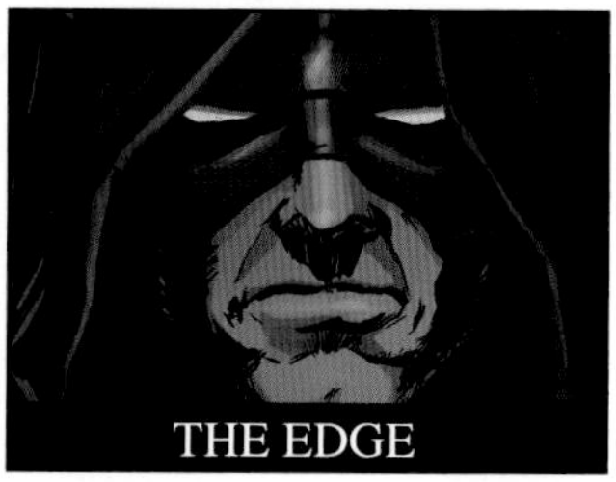

THE EDGE

EDGE:
Capitol City's Nocturnal Solider

The hardest working superhero in the business today. Also, might be the one with the least respect. Word is assistant number 27 is writing a tell-all.

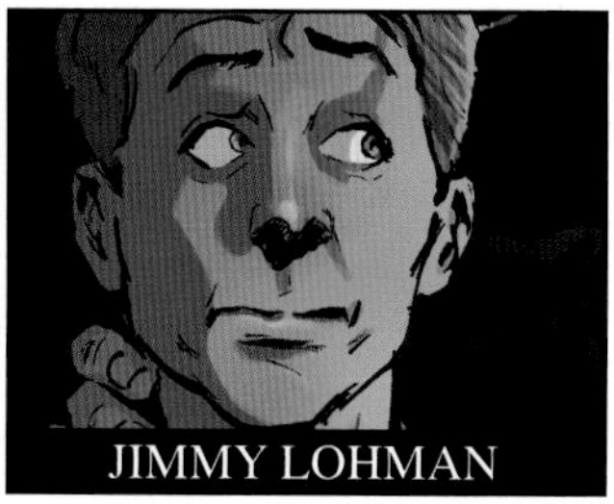

JIMMY LOHMAN

JIMMY LOHMAN:
Journalism's Young Turk

Has come to Capitol City to realize his dream of being the next Edward R. Murrow. Probably the only one his age who knows who Edward R. Murrow is.

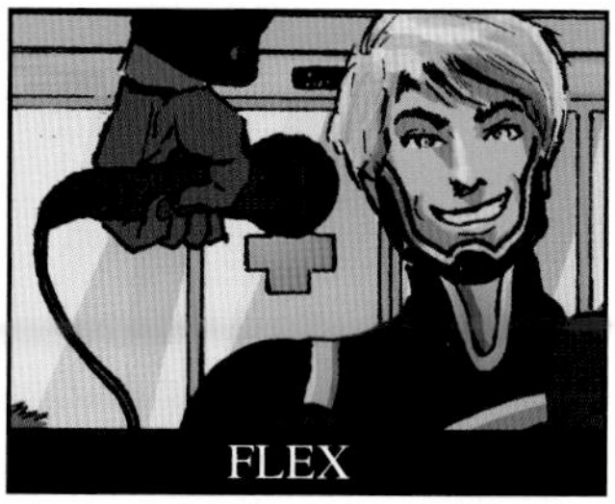

FLEX

FLEX:
The Golden Boy of the Capes and Tights crew

A favorite in City Hall as much as he is with the teeny-bopper demographic (although admittedly, it's sometimes hard to tell the difference between the two).

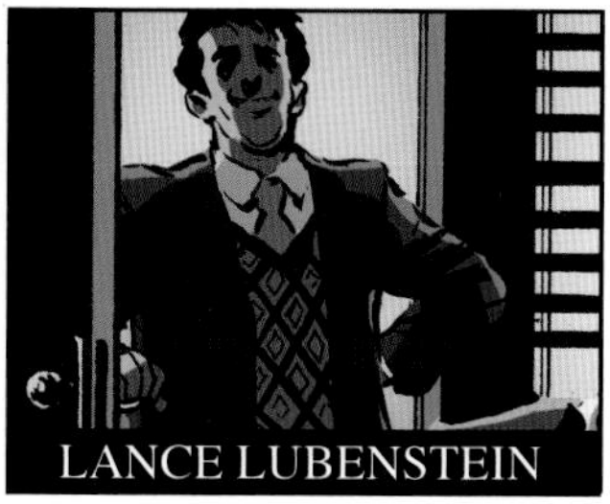

LANCE LUBENSTEIN

LANCE LUBENSTEIN:
More Money than God's Agent

The recession means he's now only a mutli-bajillionaire. How will Grant Godfried do working under this media mogul? Will he lose his edge?

PASSED OVER FOR YET ANOTHER **GLAAD** AWARD.

HIRED AS HIGH-LEVEL CONSULTANT AT GOOGLE.

HAS HER CAPE GAINED WEIGHT?

CURRENTLY ON CAPED...

CAPED TEAM

STORY
Josh Lobis and Darin Moiselle

ART
Yair Herrera

COLORS
Renato Faccini

LETTERS
Johnny Lowe

EDITS
Ian Brill

COVERS
Saumin Patel
Joe Quinones

SPECIAL THANKS
Caleb Cleveland
Tony Parker
Jose Macasocol, Jr.

BOOM STAFF:

FOUNDERS
Andrew Cosby
Ross Richie

EDITOR-IN-CHIEF
Mark Waid

VICE PRESIDENT NEW BUSINESS
Adam Fortier

MARKETING & SALES DIRECTOR
Chip Mosher

MANAGING EDITOR
Matt Gagnon

DESIGNER
Ed Dukeshire

SUBSCRIBE TO Caped

New: Breaking news and daily top stories via email
476 Subscribers

EDGE

EDGE:
Capitol City's Nocturnal Soldier

The mayor thinks he's yesterday's news. If the papers still cover his failures is that true?

JIMMY LOHMAN

JIMMY LOHMAN:
Journalism's Young Turk

Just got the job of a lifetime. Granted, that life-time might have lost thirty years.

FLEX

FLEX:
The Golden Boy of the Capes and Tights Crew

Anointed the new golden boy of Capitol City's crimefighters. That's a bit like being the world's tallest midget.

LANCE LUBENSTEIN

LANCE LUBENSTEIN:
More Money than God's Agent

Is ready to put Grant Godfried out to pasture. Why does that guy and Edge seem to have the same problems?

STILL RECOVERING FROM
PERFORMING THE
BOULDER'S HIGH COLONIC.

THE ONLY OFFICIAL IN
CAPITOL CITY WHO'S NOT
SUPERHERO OBSESSED...
AS FAR AS WE KNOW.

THINKS EDGE IS
RIPPING OFF HIS STYLE.
MIGHT SUE.

CURRENTLY ON CAPED...

CAPED TEAM

STORY
Josh Lobis and Darin Moiselle

ART
Sebastiãn Piriz

COLORS
Digikore Studios

LETTERS
Johnny Lowe

EDITS
Ian Brill

COVERS
Saumin Patel
Joe Quinones

SPECIAL THANKS
Caleb Cleveland
Jose Macasocol, Jr.

BOOM STAFF:

FOUNDERS
Andrew Cosby
Ross Richie

EDITOR-IN-CHIEF
Mark Waid

**VICE PRESIDENT
NEW BUSINESS**
Adam Fortier

**MARKETING &
SALES DIRECTOR**
Chip Mosher

MANAGING EDITOR
Matt Gagnon

DESIGNER
Ed Dukeshire

SUBSCRIBE TO Caped

**New: Breaking news and
daily top stories via email
476 Subscribers**

EDGE

**EDGE:
Capitol City's Nocturnal Soldier**

Just a superhero looking for some respect, is
that so much to ask?

JIMMY LOHMAN

**JIMMY LOHMAN:
Journalism's Young Turk**

Just an assistant looking not to die today. That
might be too much to ask.

FLEX

**FLEX:
The Golden Boy of the Capes and
Tights Crew**

You know when beloved child stars grow up,
get bitter and commit crimes? Yeah, this is kind
of like that.

LANCE LUBENSTEIN

**LANCE LUBENSTEIN:
More Money than God's Agent**

Hates Edge as much he hates Grant Godfried,
and he HATES Grant Godfried.

DR. FIELDING
STILL PREFERS WORKING
WITH SUPERHEROES THAN
HMOs.

MAYOR ZIEGLER
NOT TOO HAPPY TO BE
CONFUSED WITH
COMMISSIONER BLAKE
LAST MONTH.

DEATH
HAS COME FOR THIS SERIES.

CURRENTLY ON CAPED...

CAPED TEAM

STORY
Josh Lobis and Darin Moiselle

ART
Sebastiãn Piriz

COLORS
Digikore Studios

LETTERS
Johnny Lowe

EDITS
Ian Brill

COVERS
Saumin Patel
Joe Quinones

SPECIAL THANKS
Caleb Cleveland
Jose Macasocol, Jr.

BOOM STAFF:

FOUNDERS
Andrew Cosby
Ross Richie

EDITOR-IN-CHIEF
Mark Waid

VICE PRESIDENT
NEW BUSINESS
Adam Fortier

MARKETING &
SALES DIRECTOR
Chip Mosher

MANAGING EDITOR
Matt Gagnon

DESIGNER
Ed Dukeshire

SUBSCRIBE TO Caped

New: Breaking news and
daily top stories via email
476 Subscribers

CHARACTERS

EDGE

EDGE:
Capitol City's Nocturnal Soldier

Could he be facing his greatest challenge
yet? Other than that one lawsuit...which was
dismissed by the way, the kid wasn't his.

JIMMY LOHMAN

JIMMY LOHMAN:
Journalism's Young Turk

Has learned a lot from Edge. Amazingly enough,
some of it might be useful.

FLEX

FLEX:
The Golden Boy of the Capes and
Tights Crew

Dead. Didn't you read the last issue?

LANCE LUBENSTEIN

LANCE LUBENSTEIN:
More Money than God's Agent

Not dead. Although if Edge has his druthers...